MASS COMMUNICATION LAW

IN A NUTSHELL

Fourth Edition

By

T. BARTON CARTER

Associate Professor of Mass Communication
College of Communication
Boston University

JULIET LUSHBOUGH DEE

Associate Professor of Communication
College of Arts and Science
University of Delaware

MARTIN J. GAYNES, ESQ.

Member, Schmeltzer, Aptaker and Shepard
Washington, D.C.

HARVEY L. ZUCKMAN

Professor of Law, The Catholic University of America
Director, Institute for Communications Law Studies,
Washington, D.C.

ST. PAUL, MINN.
WEST PUBLISHING CO.
1994

Nutshell Series, In a Nutshell, the Nutshell Logo and the WP symbol are registered trademarks of West Publishing Co. Registered in U.S. Patent and Trademark Office.

COPYRIGHT © 1983, 1988 WEST PUBLISHING CO.
COPYRIGHT © 1994 By WEST PUBLISHING CO.
610 Opperman Drive
P.O. Box 64526
St. Paul, MN 55164–0526
1–800–328–9352

Library of Congress Cataloging-in-Publication Data

Mass communication law in a nutshell / T. Barton Carter ... [et al.].
— 4th ed.
    p.   cm. — (Nutshell series)
  Includes index.
  ISBN 0-314-04081-1
  1. Mass media—Law and legislation—United States.   I. Carter, T. Barton.   II. Series.
KF2750.Z9M37   1994
343.7309′9—dc20
[347.30399]   94–12723
                                                                    CIP

ISBN 0-314-04081-1

For Richard, Gregory,
Barbara and Charlotte

*

PREFACE

To appreciate the interrelationship of law and mass communication, look at a daily newpaper. Each day one is likely to find news of important court decisions, news of new legislation and news about the judiciary. Even the sports page may contain as much news about law suits between team owners, unions and players as about team performance. There has been a veritable explosion in media coverage of legal issues since the early 1960s. The media's increasing influence has resulted in more problems for them, especially in the areas of First Amendment protection and Federal Communication Commission regulation, deregulation and re-regulation of broadcasting and cable, and the emergence of the information superhighway.

In this book we attempt to meet a continuing need for a basic text in communication law, not only for law students but journalism and communication students as well.

Readers will note that the authors have made every effort to achieve gender neutral exposition in this edition. We believe the time has long since passed when we might ignore the need for equality of opportunity and the achievements of both men and women in the fields of law and communication. In this regard, Professor Zuckman is proud to report that his daughter was recently appointed Congressional correspondent for a large Eastern newspaper.

PREFACE

We wish to acknowledge our heavy debt to the following individuals and organizations in the preparation of this text: Professors Donald M. Gillmor and Jerome A. Barron, authors of the casebook "Mass Communication Law," for allowing their organizational scheme to be followed here; Professor Thomas I. Emerson, whose many writings greatly influenced our thinking on First Amendment issues, and the editorial board of Law and Contemporary Problems for permitting us to reprint material from Professor Emerson's article "The Doctrine of Prior Restraint," appearing in a symposium on Obscenity and the Arts in Law and Comtemporary Problems (Vol. 20, No. 4, Autumn, 1955), published by Duke University School of Law, Durham, North Carolina, copyright 1955, by Duke University; the late Dean William L. Prosser, founding author of the Handbook of the Law of Torts, whose works greatly shaped our thinking in Chapters II and III on the law of defamation and privacy; Professor Dan B. Dobbs, author of the Handbook of the Law of Remedies (now in its second edition), for his guidance on the law of damages in defamation actions; the late Professor Melville B. Nimmer, without whose brilliant thinking on the law of copyright infringement actions no rational discussion of those subjects could be presented; the editorial board of the Texas Law Review for permission to paraphrase portions of the article by Donna Murasky, Esquire, "The Journalist's Privilege: Branzburg and Its Aftermath," 52 Texas Law Review 829 (1974); the editorial board of the Washington Law Review for permission to para-

PREFACE

phrase portions of the article by Professors Don R. Pember and Dwight L. Teeter, Jr., "Privacy and the Press Since Time, Inc. v. Hill," 50 Washington Law Review 57 (1974); Charles B. Blackmar, distinguished jurist and former teaching colleague and cherished friend of Professor Zuckman for his insights into First Amendment problems engendered by lawyer advertising (he argued and won In re Matter of R _____ M. J. _____ in the United States Supreme Court); West Publishing Company for its new computerized storage and retrieval system that made the progression from galley to page proof to publication so much easier for the authors and helped keep typographical errors to a minimum; office coordinator Myrna Hofmann and secretary Laura Sowers in the University of Delaware Department of Communication for their administrative support; law student Johnna Moyer and Head of Public Services Ilene Haym and reference librarians Mary Jane Mallonee, David King and Mary Marzolla at the Delaware Law School Library for their research assistance.

T. BARTON CARTER
JULIET L. DEE
MARTIN J. GAYNES
HARVEY L. ZUCKMAN

July 1994

*

OUTLINE

IX

Chapter VIII. Newspersons' Privilege, Subpoenas, Contempt Citations and Searches and Seizures 258

OUTLINE

PART TWO. REGULATION OF THE ELECTRONIC MASS MEDIA

Chapter X. The Federal Communications Commission—What It Does and Does Not Do

XXI

TABLE OF CASES

References are to Pages

XXIII

XXIX

TABLE OF CASES

XXXIII

TABLE OF CASES

TABLE OF CASES

TABLE OF CASES

MASS COMMUNICATION LAW

IN A NUTSHELL

Fourth Edition

*

PART ONE

THE FIRST AMENDMENT AND MASS COMMUNICATIONS

CHAPTER I

THE FIRST AMENDMENT IN PERSPECTIVE

A. INTRODUCTION

The development of mass communications throughout the western world and particularly in the United States in the twentieth century is a product of both science and law. Science has given us the technology by which individuals may communicate information, ideas and images across time and space to other individuals. And for this we owe a debt of gratitude to scientists and inventors such as Edison, Bell, Marconi, DeForest, and Zworykin.

But technology does not exist in a vacuum. It operates in organized societies governed by laws. These societies may be open ones in which the members are relatively free to express themselves and to communicate with others by whatever means available, or they may be relatively closed, with the modes of communications tightly controlled by a very few persons. Gutenberg's invention of moveable type gave promise of spreading both literacy and ideas to the masses, but in Elizabethan England and beyond, licensing acts severely limited access to the printing press to a few printers considered "safe" by the ruling authorities. It was this legal restriction on the utilization of the first technology of mass communication that led the great poet John Milton to make his stirring call for a free press in "Areopagitica." In our own time the vast promise of cable television was retarded for years because of the complex of statutes and Federal Communications Commission regulations designed to reign in this new technology in order to protect existing economic interests.

Thus, while technology is the necessary antecedent to mass communication, a society's laws ultimately determine how the technology will be developed and how "mass" will be its reach.

In our country the fountainhead of the law governing mass communication is the First Amendment to the Constitution which says in spare but sweeping language "Congress shall make no law ... abridging the freedom of speech or of the press; ..." The way this mandate is carried out tells us much about the kind of society we have. For as that giant of electronic journalism Edward R. Murrow once noted, what distinguishes a truly free society from all others is an independent judiciary and a free press.

B. BACKGROUND, THEORIES
AND DIRECTION OF THE
FIRST AMENDMENT

1. Background

At the time Madison was directed by Congress to draft the amendment to the Constitution expressly protecting free speech and press from governmental encroachment, he and the other founders of the Republic were acutely aware of the long history of suppression in England and the Colonies of free expression, particularly that concerning the affairs of government. Even after Parliament refused to renew the last of the licensing acts in 1695, the Crown was largely able to retain its control over the press by the imposition of heavy taxes on periodicals in England, by the refusal to permit the introduction of printing presses in many of the American colonies and, most importantly, by vigorous enforcement of the criminal law of seditious libel everywhere.

Under that law printers and publishers who offended the government and its ministers could be severely punished even when their statements were true. The maxim at common law was "the greater the truth the greater the libel." The journalistic exposure of a Watergate or Teapot Dome style scandal would have been virtually impossible under that law. Worse yet for the defendant, it was the Crown's judges who determined whether the utterance or writing was defamatory to the government. Needless to say, the prosecutors won nearly all of their cases, including one against Daniel Defoe for a satirical essay "Shortest Way with Dissenters." For his efforts Defoe was fined, pilloried and imprisoned.

Much the same fate befell a number of colonial printers and publishers until the royal governor of New York, William Cosby, instituted a prosecution for seditious libel against a New York printer, John Peter Zenger. Zenger had had the temerity to criticize Cosby's administration of the colony in the pages of his Weekly Journal. In the face of the uncontested fact of publication by Zenger and the common law of libel previously described, the jury refused to convict and the seed of a free press was planted in America.

Doubtless, then, with this history in mind, the press guarantee of the First Amendment was aimed at the very least at the abuses of licensing, censorship and punishment of political expression. Indeed, when Alexander Hamilton asked what was meant by freedom of the press, Madison responded that it meant freedom from despotic control by the federal government. Beyond this, the drafters failed to hand down to us any clear theory of the Amendment.

Only after the outbreak of World War I and the consequent increase in radical agitation in the country, did the Supreme Court and constitutional scholars begin to search for coherent theories to explain the allowance or suppression of expression in specific cases. This search for theory was further encouraged by the ruling in Gitlow v. New York (1925) that the constraints of the First Amendment applied to the states through the operation of the due process clause of the Fourteenth Amendment.

2. Theories and Tests of the First Amendment

Over the years a number of general theories have been espoused to justify the existence of the First Amendment guarantees of free speech and free press. The most famous of these is the "free trade of ideas" espoused by Justices Holmes and Brandeis in their dissenting opinion in Abrams v. United States (1919) and their concurring opinion in Whitney v. California (1927). By this theory the First Amendment stands as a protector of truth emerging from the public discussion of competing ideas.

Another major theory is the so-called Meiklejohn interpretation of the First Amendment. Named after its leading proponent, Professor Alexander Meiklejohn, this interpretation, broadly stated, holds that ours is a self-governing society and the First Amendment protects the freedom of thought and expression directed to the process by which we govern ourselves. Thus, it is concerned with the need for the citizenry to acquire such qualities of mind and spirit and such information as will make possible responsible self-governance. Implicit in this form of government is the idea that while the people delegate certain responsibility to their elected representatives, they reserve for themselves the means to oversee their government and that the elected representatives may not abridge the freedom of the people in maintaining this oversight. Thus, in the Meiklejohn view, the central meaning of the First Amendment is the protection it affords to the public power of the people collectively to govern themselves. See Meiklejohn, "The First Amendment is an Absolute," 1961 Sup.Ct.Rev. 245, 253–263.

Practically, what this thesis translates into is absolute protection for all thought, expression and communication which bears on the citizen's role of self-government. Major emphasis is placed on political expression: punishment for seditious libel becomes an impossibility. But Meiklejohn would also include within the coverage of the First Amendment all aspects of educational, philosophical, scientific, literary and artistic endeavors because sensitivity to humanistic values and rationality in judgment are dependent upon these pursuits. Other expression not directly or indirectly related to the process of self-government would be beyond the pale of the First Amendment, as perhaps horror comic books.

Although no Supreme Court decision has completely accepted the Meiklejohn thesis, it has been embodied to some extent in the law of defamation. See e.g., New York Times Co. v. Sullivan (1964). There, the Court found the state's defamation law constitutionally deficient in failing to provide safeguards for freedom of speech and press in libel actions brought by public officials against critics of their official conduct. Justice Brennan, speaking for the Court, quoted James Madison. "If we advert to the nature of Republican Government, we shall find that the censorial power is in the people over the Government, and not in the Government over the people." This idea is, of course, at the heart of the Meiklejohn interpretation. See also Near v. Minnesota (1931) for an earlier Supreme Court expression of the same idea.

Other general theories of the First Amendment include the somewhat cynical "safety valve" idea of permitting individual members and groups in society to "let off steam" without seriously affecting the status quo, and the more idealistic belief that free expression is a necessary aspect of individual development and growth.

a. Absolutism

But these general theories and principles do not resolve hard cases. Thus, the quest has been for operative or functional tests permitting reasonably consistent decisions in the field of free expression.

The most extreme approach is the idea that the First Amendment provides a central core of protection for expression in all circumstances—the so-called absolutist approach. While this approach has been characterized as holding that the "no law" injunction of the First Amendment *means* no law, the absolutist schools of thought are more complex than that.

The absolutists agree that the First Amendment does provide a central core of protection, but to determine whether particular expression is protected in the face of governmental efforts at regulation, the broad language of the First Amendment must be defined. What does "no law" mean? What constitutes abridgment? And what is the expression that is to be protected? "No law" is defined generally to include not only statutes but administrative regulations promulgated pursuant to statutes, municipal ordinances, executive orders and court orders. Insofar as abridgment is concerned, the absolutists would permit limitations on free expression incidental to reasonable regulation promulgated pursuant to a "law" directed solely to controlling the time, place and manner of expression. In determining whether a challenged regulation is reasonable, the absolutists would reject any regulation based on a law that does not contain appropriate safeguards to limit administrative discretion. If such safeguards are present the absolutists would then look to see whether the regulation has created a sufficient inroad on expression by its nature, degree and impact so as to constitute an "abridgment" of free expression.

The key to understanding the absolutist's view of abridgment is recognition that regulation must relate only to time, place and manner of the presentation of expression and that such regulation must not be so restrictive as to interfere with the *substance* of expression. See, e.g., Saia v. New York (1948), in which Justice Douglas, an adherent of absolutism, while conceding that some narrow regulation of sound trucks to prevent abuses would be constitutionally permissible, held unconstitutional a local ordinance which forbade the use of sound amplification devices except with the permission of the chief of police. The grant of such permission was placed in the chief's sole discretion and thus under the ordinance he was in a position to determine not only the time, location and volume of operation but the kind of speech that might be amplified and the particular groups that might use amplification equipment.

Of the various absolutist views of the scope of the First Amendment, perhaps the most celebrated is that held by the late Justice Hugo Black. Justice Black was an adherent of the Holmes–Brandeis view of the First Amendment as primarily a protector of the free market in ideas. But he was wary of their "clear and present danger test" discussed below, because judges could hold that certain expression in certain circumstances failed the test for First Amendment protection. Rather, Justice Black came to believe that all ideas and their expressions, including the libelous and the obscene, are to be given absolute protection. This view of the scope of the First Amendment is, of course, more expansive than that taken by Meiklejohn and has never commanded majority adherence on the Court.

While Justice Black was an implacable foe of any infringement of free expression except the most incidental occasioned by reasonable "time, place and manner" regulation, "speech" and "press" were to him technical terms and only expression encompassed within those terms was to be protected. Justice Black normally defined "speech" and "press" more broadly than anyone else on the Court, but in the context of public demonstrations he defined "speech" very narrowly so as to exclude expression bound up with essentially physical conduct. For instance, in Adderley v. Florida (1966), he spoke for the Court in upholding the convictions of 32 students who demonstrated in a nonviolent manner on a nonpublic jail driveway to protest the arrests of fellow students and local segregation policies. The 32 were among 200 students who had apparently blocked the driveway and had engaged in singing, clapping and dancing to protest what they believed to be an unjust situation. Among the dissenters in the Adderley case were Justice Black's usual allies in First Amendment cases, Justices Douglas and Brennan and Chief Justice Warren.

At bottom, whatever their differences as to the reach of the First Amendment, the late Justice Black and the other absolutists were attempting to remove from the judiciary the power to balance the interest in free expression against the exigencies of the times. For them, the balance was struck once and for all in favor of freedom of speech and press by the drafters of the Bill of Rights and that balance may not be disturbed.

b. The "Clear and Present Danger" Test

Another approach reflective of the free trade of ideas approach, was the "clear and present danger" test. Proposed by Justice Holmes in Schenck v. United States (1919), the test permitted the punishment of expression when "the words used are used in such circumstances and are of such a nature as to create a clear and present danger that they will bring about the substantive evils that Congress has a right to prevent. It is a question of proximity and degree."

In Schenck, the expression was in the form of a leaflet authorized by the American Socialist Party attacking the Conscription Act of World War I and urging recent conscripts to resist serving in the armed forces by asserting their alleged rights under the Thirteenth Amendment. Defendant, an officer of the party, was indicted, inter alia, for conspiracy to violate the Espionage Act of 1917 by causing and attempting to cause insubordination in the military forces and obstruction of the recruiting and enlistment service during a period of war. In the circumstance of war time, Holmes, who had himself been an officer in the Union Army during the Civil War, found that the leaflet created a danger of disruption of the war effort of sufficient proximity and magnitude to permit punishment in the face of the sweeping guarantees of the First Amendment.

Aside from the problem that it frankly permits the Congress in certain circumstances to legislate punishment of expression, the test is vague and difficult to apply. As Brandeis and Holmes admitted in their concurring opinion in Whitney v. California (1927), the Supreme Court had not yet "fixed the standard by which to determine when a danger shall be deemed clear; how remote the danger may be and yet be deemed present; and what degree of evil shall be deemed sufficiently substantial to justify resort to abridgement of free speech and assembly as the means of protection."

Moreover, even if there were a common understanding of the meaning of the test, the results of its application to challenged legislation directly or indirectly prohibitive of expression would vary according to extrinsic circumstances such as war or peace, cold war or detente, and prosperity or depression. Expression that might be afforded First Amendment protection from legislative repression in one social context might be denied it in another, and the speaker or publisher would not know whether his particular expression was safeguarded until the courts passed upon it. Thus, the test might have the effect of discouraging borderline writings or utterances.

In recent years, doubts about the test by civil liberties oriented justices and constitutional scholars and the hostility of those more state security oriented, have sapped "clear and present danger" of its vitality as constitutional doctrine. For instance, Brandenburg v. Ohio (1969) involved a prosecution for violation by certain members of the Ku Klux Klan of the Ohio criminal syndicalism statute. Although this prosecution was much like earlier prosecutions in which the "clear and present danger" test had been employed (compare Whitney v. California (1927) involving a similar state criminal syndicalism statute), the per curiam opinion of the

Supreme Court striking down the state law as an infringement of the First Amendment did not mention the test. Rather, the Court simply drew a distinction between advocacy of forcible or illegal political action in the future and advocacy directed to inciting *imminent* lawless action and likely to produce just such action. Only the latter is unprotected speech.

In the field of political speech akin to seditious libel, the test now appears to be inoperative. But it may retain vitality in the narrow area of criminal contempt of court. Beginning with Bridges v. California (1941), the Supreme Court applied the test to determine whether out-of-court utterances or writings attempting to influence the outcome of pending judicial matters or to criticize or ridicule members of the judiciary for their conduct on the bench could be punished through contempt of court proceedings. The substantive evil to be guarded against by the judiciary's exercise of the contempt power in these cases was the subversion of the fair administration of justice. The question in each case then was whether the out-of-court expressions created a clear and present danger to the proper administration of justice. The Supreme Court held that under the circumstances of the cases the out-of-court attacks on the judiciary and their handling of pending matters did not pose the requisite danger and thus the contempt citations were violative of First Amendment guarantees. See Bridges v. California, supra; Pennekamp v. Florida (1946); Craig v. Harney (1947); Wood v. Georgia (1962). An important

theme in these cases is that judges are made of
sturdy stuff and will not be affected by such expression. It must be borne in mind, however, that the
last explicit application of the "clear and present
danger" test in a contempt case was in 1962.

c. Ad Hoc Balancing of Interests

In Justice Frankfurter's dissent in Bridges is the
seed of another general approach to First Amendment cases. In his opinion Justice Frankfurter
emphasized that other interests protected by the
Bill of Rights were also at stake—the interests of
due process of law and fair trial. He would not give
any special deference to the interests protected by
the First Amendment. "Free speech is not so absolute or irrational a conception as to imply paralysis
of the means for effective protection of all the
freedoms secured by the Bill of Rights.... In the
cases before us, the claims on behalf of freedom of
speech and of the press encounter claims on behalf
of liberties no less precious." Bridges v. California
(1941).

Frankfurter would resolve competing claims by
weighing their relative importance in each case. In
Bridges, he came to the conclusion that the interest
in the impartial administration of justice outweighed the competing interest in allowing the Los
Angeles Times through its editorial pages to attempt to prevent a judge from granting a request
for probation from several labor organizers convicted of strong arm tactics, or in allowing Harry
Bridges, a Pacific Coast longshoremen's union lead-

er, to proclaim in the newspapers his threat to tie up the entire Pacific Coast shipping business if a court order of which he disapproved was enforced.

Frankfurter's approach formed the basis for the ad hoc balancing of interests. This balancing of First Amendment interests was embraced by a majority of the Court in American Communications Association v. Douds (1950), in which certain labor unions attacked a provision of the Labor Management Relations Act barring unions from access to procedures important to the collective bargaining process unless their officers executed affidavits declaring, among other things, that they were not members of or affiliated with the Communist Party. The unions contended that the provision violated union leaders' fundamental rights guaranteed by the First Amendment such as the right to hold and express whatever political views they choose and to associate with whatever political groups they wish. In concluding that the section of the act was compatible with the First Amendment, Chief Justice Vinson weighed First Amendment interests against the interest to be fostered by the statute in question, i.e., interstate commerce free from the disruption of political strikes.

Perhaps the most explicit statement of this approach was made by Justice Harlan in Konigsberg v. State Bar of Cal. (1961). There Konigsberg, a candidate for admission to the California Bar, was denied a license to practice law because he had refused to answer questions put to him by a bar committee (acting as a state agency) concerning his alleged membership in the Communist Party. Konigsberg challenged the state's action on several grounds including violation of protected rights of free speech and association. In rejecting this challenge Justice Harlan said, "Whenever ... these constitutional protections are asserted against the exercise of valid governmental powers a reconciliation must be effected, and that perforce requires an appropriate weighing of the respective interests involved [citations omitted].... With more particular reference to the present context of a state decision as to character qualifications, it is difficult, indeed, to imagine a view of the constitutional protections of speech and association which would automatically and without consideration of the extent of the deterence of speech and association and of the importance of the state function, exclude all reference to prior speech or association on such issues [concerning bar membership] as character, purpose, credibility or intent." Following this standard, a majority of the Court found that the state's interest in safeguarding the bar from possible subversive influence outweighed interests protected by the First and Fourteenth Amendments.

The ad hoc balancing approach has the virtue of pragmatism. It recognizes the importance of First Amendment interests but permits the making of pragmatic judgments as to when those interests should prevail over other and conflicting interests, often of a state security nature. But this virtue may also be a vice, for the protections afforded by the First Amendment are stated in absolute terms and the Amendment makes no provision for restricting freedom of speech and press when other interests are in conflict. This approach also suffers from vagueness. Because it is ad hoc, no consistent weight can be given to conflicting interests and the lower court judges are left on their own to determine when First Amendment interests are outweighed. Under such an approach a judge's predilections either for state security or individual liberties may be easily rationalized and, as with the "clear and present danger" test, the individual can never have any advance notice whether his interest in freedom of expression will outweigh some competing interest of the state expressed in its legislation. See Frantz, "The First Amendment in the Balance," 71 Yale L.J. 1424, 1440–1443 (1962).

d. *Definitional Balancing*

Another approach to the balancing of government and speech interests was first enunciated in Chaplinsky v. New Hampshire (1942), which addressed the constitutionality of a New Hampshire statute construed to ban "words likely to cause an average addressee to fight."

In upholding the statute, the Court stated that certain classes of speech had never been thought to raise a constitutional problem. They included the lewd and obscene, the profane, the libelous and insulting or "fighting words."

At first glance this approach, placing entire classes of speech outside the protective ambit of the First Amendment, gives much more guidance for future decisions than the ad hoc approach. Often however, it creates a different uncertainty due to the difficulty of defining these classes of speech. Thus, the court has struggled for more than thirty years to define obscenity, a struggle that reduced Justice Stewart to declaring in Jacobellis v. Ohio (1964), that he couldn't define hard core pornography but he knew when he saw it. Similar problems exist with the definition of commercial speech. See, e.g., Central Hudson Gas & Electric Corp. v. Public Service Commission of New York (1980) (Justice Steven's concurring opinion).

The other problem with definitional balancing is that there is a danger of overreaching. Essentially, definitional balancing is a finding that the societal interest in restricting a certain type of speech always outweighs the value of that speech, regardless of context or circumstances. Thus, prior to 1964, there was no constitutional protection for libel, even for discussions of the performance of public officials. This, of course, was changed by New York Times Co. v. Sullivan.

The preceding approaches or tests have not been consistently applied by their proponents to all First Amendment problem areas and when they are applied the competing approaches do not always yield results in conflict with each other. But, again with the caveat that tests or theories cannot always be relied upon to predict the outcome of specific cases, an understanding of them is useful in predicting the direction of the Supreme Court in relation to the First Amendment.

3. Present Direction of the Supreme Court

The transition from the Burger Court to the Rehnquist Court has not presented anywhere near the radical change in direction that occurred between the Warren and Burger courts. Even though many of the Justices, especially the four newest (Kennedy, Souter, Thomas and Ginsburg) have not clearly articulated their approach to the First Amendment, it is possible to make some tentative judgments about the direction of the current Supreme Court regarding First Amendment philosophy.

It appears that the entire Court has embraced an ad hoc balancing approach, some justices perhaps more completely than others. This ad hoc balancing approach has produced a more limited view of the First Amendment than existed in the Warren era.

Often, as part of its attempt to balance the particular interests at stake, the Court will apply a "test" or set of guidelines to the specific facts of the case. For example, in Central Hudson Gas & Electric Corp. v. Public Service Commission of New York (1980), Justice Powell enunciated a four-part test to determine the constitutionality of restrictions on commercial speech. First, is the commercial speech protected by the First Amendment? (At a minimum, it should not involve illegal activity, nor should it be false or misleading.) Second, is there a substantial government interest in restricting the speech? Third, does the regulation directly advance the asserted government interest? Fourth, is the regulation no broader than necessary to serve the asserted government interest?

This "test" is typical of the Court's approach in that it forces the government to articulate a competing public interest that justifies restricting First Amendment rights, recognizes that such competing interests can outweigh First Amendment rights, and requires the government to narrowly tailor its restrictions. See also Press–Enterprise Company v. Superior Court (II) (1986).

Obviously, whenever ad hoc balancing is used, one of the keys is the weight given to the First Amendment interest involved. In the Court's eyes all First Amendment rights are not created equal. Rather, the Court has established at least three distinct hierarchies of speech that are used to determine the degree of First Amendment protection involved.

One hierarchy is based on the actual content of speech. In what is essentially a refined version of definitional balancing the Court has taken the position that protected expression is not monolithic but divisible into categories with the extent of First Amendment protection dependent upon the intrinsic worth of the expression in each category. See Young v. American Mini Theatres (1976); Federal Communications Commission v. Pacifica Foundation (1978) (opinion of Justice Stevens joined by Chief Justice Burger and Justice Rehnquist); Posadas de Puerto Rico Associates v. Tourism Company of Puerto Rico (1986). This position raises some very thorny questions for the courts: what criteria should they use in categorizing protected speech; how will individual judges be able to cast aside their own personal value systems in determining objectively the comparative worth of particular expression; and finally, what degree of First Amendment protection will be afforded each of the categories of expression?

The mode of transmission of speech is also used to determine the degree of First Amendment protection available. The Court has long held that differences in the characteristics of new media justify the application of different First Amendment standards. Thus, in Miami Herald Publishing Company v. Tornillo (1974) the Court declared unconstitutional a statute granting an individual attacked by a newspaper the right to have a response printed in that newspaper; yet the Court upheld a similar regulation applying to broadcasters in Red Lion Broadcasting Company v. FCC (1969). The Court reaffirmed its support of different standards for different media in City of Los Angeles v. Preferred Communications, Inc. (1986) (a case involving the constitutionality of cable franchising rules), but left the determination of the standard for cable to a future case. As new communication technologies proliferate, the Court may find it more and more difficult to differentiate them in terms of appropriate First Amendment standards.

Finally, recognizing that the right to publish news can be seriously restricted by limitations on the right to gather news, the Court has extended some First Amendment protection to newsgathering, often under the rhetoric of a right of access. See Branzburg v. Hayes (1972); Richmond Newspapers, Inc. v. Virginia (1980). However, the degree of protection afforded newsgathering is nowhere near as extensive as that given dissemination of news, a situation unlikely to change given Chief Justice Rehnquist's strong opposition to protection for newsgathering. See Gannett Co., Inc. v. De-Pasquale (1979).

The good news for advocates of strong First Amendment protection is that the decisions produced by the ad hoc balancing approach tend to make small adjustments in the law as opposed to sweeping changes.

The bad news is that because the ad hoc approach depends so heavily on the value that each Justice attaches to the government interest asserted, as well as to the speech involved, there is much less guidance for the lower courts. In addition, several of the Justices are increasingly evincing a willingness to accept state assertions as to the validity and importance of its interest without any requirement of proof. The increasing deference to the state's judgment clearly tilts the scales in favor of the restrictions at issue. See Posadas de Puerto Rico Associates v. Tourism Company of Puerto Rico (1986).

Further, predicting Supreme Court decisions has become very difficult. It appears that there now exists considerable reluctance upon the part of important segments of the media to chance litigation in the Supreme Court because of the Court's embrace of the ad hoc balancing philosophy. See, e.g., Street v. NBC (1981), in which NBC successfully defended a libel action in which a central issue was whether the rape prosecutrix in the famous "Scottsboro Boys" case of the 1930s was still a public figure more than 30 years later. The Sixth Circuit answered affirmatively, but when the Supreme Court granted Mrs. Street's petition to review that ruling, NBC, which had prevailed below, settled the suit, paying her a substantial sum of money, rather than face the Burger Court.

Other trends in the Court's approach to the First Amendment include a continued departure from the idea that time, place and manner restrictions on protected expression may not be influenced by the content of the expression except where captive or juvenile audiences are involved, i.e., the restrictions must be "content neutral." In Young v. American Mini Theatres, Inc. (1976), a five-justice majority upheld a Detroit zoning ordinance that required dispersal of "adult" bookstores and motion picture theatres but not other bookstores and theatres in order to protect established commercial and residential neighborhoods. This "place" restriction was justified on the basis of the type of books sold and the motion pictures exhibited. In other words, the majority "peeked" at the content of the expression here and, having peeked, upheld the place restriction embodied in the ordinance because of the content. See also City of Renton v. Playtime Theaters, Inc. (1986).

Also, in the past, the Court, perhaps to conserve judicial energy, occasionally avoided the philosophical struggle over the proper approach to the First Amendment by nullifying statutes, ordinances and governmental regulations infringing free expression simply on the basis of their "vagueness" or "overbreadth." See, e.g., Erznoznik v. Jacksonville (1975) (ordinance making it a public nuisance and a criminal offense for a drive-in movie theater to exhibit any film containing nudity if the screen is visible from the street held overbroad and struck down as violative of the First Amendment). But the Court now seems to be narrowing the application of the "vagueness" and "overbreadth" devices. See, e.g. Young v. American Mini Theatres, Inc. (1976) (all opinions); New York v. Ferber (1982) (statute prohibiting the promotion of a sexual performance by a child by distributing material which depicts such performances held not substantially overbroad).

Finally, the Court's application of the overbreadth doctrine may have changed considerably. The majority opinion in R.A.V. v. City of St. Paul, Minnesota (1992), written by Justice Scalia, has introduced an entirely new element to definitional balancing and overbreadth analysis. A city ordinance construed to apply only to fighting words was nevertheless unconstitutional on its face because it only applied to those arousing "anger, alarm or resentment in others on the basis of race, color, creed, religion or gender." According to Scalia, even categories of speech "not within the area of constitutionally protected speech," cannot be subjected to "content discrimination unrelated to their distinctively proscribable content." Because the antibias ordinance did not apply to other types of fighting words, it constituted impermissible content regulation. The four Justices who rejected this new approach to definitional balancing nevertheless found the ordinance substantially overbroad and thus, unconstitutional.

C. THE DICHOTOMY BETWEEN PRIOR RESTRAINT AND SUBSEQUENT PUNISHMENT OF EXPRESSION

On one point adherents of all schools of thought appear to agree. At a minimum the First Amendment was adopted to prevent the federal government—and later the state governments through the Fourteenth Amendment—from instituting a general system of prior restraint on speech or press similar to that employed in England and the Colonies in the seventeenth and eighteenth centuries, i.e., licensing of the press and censorship of expression.

There were those, including Blackstone in his Commentaries on the Laws of England, who believed that freedom of the press consisted only in proscribing prior restraints upon publication and that once publication was made the publisher had to accept the consequences which might be imposed upon him by an offended government or individual.

That First Amendment protection extended also to attempts by government to punish completed utterances and publications through imposition of criminal sanctions was not fully settled until the formulation of the "clear and present danger" test in Schenck v. United States (1919). And that the Amendment further provided the publisher or speaker some protection against subsequent civil defamation actions was not recognized until New York Times Co. v. Sullivan, supra.

Despite the fact that the threat of subsequent criminal punishment and civil judgments for damages may have a substantial deterrent effect upon free expression, the Supreme Court has not, as indicated in the preceding sections, achieved anywhere near the consistency of doctrine that it has regarding the condemnation of administrative and judicial prior restraints.

There are many reasons besides the historical for the Court's hostility toward governmental action smacking of prior restraint. Professor Emerson in his classic article "The Doctrine of Prior Restraint," 20 Law and Contemporary Problems 648 (1955), provides us with a modern catalogue of these reasons. A system of prior restraint is broader in its coverage, more uniform in its effect and more easily and effectively enforced than subsequent punishment. Everything which is published or publicly uttered would be subject to scrutiny. Then, too, expression which is banned never sees the light of day and that which is not banned may be so delayed in the administrative mill that it becomes superfluous or obsolete when it is "cleared." The procedural safeguards of the criminal judicial process, including public scrutiny, are not present to the same degree in the administrative censorial process. Finally, the entire process is geared toward suppression and the censor will be impelled to find things to suppress.

The landmark case recognizing the dangers of prior restraint is Near v. Minnesota (1931). There, a state statute provided for the abatement as a public nuisance of "malicious, scandalous, and defamatory" publications. The statute further provided that all persons guilty of such a nuisance could be permanently enjoined from further publication of malicious, scandalous and defamatory matter. A county attorney brought an action under the statute to enjoin The Saturday Press on the ground that it accused law enforcement agencies and officials of the city of Minneapolis with failing to stop vice and racketeering activities allegedly controlled by a "Jewish Gangster." In the face of the publisher's claim that his activities were protected by the First and Fourteenth Amendments, the trial court perpetually enjoined him from conducting a public nuisance under the name of The Saturday Press or any other name. The state supreme court affirmed the injunctive order. The United States Supreme Court reversed. Cutting through the peculiar procedures of the statute, the Court indicated that its object and effect was to suppress further publication. This they equated to prior restraint of the press. Moreover, if the person enjoined were so bold as to resume his or her publishing activities, he or she would have to submit the material to the appropriate judicial officer for clearance prior to publication in order to avoid being held in contempt of court for violation of the injunctive order. To the Court this constituted effective censorship prohibited by the due process clauses of the First and Fourteenth Amendments.

This decision stands out for many reasons. It was the Court's first definitive statement concerning the constitutionality of prior restraint on expression. More than this, it made clear that what was important was not the form governmental action took but its effect on speech and press. And because it indicated that the constitutional ban on prior restraints was not absolute and did permit certain narrow exceptions, it opened up the question of the precise limits of the First Amendment in this area. Finally, it made the point very clearly that while expression was generally protected from prior restraint, it might subsequently be punished if it were determined that the expression was unlawful. This dichotomy drawn by the Court in Near persists today. It was relied upon expressly by four of the Justices in their separate opinions in New York Times Co. v. United States (1971) (the "Pentagon Papers" case). See also Vance v. Universal Amusement Co., Inc. (1980).

D. INFORMATION AS PROPERTY

As the United States moves further towards an information-based economy, there is an increasing

conflict between the property rights in information
and the free flow of ideas protected by the First
Amendment.

1. Conflict Between Economic Interests and Information Flow

The primary motivation for information owners
restricting others' First Amendment rights is an
economic one. Often it is simply a question of
seeking compensation for what is seen as the use of
someone else's property. In other words, anyone
who is willing to pay can disseminate the information. Other times the purpose is to obtain a competitive edge through exclusive coverage of a news
or entertainment event. For example, ABC originally claimed exclusive rights to some of the July 4,
1986 Statue of Liberty festivities.

Sometimes, however, the primary motivation is
not an economic one. For example, a Boston cable
news channel attempted unsuccessfully to prevent
Congressional candidate James Roosevelt from using an unauthorized tape of its interview with his
opponent, Joseph Kennedy, in his campaign advertisements. The cable channel claimed that this
particular use of its programming would damage its
credibility as a news organization.

In another case author J.D. Salinger sought to
enjoin a biography of him containing excerpts from
personal letters that he had donated to various
school libraries. Here, the issue was not who would
get to distribute the information or profit from it,
but whether it would be distributed at all.

The conflict between information rights and First Amendment values can take place within the framework of many different areas of the law including right of publicity, trademark law, trade secret law, and contract law. However, copyright law is probably the best illustration of the problems raised by the conflict and attempts to strike an accommodation between these competing interests.

2. Copyright and the First Amendment

The legal concepts of American copyright law and the provisions of the Copyright Act of 1976, 17 U.S.C.A. § 101 et seq., 90 Stat. 2541 (1976) are summarized in another volume of the "Nutshell" series and will not be generally repeated here. It is enough to say that the Congress, pursuant to constitutional authority, can and does protect the owners of intellectual property in fixed form such as writings, photographs, and sight and sound recordings from having their creations copied and appropriated by others. Such copying and appropriation of copyrighted works constitutes infringement for which the copyright holder may seek civil remedies and the federal government may in certain cases seek criminal sanctions.

Although the aim of copyright law to encourage the production of intellectual property is laudable, it can have the effect of limiting distribution of copyrighted material even in the face of First Amendment claims by the news media.

Thus in Roy Export Co. v. Columbia Broadcasting System, Inc. (1982), CBS's claim of First Amendment protection in the use, on the occasion of Charlie Chaplin's death, of a special compilation of excerpts from Chaplin's motion pictures in which Roy Export Co. held the copyright was rejected by the United States Court of Appeals. In affirming that CBS had been guilty of copyright infringement in using "the compilation" originally prepared for the 1972 Academy Award Presentations during which Chaplin received a special "Oscar," the Second Circuit made clear that it would be a very rare case in which copyrighted material was so imbued with news value as to subordinate the copyright holder's protection to First Amendment claims.

It should be noted, however, that raw news and information are not subject to copyright and are in the public domain for anyone to disseminate. See International News Service v. Associated Press (1918) in which the Supreme Court recognized that the substance of the news of the day was not copyrightable because of the obvious public policy that such history should be made freely available to all. But the way news or information is organized, including the words used and the manner chosen by the reporter or publisher to express the news or information gathered, is copyrightable.

Sometimes the line between the news and someone's expression of the news is a difficult one to draw. The determination of when two descriptions of an event are similar enough to constitute copyright infringement is not governed by any clear guidelines.

It should be obvious that copyright protection provides a serious limitation on the use of existing material by the news media. But the nonconstitutional "fair use" defense to copyright infringement suits provides at least limited protection for First Amendment values by affording journalists some right to publish copyrighted material.

This defense is not statutory in origin but was created by the courts, apparently in the belief that public policy requires persons other than the copyright owner to be able to use the owner's work under strictly limited conditions in certain contexts in which it will be of value to the public. This defense has often been misunderstood by the courts and has not been defined with any great precision. Nevertheless, certain features of the defense can be discerned. One may be protected in copying another's copyrighted work where the copying is not likely to hurt the present and potential markets for the copyrighted work and where the copying is likely to be of substantial benefit to the public. In determining whether the use of another's creation is a "fair use," the purpose of the defendant's work, the amount of copying involved, the public interest in the copyrighted material, the nature of the media involved and the effect of the copying on the market value of the plaintiff's work are all factors to be considered. An example of the balancing of these factors is Time, Inc. v. Bernard Geis Associates (1968), in which a book publisher reproduced several frames of the Zapruder home movie of the Kennedy assassination in a book about the assassina-

tion. In holding the reproduction of the frames a
fair use, the court balanced the great public interest
in information concerning the assassination against
the doubtful effect of the reproduction on the market value of Time, Inc.'s copyright in the entire
film.

These principles have now been given explicit
statutory recognition in § 107 of the 1976 Copyright Act which states that in determining whether
the use made of a work in any particular case is a
fair use, the following four factors shall be considered:

  1. the purpose and character of the use, including whether such use is of a commercial
  nature or is for nonprofit educational purposes;

  2. the nature of the copyrighted work;

  3. the amount and substantiality of the portion used in relation to the copyrighted work as a
  whole; and

  4. the effect of the use upon the potential
  market for or value of the copyrighted work. 17
  U.S.C.A. § 107.

The public interest is central to a successful invo-
cation of the fair use defense. Statutory protection
of expression encourages authors and artists to continue to produce original works; continued production and dissemination of these works aids the flow
of ideas throughout society. But statutory protection can also retard the flow of ideas, offering a
work so much protection that the ideas contained

therein are no longer free to enter the marketplace. The fair use defense moderates this overprotection, thus stimulating the circulation in society of the ideas and information that the copyrighted work contains. This rationale for the defense explains some of the more common examples of fair use, such as the quotation or paraphrase of passages from books in book reviews and the limited quotation of copyrighted materials in news stories.

At bottom, then, two elements predominate in determining the availability of the fair use defense: (1) the intensity of the public interest in the free dissemination of portions of particular copyrighted works (e.g., the desire of the public for as much opinion and information about the Kennedy assassination as possible); and (2) the effect such free dissemination will have on the property value of or income from the particular copyrighted work (e.g., parody of a literary work or motion picture in such detail that an audience exposed to the parody will have little desire to pay for the privilege of reading or viewing the original).

Harper & Row Publishers, Inc. v. Nation Enterprises (1985) is a good example of the difficulty of applying the fair use defense in a "news" context. Harper & Row had contracted for various exclusive rights to President Gerald Ford's memoirs, "A Time to Heal," including the right to license prepublication excerpts. Harper & Row had then granted Time Magazine the right to excerpt 7,500 words from President Ford's account of his decision to pardon President Nixon in return for $25,000 (half in advance), such publication to take place one week before the publication of the book. Prior to Time's scheduled publication, Victor Nevasky, editor of The Nation Magazine, obtained an unauthorized copy of "A Time to Heal." Working directly from this manuscript, he produced a 2,250 word article consisting exclusively of quotes, paraphrases and facts drawn from the Ford manuscript. This article appeared before the scheduled publication of the Time article. As a result Time did not publish its article and refused to pay Harper & Row the remaining $12,500.

In the ensuing copyright action, The Nation relied on fair use and the First Amendment to defend its actions. In a 6 – 3 decision the Court held that The Nation's excerpt was not a fair use. In applying the four factors of fair use, the Court first held that the general purpose was indeed news reporting, but that the more specific purpose was to supplant "the copyright holder's commercially valuable right of first publication."

In examining the nature of the copyrighted work, the Court acknowledged that it was a factual work and that the need to disseminate factual works is greater than that for fictional works. Having done so, however, the Court then focused on the unpublished nature of the work and decided that fair use has a more limited application to *unpublished* works.

A key issue was the amount and substantiality of the portion used. Here, although there was some dispute as to exactly how much of The Nation's article consisted of infringing material, it was clear that overall it was a very small amount when compared to the entire text of "A Time to Heal." The Court, however, viewed this as a qualitative as well as a quantitative issue, and found that the material on the Nixon pardon was the heart of the book and that the quotes used in The Nation's article were the essence of that article. In that sense the portion used was substantial.

For the Court, the easiest part of the test was the effect on the market for the copyrighted work. Harper & Row had lost $12,500 when Time cancelled its projected article as a result of The Nation's article. When considered in conjunction with the analysis of the other three factors, the finding against fair use was clear.

Justice Brennan wrote a sharp dissent accusing the majority of extending copyright protection to information and ideas. In his view the purpose of the work—news reporting—and the nature of the copyrighted work—historical and factual—supported a fair use defense. He found the amount taken not to be excessive even though it dealt with the most important part of the book. Because he believed that the cancellation by Time was as much a result of information contained in The Nation article as expression appropriated from Ford's book, he did not find that the infringement had any serious effect on the market for the copyrighted material.

The significance of this case is in some ways difficult to determine. Some would argue it is limited to the rather unusual facts of the case. Although there was no proof the manuscript was stolen, the Court appeared to assume that it was. Also, the infringing work was published prior to the copyrighted work, a fact emphasized by the Court. Given that most fair use cases involve someone copying an already published work, it may be relatively easy to distinguish Harper & Row.

On the other hand, if it operates, as Justice Brennan suggests, to restrict the fair use defense to a point where information itself acquires some copyright protection, then it presents a serious threat to the free flow of information protected by the First Amendment.

The limitations of fair use as a vehicle for First Amendment protection became even more apparent in Salinger v. Random House, Inc. (1987). Author J.D. Salinger sought to restrain the publication of a biography of him on the grounds that it contained excerpts from copyrighted letters that he had written. The biographer, Ian Hamilton, had obtained copies of the letters from various college libraries to which they had been donated by their recipients. As in Harper & Row the case was treated strictly as a copyright case with no real First Amendment issues. For the court of appeals, the key question was whether or not the use of the excerpts from the letters constituted fair use.

The court of appeals relied heavily on Harper & Row for its fair use analysis because it was "the court's first delineation of the scope of fair use as applied to unpublished works."

In considering the application of the four fair use factors to Hamilton's use of the Salinger letters, the court started by categorizing the purpose of the use alternatively as "criticism," "scholarship," or "research." All of these categories are viewed as appropriate to a fair use. The court went on, however, to specifically reject the idea that a biographer is entitled to an especially generous application of the defense.

The court noted that as long as the biographer took only the factual content of the letter, there was no copyright problem. But the court did not recognize any need to take the expression contained in the letter.

Turning to the second factor, the court focused on the unpublished nature of the work as being of critical importance. In essence, the court viewed it as creating a heavy presumption against a finding of fair use.

With regard to the amount and substantiality of the use, the court of appeals found that copyrighted expression was used on at least 40% of the book's 192 pages.

Finally, the court found that due to the substantial amount taken by Hamilton and his extensive use of the phrases "he wrote" and "he said" that at least some members of the public might be misled into believing that they had read the essence of Salinger's letters, thus reducing the potential market for a book of his letters. This led the court of appeals to conclude that the fourth fair use factor—effect on the potential market for the work—weighed slightly in Salinger's favor. Based on this analysis the court ordered an injunction prohibiting the sale of the biography.

Similarly, the court of appeals reversed a district court's finding that the First Amendment precluded an injunction against an infringing work in New Era Publications International v. Henry Holt & Co. (1989). The case involved a biography of L. Ron Hubbard, the founder of the Church of Scientology. Russell Miller, the author of "Bare–Faced Messiah," had used quotations from Hubbard's own unpublished letters and diaries to support his contention that Hubbard was a bigot and a hypocrite. The district court, despite finding that the quotations exceeded the bounds of fair use, had denied a request for an injunction. Noting the "abhorrence of the First Amendment to prior restraint," the district court concluded that the damage remedy would adequately protect the copyright holder's interests.

The court of appeals upheld the denial of the injunction, but only on the ground of laches. With regard to the First Amendment question the court concluded that all First Amendment claims were encompassed by the fair use doctrine and thus, no separate First Amendment analysis was warranted.

In Wright v. Warner Books, Inc. (1991), the court of appeals seemingly retreated somewhat from its position on the application of fair use analysis to unpublished works, when it upheld a district court finding that the use of excerpts of unpublished letters in a biography of Richard Wright was a fair use. However, the court once again failed to apply a separate First Amendment analysis.

Just to be certain that the judges of the Second Circuit did not regress to their earlier approach, the Congress in 1992 enacted, and President Bush signed, legislation adding the following language to the Fair Use Section of the Copyright Act. 17 U.S.C.A. § 107: "The fact that a work is unpublished shall not by itself bar a finding of fair use if such finding is made upon consideration of all the above factors."

Perhaps the most important conclusion that can be drawn from Salinger, New Era and Wright is that courts are unwilling to examine any copyright case for First Amendment problems. The assumption is that the idea-expression dichotomy and the defense of fair use provide a proper accommodation between the sometimes competing interests. The distinction between prior restraint and subsequent punishment recognized by the Supreme Court in Near and the "Pentagon Papers" case does not apply to copyright cases.

Thus in Salinger and New Era the court of appeals was not concerned that the expression in Salinger's letters or the evidence for Miller's assertions about Hubbard might be withheld from the public for many years. Nor did the court address the fact that the real interests of the copyright holders (privacy in Salinger and limiting criticism in New Era) would have been insufficient to justify an injunction had the cases been subjected to First Amendment as opposed to copyright analysis.

Parodies present another troubling conflict between the property rights protected by copyright and the free flow of ideas protected by the First Amendment. In Campbell v. Acuff–Rose (1993), the Sixth Circuit, rejecting a claim of fair use, found 2 Live Crew's song "Pretty Woman" had infringed the copyright for Roy Orbison's "Oh, Pretty Woman." The Supreme Court reversed, holding that the court of appeals' fair use analysis was flawed.

The first error was holding that the parody was presumptively unfair because of its commercial nature. The Court held that § 107 does not set out bright line rules, but rather calls for case-by-case analysis. Thus, in terms of the purpose of the use, the fact that the song was a parody weighed in favor of fair use, while the fact that it was commercial weighed against it.

A second error was holding that because the parody took the heart of the song, the amount and substantiality taken from the original was too great. As the Court noted, in order for a parody to be effective, it must take enough so as to make it clear what work is being parodied. Sometimes this makes it necessary to take the heart of the work, in this case the opening bass line. Thus, in applying the third fair use factor, it is necessary to examine the context. Taking only the amount necessary to conjure up the original favors a finding of fair use.

The final error was presuming from the commercial nature of the parody that it had harmed the market for the original. The Court explained that there are two ways a parody can harm the market for the parodied work. The first, offering a substitute for the original work or for any potential derivative work (such as a rap version of the original), weighs heavily against a finding of fair use. Damage to the original resulting from the criticism expressed in the parody, however, does not weigh against fair use. The case was remanded for further proceedings consistent with the Court's opinion.

As illustrated by these recent copyright cases, there is an increasing conflict between property rights in information and the free flow of ideas protected by the First Amendment. Courts attempting to balance these sometimes competing interests have so far produced inconsistent results.

In the chapters that follow, the First Amendment will be considered in several specific contexts. These include the permissible scope of defamation and invasion of privacy actions in tort, the efforts of government to suppress pornography, the possible conflict between protection of a free press and the

Fifth and Sixth Amendment guarantees of a fair and impartial trial, the existence, or non-existence of a newsperson's privilege not to reveal his or her sources of information when compelled to do so, and the permissible limits of governmental regulation of advertising.

Traditionally, these First Amendment problem areas have involved questions concerning the limitation on the power of government or its agencies to act in certain ways, e.g., the power of courts to enter judgments in defamation actions. But we will also advert to a theory largely developed by Dean Jerome A. Barron that the First Amendment actually compels the government to act affirmatively to insure freedom of expression by requiring citizen access to the mass media. While this theory has been rejected by the Supreme Court with regard to the print media, it has been instrumental in forcing a wide ranging re-examination of the nature of the First Amendment in the late twentieth century.

CHAPTER II

DEFAMATION AND MASS COMMUNICATION

A. INTERESTS IN CONFLICT

One of the interests that has competed with the interest in freedom of expression down through the centuries is that of reputation, both personal and proprietary. The importance of this interest should not be minimized. As Justice Stewart said in his concurring opinion in Rosenblatt v. Baer (1966), "The right of a man to the protection of his own reputation from unjustified invasion and wrongful hurt reflects no more than our basic concept of the essential dignity and worth of every human being— a concept at the root of any decent system of ordered liberty."

The early common law courts considered reputation to be an interest deserving of protection by recognizing an action for money damages to compensate for injury resulting from defamatory communications. This action has evolved into the complex (some would say "confused and confusing") twin tort actions of libel and slander. There is no doubt that the ever present fear that one may have to respond in damages for what one publishes has a limiting effect on the work of the modern journalist or public speaker. It has been reported that one of the reasons for the demise of Pulitzer's New York World was the drain on its resources from numerous libel actions brought against the paper.

The thrust of the recent significant cases in the field of defamation has been the recognition of the unavoidable conflict between these two interests and the attempt to provide a measure of legal protection for both.

B. COMMON LAW DEFAMATION

1. Definition and Elements

Defamation has been defined as the injury to reputation by words that tend to expose one to public hatred, shame, contempt or disgrace, or to induce an evil opinion of one in the minds of right-thinking persons and to deprive one of their confidence. Kimmerle v. New York Evening Journal (1933). While this definition provides a good starting place for understanding the nature of defamation, it fails to place any emphasis on loss of reputation in one's business or profession. Moreover, the loss of reputation need only be with regard to a small but significant segment of the community, whether "right-thinking" or not. Finally, as the late Dean William L. Prosser pointed out, one may be defamed by imputations of insanity or poverty, which would instead arouse pity or sympathy—feelings that diminish esteem and respect. W. P. Keeton, editor, Prosser and Keeton on the Law of Torts 773 (5th Ed. 1984). An example of this would be a false statement that an individual is a hopeless alcoholic.

In the past, defamation actions have been either criminal or civil in nature. But in recent years, with the notable exception of the state's prosecution of New Orleans district attorney James Garrison for his verbal attacks on certain sitting criminal court judges (Garrison v. Louisiana (1964)), the criminal action has largely fallen into disuse. Perhaps this is because of its odious historical association with prosecutions for political sedition. In any event, the focus of this chapter will be the modern civil actions of libel and slander.

The essential elements common to both libel and slander actions are (1) the making by the defendant of a defamatory statement; (2) the publication to at least one other than the plaintiff of that statement; and (3) the identification in some way of the plaintiff as the person defamed.

a. The Defamatory Statement

The words complained of must be such as will injure the reputation of a living person or existing organization because only the injured party may sue for defamation. Some words such as "thief," "cheat," "murderer" or "whore" are almost universally understood to hurt someone's reputation. Other words may have that effect in relation to the times and the victim's position. Falsely labeling one a Communist during the World War II period of United States–Soviet cooperation was not actionable. But the same false label was considered defamatory after the commencement of the "Cold War."

In general, defamation suits tend to involve false charges that fall into the following categories:

1. accusation of a crime
2. sexual impropriety or other immoral behavior
3. having a loathsome disease or being mentally ill
4. professional incompetence or misconduct in one's business
5. bankruptcy, financial irresponsibility or dishonesty
6. disgraceful behavior such as child abuse or substance abuse
7. criticism of a product (trade libel).

The plaintiff's situation in life may also give a damaging effect to otherwise innocent words. The selling of pork is normally a respectable occupation, but suggesting that a kosher butcher sells bacon has been considered defamatory, for clearly it would cause religiously oriented customers to think less of the butcher and to take their business elsewhere. See Braun v. Armour & Co. (1930).

Defamatory words can be presented in numerous ways. One need not attack with a verbal axe. The stiletto of ridicule may suffice. Provided that even one person other than the plaintiff understands the communication to be defamatory and such understanding is reasonable, given its content and context, a court may accept the plaintiff's argument that it is defamatory. Of course, the defendant may attempt to show that the communication had at least one nondefamatory meaning and others understand it in that sense, or that the communication was made in jest and could not reasonably be taken seriously. Courts in Illinois, for example, have fashioned the "innocent construction rule" which gives defendants the benefit of the doubt; in other words, if there are two reasonable ways to interpret a statement, one defamatory and the other nondefamatory, the court will choose the "innocent" meaning. But the great majority of states do not follow this rule.

b. Publication

Publication is a legal term of art meaning that the defamatory communication, whatever its form, has been perceived by someone other than the person defamed. Publication in the sense of printing and distribution of printed matter is not required. For example, publication occurs if a patient makes a serious statement in a loud voice in a crowded waiting room directly to a licensed physician that he or she is a "quack" and the statement is overheard by one or more of the other patients.

In this situation, it is clear that the communicator either intends that others overhear his or her accusation or is so uncaring whether it is overheard as to be deemed reckless in his or her conduct. But where one does not intend the communication to be conveyed to anyone other than the target of his or her attack, and the means chosen to convey the communication will in the normal course prevent reception by third persons, there is no publication. For instance, Able writes his former business partner Baker a letter in which he accuses Baker of causing the downfall of their business by "stealing the company blind." Able places the letter in a sealed envelope, marks it "personal," addresses it to Baker and mails it to his house. Baker's son, curious about the letter from his father's former associate, opens and reads the letter prior to Baker and without authority. There is no publication here and hence, no actionable defamation.

Moreover, since it is the *defamer* who must intentionally or recklessly promote publication, the requirement is not met by the victim himself or herself publicizing the communication to others. If in the above hypothetical, Baker opened the letter and then showed the letter to his son, the result would be the same—no publication. Where there is publication, however, repetition of the original defamation by persons other than the victim constitutes republication for which the original communicator will also be held liable provided the republication is foreseeable. Of course, the person who does the republishing may also be held liable.

A question of special significance to the print media is whether the distribution of each copy of a press run is a separate publication providing the basis for multiple defamation actions or whether the press run is to be viewed as constituting one publication. The early English cases suggested the first alternative but they were decided before the advent of high speed presses, large press runs and mass distribution. Shortly before World War II American courts began to move toward what has become known as the "single publication rule." The rule provides that only one cause of action for defamation arises when the product of a press run or printing is released by the publisher for distribution, no matter how many separate transactions may result. A corollary is that the statute of limitations for defamation commences to run from the moment of first release. See Gregoire v. G.P. Putnam's Sons (1948), the leading case for the single publication rule, holding that a libel action based on the sale of a single copy of a book whose last printing was more than two years prior to the sale was barred by New York's one-year statute of limitation. Reinforcing this judicial trend is the Uniform Single Publication Act (see Restatement (Second) of Torts § 577A) promulgated by the National Conference on Uniform State Laws in 1952. This model legislation extends the single publication concept to radio, television and motion pictures. The act has been adopted by statute in nine states, including California, Illinois and Pennsylvania, and has been adopted by judicial decision in 17 states. See Keeton v. Hustler Magazine (1988).

c. *Identification*

Published defamation is not actionable unless the complaining party can establish that it was he or she who was defamed. Very often the target of a defamatory communication is not clearly named therein and thus the identification of the complaining party with the communication becomes a problem of analyzing extrinsic circumstances.

Identification may also be difficult when a group is defamed. In the past it was possible to criminally libel a large group or race of people, as in Beauharnais v. Illinois (1952). In this case white racist Joseph Beauharnais was fined $200 for distributing pamphlets insulting to blacks who were integrating the white Chicago suburb of Cicero. The Supreme Court upheld Beauharnais' conviction on the grounds that such libelous speech was not protected by the First Amendment. Most legal scholars would probably agree that the Beauharnais ruling is no longer viable, however, in light of New York Times Co. v. Sullivan, discussed below. The recent case of R.A.V. v. City of St. Paul, Minnesota (1992), in which the Supreme Court struck down a St. Paul ordinance against hate speech, further suggests that Beauharnais may no longer be viable.

In the four decades since Beauharnais, the general rule has changed so that the courts will not entertain an action for group libel when the complainant is a member of a large group which has been defamed. In the case of defamation of small homogeneous groups, the courts will permit actions by the individual members of the group. But how many people constitute a small group? There is no magic number, but any group under 100 may be small enough for a court to find that one or more members have been identified. The inclusiveness of the language affects identification; generally, a court will ask a jury to determine the degree to which other people would find a defamatory statement attaching to an individual or to everyone in the group. For example, in Fawcett Publications v. Morris (1962), a member of the 1956 University of Oklahoma football team sued *True* magazine when it published an article implying that the Sooners had used stimulative drugs. Although no players were named in the article and over 60 were on the squad, the Oklahoma Supreme Court held that the suit could be maintained, concluding that the article defamed every member of the team, including the plaintiff. Some courts will allow individual actions by certain members of small groups when the defamatory communication is directed to a segment of the group. Of course, in this last case the plaintiff must convince the finder of fact (normally the jury) that he or she was a member of the segment attacked. See Neiman–Marcus Co. v. Lait (1952) for an application of these rules regarding civil actions for group defamation, and Hudson v. Guy Gannett Broadcasting Co. (1987).

d. Economic Loss

In addition to establishing the defamatory nature of the communication, its publication and the necessary identification, the plaintiff in certain cases must also plead and prove that he suffered actual pecuniary or economic loss (special damages). In determining when this additional requirement must be met, we are confronted with the herculean task of sorting out libel from slander, libel per se from libel per quod and slander per se from all other slander.

2. The Contrast Between Libel and Slander

Broadly differentiated, the tort of libel includes defamatory communications of a more or less permanent sort such as printed material, photographs, paintings, motion pictures, signboards, effigies and even statuary, while slander includes more ephemeral communications such as the spoken word, gestures and sign language. The distinction arises out of the historical development of common law court jurisdiction. In wresting jurisdiction from the ecclesiastical courts of England, which heard cases of slander, and in succeeding to the jurisdiction of the notorious Star Chamber over printed defamation, the common law courts kept the two types of defamation separate. See Donnelly, "History of Defamation," 1949 Wis.L.Rev. 99.

While classification of communications as slander or libel might not have been too difficult in the late seventeenth century with the limited communications then available, it becomes troublesome in an electronic age with its dependence on telephones, radio, television and even computers for communication. Indeed, the courts have never agreed on the taxonomy of radio and television defamation. For example, in eight states including California, a defamatory broadcast is considered to be slander. Connecticut and Tennessee, seeking greater discrimination, classify it as libel if read from a script and slander if the remark is ad libbed. Courts in 13 states have held that broadcasting is libel. But the majority of states do not distinguish between libel and slander with regard to broadcasting; instead, they simply refer to "broadcast defamation" and courts deal with it under the general laws of defamation in those states. See H. R. Kaufman, ed., Libel Defense Resource Center, 50 State Survey: Current Developments in Media Libel and Invasion of Privacy Law, Vol. 9, 1993.

What too many courts appear to do when they are confronted with defamation via a new medium is to fix their gaze on the medium rather than on the interest the law is trying to protect and the reasons supporting the libel-slander dichotomy. The interest is, of course, reputation and the sting of defamation is its injury to reputation. Initially, the main justification for labeling writings as libelous, with concomitantly more serious consequences, including fine or imprisonment, was the greater permanence of the defamation and the correspondingly greater potential for wider distribution and greater injury to the victim. Today, no medium surpasses radio, television and cable in wide distributive power. The potential injury to reputation from electronic defamation is devastating and on principle justifies the libel classification whether the defamation is read from a script or made extemporaneously.

There is no real way to avoid the troublesome task of classifying defamation since the requirement of special damages rests upon that classification. Generally, if the defamatory communication is held to constitute libel, the complaining party is not required to plead and prove as part of his or her case actual pecuniary loss resulting from the libel. On the other hand, if the communication is categorized as a slander, the complaining party generally has to establish such loss. As a practical matter many slander suits are quashed in the law office when the angry prospective plaintiff is informed by his or her own attorney to forget a lawsuit because he or she has no out-of-pocket loss. There is, however, a qualification to the requirement of financial sting in slander actions.

a. The Special Cases of Slander

As another matter of jurisdictional development, the common law courts established three special categories of slander which were to be actionable without regard to the existence of special damages: (1) imputation of crimes recognized by the common law courts; (2) imputation of certain loathsome diseases (limited to sexually transmitted diseases, leprosy and the black plague); and (3) imputations affecting the victim in his or her business, trade, profession or office. Later, by statute or common law decision a fourth category, the imputation of unchastity to a woman, was created. These four categories of slander continue to be recognized by most courts as permitting a plaintiff to sue his or her slanderer without establishing special damages. The scope of the categories has not changed greatly over the years, despite the fact that the fourth category reflects our society's double standard: calling a woman unchaste is slander *per se*, but accusing a man of promiscuity is slander but not slander *per se*. The present day test for the imputation of criminal conduct is whether the conduct involves moral turpitude. Thus today, a false oral allegation to a third party that "X" embezzles from his employer would be actionable in most American jurisdictions without the need for "X" to establish pecuniary loss.

While from a plaintiff's perspective the existence of these special categories provides a liberalizing force in the law of slander, a somewhat parallel development in the law of libel has had the opposite effect.

b. *Libel Per Se and Per Quod*

As the tort of libel developed, the rule became fixed that in contrast to slander actions, special damages need not be pleaded and proven by the plaintiff in order for him or her to recover. An explanation often given for this distinction is that the written communication once had greater potential for mischief because of its more permanent form. Therefore, some injury to the victim could be conclusively presumed.

No distinction was drawn by the courts between those libelous communications plain upon their face (libel *per se*) such as "John Doe is a bastard" and those which require reference to extrinsic circumstances to give them the necessary defamatory meaning (libel *per quod*). The classic example of libel per quod is the erroneous newspaper story stating that Mary Doe of 1234 Shady Lane has just given birth to twins at a local hospital. The story is libelous because of the extrinsic fact that Mrs. Doe has been married only one month before and several persons reading the story know this fact.

Originally, then, if the defamatory communication was broadly classified as libel, special damages were not essential to a successful action. This is still stated to be the majority rule by the American Law Institute's Restatement of the Law of Torts Second, Section 569. But the late Dean William L. Prosser noted that at least 35 American jurisdictions draw a distinction between libel per se and per quod and hold that libel per quod is to be treated like slander, meaning that it is actionable only with the pleading and proving of special damages unless the libel falls within one or more of the four special categories associated with slander. W. Prosser, Handbook of the Law of Torts (4th ed. 1971) 763. Moreover, the presumption of damage required by libel per se is now constitutionally suspect with regard to libelous communication of public concern not made with actual malice. See Gertz v. Robert Welch, Inc. (1974); W. Prosser and W. Keeton, Handbook of the Law of Torts (5th ed. 1984) 796, 843. A major reason for this apparent change in the common law appears to be the reluctance of courts to hold newspapers and other media broadly liable for communications which they may not even be aware are defamatory.

To summarize:

1.   Slander is actionable only with a showing of special damages . . .

2.   . . . unless the slander imputes to the complaining party (1) criminal conduct recognized as involving moral turpitude; (2) infection with a sexually transmitted disease, leprosy or the plague; (3) misconduct or mismanagement in business, trade, profession or office; or (4) unchastity (if the victim is a female).

3.   Libels per se in all jurisdictions and libels per quod in a large number of jurisdictions (including New York) are actionable without the need for special damages.

4.   Libels per quod in other jurisdictions are now actionable only with a showing of special damages unless they fall into one of the four special categories established originally for slander.

The above rules and the proper classification of defamation cases under them are extremely important since the establishment of special damages, meaning pecuniary loss as a result of the defamatory communication, is often very difficult for the plaintiff.

3. Theories of Liability

At common law, so long as the defendant intended to publish to a third person that which is ultimately adjudged to be defamatory toward the plaintiff, the defendant is strictly liable in tort, absent a valid defense. The plaintiff need only establish the intention of the defendant to publish and need not establish that the defendant intended the publication to be defamatory. Peck v. Tribune Co. (1909). Thus, a publisher under this rule "published at his own peril" and would be held liable for coincidences and honest errors as well as for intended defamatory attacks. Strict liability for the media was ended by the Supreme Court decisions in New York Times Co. v. Sullivan (1964) and Gertz v. Robert Welch, Inc. (1974), discussed infra at pp. 76–89.

4. Remedies

Once the plaintiff has established his or her cause of action and assuming the defendant has not interposed any valid defense (see infra, pp. 62–74, the focus of the defamation suit shifts from the question of liability to the question of remedies available to the defamed person. The major remedy for injury to reputation is the award of monetary damages.

a. Damages

We have already seen that in cases of libel per quod in perhaps a majority of jurisdictions and in cases of slander, excluding the four special categories, proof of special damages is necessary for liability. Of course, such damages may be established in any defamation action. Such damages require rather specific pleading and proof by the plaintiff of pecuniary or economic loss actually resulting from the defamatory communication and reasonable foreseeability of the plaintiff's loss by the defendant. Obvious cases are the loss of one's employment, the loss of opportunity for business profits and impaired credit rating because others are influenced by the defamation.

The existence of special damages may influence the jury's award of general damages. These are damages awarded for actual losses to the plaintiff from the defamation and cover both proven and unproven pecuniary and nonpecuniary loss for such injuries as hurt feelings, embarrassment, mental and emotional distress and physical consequences. Unless the action is one which specifically requires the showing of special damages, such damages are not a prerequisite for the award of general damages.

Many factors may be considered by the jury in attempting to determine reasonable and appropriate general damages. These are catalogued by a leading authority as including (1) the nature of the defamation (irrational name calling or insinuation of serious wrongdoing); (2) the form and permanency of the publication (oral conversations between individuals or communication by the mass print or electronic media); (3) the degree of dissemination; (4) the degree to which the defamatory communication is believed; (5) the nature of the plaintiff's reputation; (6) in certain cases, the good faith of the defendant in publishing the defamatory matter and (7) the defendant's subsequent conduct in retracting the complained of communication or in making apology. D. Dobbs, Law of Remedies: Damages–Equity–Restitution 259–276 (1993).

If spite, evil motive or reckless disregard for the truth is present, the jury will be instructed that it may, but need not, award the plaintiff punitive damages. As the term implies, such damages are designed to punish the defamer and are not compensatory in nature. If such damages are to make the defendant "smart" for his or her indiscretion and deter him or her in the future, the jury must be entitled to know the defendant's net worth and to reduce it to where it hurts.

Punitive damages may have too great a deterrent effect. One lower court has suggested that when First Amendment interests are balanced against the interests of the state in punishing defamers, the "chilling effect" of punitive damages on freedom of expression is too great a price for a free society to pay in attempting to rid itself of defamation. Maheu v. Hughes Tool Co. (1974).

An example of a staggering punitive damage award occurred in TXO Production Corp. v. Alliance Resources Corp. (1993), when the Supreme Court upheld a judgment for $19,000 in compensatory damages and $10 million for punitive damages against TXO Production Corporation, a subsidiary of USX, after a jury found TXO guilty of slander of title and of bad faith and malice in its dealings with Alliance Resources. Although the punitive damage award of $10 million was about 526 times the compensatory damage award of $19,000, the Court held that, provided punitive damages are "reasonable," they do not violate the due process clause of the Fourteenth Amendment. The TXO decision may unfortunately reinforce the chilling effect among the media, however, making them more timid than ever, due to the fact that the Supreme Court's view of what constitutes "reasonable" punitive damages can be interpreted by libel plaintiffs as "the sky's the limit."

C. THE COMMON LAW DEFENSES

Once the plaintiff has provided sufficient evidence of the elements necessary to establish a prima facie case of defamation and the consequent award of damages, the defendant is put to his or her defense. He or she may, of course, deny one or more aspects of the plaintiff's case such as the defamatory nature of the communication or the publication of the offending communication. In addition or alternatively, he or she may attempt to establish one or more of the complete common law defenses of truth, privilege and fair comment in order to defeat liability, or to attempt to establish certain incomplete defenses to reduce the award of damages. In resorting to these defenses, the defendant accepts the burden of pleading them in his or her answer and then proving them by a preponderance of the evidence at trial.

1. Truth or "Justification"

Although British common law in the American colonies held that "the greater the truth, the greater the libel," in criminal libel cases involving criticism of a public official, even British common law respected truth as a defense in civil actions for defamation.

But the defense of truth can be risky. Knowing something to be true and proving it in a court of law are, of course, two different things. In many situations only the plaintiff will have access to the necessary proof and, understandably, he or she will not make it easy for the defendant to establish the defense.

Moreover, the defense must be as broad in its reach as the communication complained of. The defense will fail if only a portion of the allegation is verified. For example, a newspaper charge that X is an habitual vice law offender is not justified by the paper establishing one conviction of X for a gambling violation. And a statement that a reliable source has informed the communicator that X is guilty of tax evasion is not justified by establishing only that someone informed the defendant about X and that someone is indeed a reliable source. The truth of the charge itself must be established even though the defendant was not the originator of the story. But this does not mean that defendants have to verify every detail of their communication. The defense is available if the substance of the communication can be established. An individual who publicly accuses his or her neighbor of embezzling $1500 from the neighborhood association treasury will escape liability by proving embezzlement of $150, for example.

2. Privilege

As with most intentional torts, the common law recognizes the defense of privilege in certain cases of defamation. Despite the fact that the plaintiff suffers harm to his or her reputation from the defamation, the defamer may be shielded from liability because the law accords supremacy to conflicting interests of the defendant in communicating the defamation or of third persons in receiving the communication or of the public generally in encouraging free expression of matters of general concern. The defense, which is relatively narrow in scope, is divided into two aspects: the absolute privilege to defame and the qualified privilege.

a. Absolute Privilege

One who possesses an absolute privilege to defame or, perhaps more accurately, an absolute immunity from suit is not required to establish his or her good faith in making the defamatory communication. Motivation is immaterial. The public proceedings in which the absolute privilege is available are divided into the legislative, judicial, executive and administrative.

All who speak in a legislative forum—U.S. Congresspersons, state representatives, city councilmembers—enjoy an absolute privilege to speak without fear of being sued for libel. But the comments must be made in a legislative forum. The Supreme Court has ruled that although a senator's speech on the floor of the Senate is completely immune from a libel suit, newsletters and press releases about the speech issued from the senator's office are not immune. Only speech which is "essential to the deliberations of the Senate" is protected by this privilege, and neither newsletters nor press releases are part of the deliberative process. Hutchinson v. Proxmire (1979).

The absolute privilege is also conferred on all communications in judicial forums such as courtrooms or grand jury rooms. Judges, lawyers, witnesses, defendants and plaintiffs are immune from a libel action provided the remark occurs during the official portions of the hearing or trial.

Finally, people who work in the executive and administrative branches of government—presidents, governors, mayors, heads of government agencies—may also enjoy absolute privilege for official communications or statements. For example, in Barr v. Mateo (1959), a department head distributed a press release explaining why two federal employees had been fired. In its decision, the Supreme Court accorded government officials an absolute privilege to make defamatory statements within the bounds of their offices.

The reasons for the absolute privilege are clear: if participants are forced to analyze their remarks for strict legal relevance and risk civil liability should they be in error, their fearlessness and independence may be impaired and their actions on the public's behalf inhibited. Unfortunately, like any privilege, the absolute privilege can be abused. One of the worst abusers of the privilege was Senator

Joseph McCarthy, who destroyed the careers of hundreds of people during the McCarthy Era when he accused them of being Communists. As long as McCarthy made his accusations on the floor of the Senate, he was immune from all libel suits.

Aside from speech by government representatives in their official capacity and communications between husband and wife, the absolute privilege does not obtain. The report of a credit rating enjoys an absolute privilege in some states but not in others.

b. Qualified Privilege

In contrast to the absolute privilege discussed above, the qualified privilege to communicate defamatory matter is defeated by the plaintiff establishing malice on the part of the defendant. This entails proving a publication was motivated chiefly by some consideration other than furthering the interest for which the law accords the privilege in the first place. The law's recognition of this lesser privilege reflects the idea that some of the interests competing with that of reputation, while not as compelling as those which justify an absolute privilege or immunity for the publisher, are still sufficiently important to justify a lesser degree of protection.

Depending on the jurisdiction, there is a qualified common law privilege for an employer to comment on an employee's performance to a manager or to someone requesting a reference for the employee, for communication to an employer regarding an employee's conduct toward a customer, and for a plant manager to tell employees that plaintiffs were terminated for theft of plant property. See Gonzalez v. Avon Products, Inc. (1985). A qualified privilege exists for a plant supervisor to tell employees that a plaintiff was demoted because he could not perform his job, and for a union member to make charges against the union's business manager. See Battista v. Chrysler Corp. (1982) and Pierce v. Burns (1962). There is also a qualified common law privilege for a physician to criticize a pharmacist's competence in talking with a patient, and for a bank officer to make a charge of forgery to a police officer. See Newark Trust Co. v. Bruwer (1958).

In the case of the media, the interests supporting the existence of the qualified privilege in reporting the proceedings of government and some private institutions and organizations are those of public oversight of governmental activity and legitimate public desire for information about matters affecting the public generally or a substantial segment thereof. And even when the oversight function is not involved the public may have some legitimate interest in being informed of public proceedings of both governmental and private organizations in order to prepare for or guard against the consequences of those proceedings.

(1) Limitations on the Scope of the Privilege

The courts have placed certain limitations on the scope or availability of the privilege to the media in reporting public proceedings. A majority of courts, for instance, led by Massachusetts, takes the position that the privilege does not extend to reporting allegations or statements contained in complaints, affidavits or other pretrial papers unless and until such papers are brought before a judge or magistrate for official action. See Sanford v. Boston Herald–Traveler Corp. (1945). Thus the reporter must be alert to the law of his or her state and, if it follows the majority view, must be wary of the content of court papers filed with the clerk of court but not yet acted upon by a judicial officer vested with discretionary authority. The minority view, exemplified by the New York case of Campbell v. New York Evening Post, Inc. (1927), is that the report of the contents of papers properly filed and served on the required parties may be privileged since the filing and serving of pleadings or other papers authorized by the rules of court are public and official acts done in the course of judicial proceedings.

Then, too, reports of the activities of executive officers or administrative agencies are generally not privileged until the officer or agency has taken some definite final action, as a district attorney filing a criminal information or obtaining an indictment. The report of a district attorney's preliminary investigation would not in most jurisdictions be privileged. Police proceedings are especially dangerous for the newsperson to report because of the significant variations from state to state regarding the point at which the privilege attaches. The status of the police blotter, the record of arrests and charges and the oral reports of police officers concerning their preliminary investigations varies according to the jurisdiction involved.

With regard to the legislative process, so long as the particular proceeding reported upon is authorized, the report itself will be privileged, assuming conformity with the general requirements discussed below.

The proceedings subject to the privilege must normally be public in nature unless a statute provides otherwise. Thus, a report of secret grand jury deliberations would not be considered privileged though such deliberations are official proceedings. Exceptions to the "public proceeding" requirement are occasionally recognized such as in Coleman v. Newark Morning Ledger Co. (1959), where a fair and accurate report of Senator Joseph McCarthy's press conference summarizing the secret proceedings of his subcommittee's investigation into alleged communist activity at Fort Monmouth, New Jersey, was held to be privileged despite the fact, pointed out in the dissenting opinion, that there was no verification of whether Senator McCarthy's report of the secret legislative proceeding was itself fair and accurate. Such exceptions are rare and the reporter should not assume from them that there is legal justification for publishing reports of secret governmental proceedings.

(2) General Requirements of the Privilege

As indicated by the Coleman case, if the qualified privilege is to attach the report must be fair and accurate and motivated by a sense of duty to make disclosure to those receiving the report. The privilege will be unavailable if it is held to be either an unfair or inaccurate account of that portion of the proceeding covered. The report need not, of course, be verbatim, but its condensation, abridgment or paraphrasing must accurately and fairly reflect what transpired. An erroneous detail will not destroy the privilege so long as it does not affect the essential accuracy or fairness of the report. A report may, of course, be literally accurate so far as it goes and yet unfairly portray the proceedings and the complaining person's involvement in them because the report ends at a critical point or omits important facts favorable to that person.

Moreover, if the defamatory report is made chiefly for a purpose other than to inform those who have a "need to know," the publication will be considered malicious and the privilege will be destroyed. Malice is found when the main reason for the publication is not the proper one of informing those the law recognizes as having a legitimate interest in the contents of the report. A fair and accurate account of a proceeding containing defamatory matter given to a friend at a party to make idle cocktail conversation could be considered malicious because the proper motivation for making the account is missing. And the privilege will not obtain if the communication is motivated mainly by some selfish objective of the reporter or publisher such as enhancing their business interests at the expense of a competitor who is unfavorably referred to in the public proceeding reported.

3. Fair Comment

The fair comment privilege was the most popular of the common law defenses. It is now made less important by the holding in New York Times Co. v. Sullivan (1964). The constitutional privilege found in that case regarding public figures is broader than the traditional fair comment privilege.

As traditionally viewed, fair comment involved the honest expression of the communicator's opinion on a matter of public interest based upon facts correctly stated in the communication. Such expression had to be free of speculation as to the motivation of the person whose public conduct is criticized unless such discussion was warranted by the stated facts. See Foley v. Press Publishing Co. (1929). Chief among the unique characteristics of this defense are (1) its emphasis upon opinion based upon fact rather than the reporting of the facts themselves and (2) its broader scope, permitting comment on all matters of public interest rather than simply proceedings of a public nature. It is these characteristics which made possible political and artistic criticism by the media prior to New York Times v. Sullivan. The courts gave broad meaning to fair comment. Commentaries containing exaggeration, illogic, sarcasm, ridicule and even viciousness were protected if at all justified by the underlying facts. Opinion is not *per se* protected by the First Amendment; thus, the rules of fair comment apply to determining whether a particular opinion is protected by the common law privilege.

Malice would negate the defense of fair comment but it could not be inferred merely from the words chosen by the publisher or speaker. Malice could only be found from an examination of the communicator's motives in publishing. The defense was also negated in a majority of the jurisdictions if the comment or opinion were based on a major error of fact. Furthermore, the defense of fair comment will not succeed unless the factual basis for the opinion is disclosed with it or is generally known to the audience. For example, if a newspaper columnist writes "Dr. Jones is a murderer," this would be defamatory if it is false. But if readers know that Dr. Jones performed euthanasia in one case, they are free to agree or disagree with the opinion that he is a murderer.

4. Incomplete Defenses

Certain defenses in defamation actions are labeled incomplete because they do not bar liability even if successful but only reduce the amount of damages recoverable by the plaintiff. Chief among them is that of retraction. If the defamer publishes a retraction of the defamatory communication punctually and with essentially the same prominence as he or she gave to the defamation, the danger of a punitive damages award will be negated and compensatory damages may be reduced.

It should be emphasized that the retraction must be complete and unequivocal. Less than full retraction or a veiled continuance of the defamation will not mitigate damages but, in fact, may increase them. It will not do to state that "John Doe hasn't the morals of a tom cat" and then be willing to "retract" by stating that "John Doe does have the morals of a tom cat." It should also be noted that the availability of the partial retraction defense, the effects of retraction and the consequences of a refusal to retract are governed in a number of states such as California by statute. The California retraction statute figured prominently in the celebrated libel suit by comedienne Carol Burnett against the National Enquirer. The statute by its terms applies to and provides partial protection for newspapers. In the Burnett case the trial court ruled that the National Enquirer was a magazine and thus, although it had published a retraction of the libelous material about Burnett, it was not protected against the imposition of punitive damages.

Somewhat akin to retraction is the idea of allowing the defamed party the right to reply to personal attack. The voluntary agreement by media defamers to allow use of their facilities by victims to reply to attacks does not necessarily establish the defamer's good faith and the award of punitive damages remains a possibility. But the actual injury to the defamed party may be reduced because of the opportunity afforded to reach and favorably influence those whose good opinion of him or her has been affected. However, any effort by government to mandate the right of reply insofar as the print media are concerned would appear to be violative of the First Amendment. See Miami Herald Publishing Co. v. Tornillo (1974). But as of this time, a distinction is made by the Supreme Court with regard to broadcasters, and they may be compelled to extend the right to reply, in certain narrow circumstances, to those personally attacked over their facilities. Red Lion Broadcasting Co. v. Federal Communications Commission (1969). The distinction between print and electronic media is a doubtful one in this context. See the discussion of the "Fairness Doctrine" infra Chapter XI, pp. 423–428.

———

This completes the discussion of common law defamation, a law in many respects quite favorable to the defamed party's interest in reputation. Witness, for instance, its theory of strict liability. Conversely, this law imposes many restrictions upon and dangers for those who seek to exercise their right of free expression under the First Amendment. Damage awards by juries are skyrocketing. The Brown & Williamson Tobacco Corporation won a $3 million damage award from CBS in 1987 that was upheld on appeal. Brown & Williamson Tobac-

co Corp. v. Jacobson (1987). Entertainer Wayne
Newton won a $19.3 million damage award from
NBC in 1986 after NBC broadcast a story linking
him with organized crime. Fortunately for NBC,
the United States Court of Appeals for the Ninth
Circuit overturned the verdict and dismissed the
case, ruling that Newton had not proven actual
malice and NBC's statements were basically true.
Newton v. National Broadcasting Co. (1990). But
even when the media win, the costs of defending
themselves are so high that self-censorship and a
chilling effect will be the inevitable result. ABC
allegedly spent $7 million defending itself against a
series of lawsuits by Synanon, and it cost CBS
several million dollars to defend itself against William Westmoreland's libel suit. Westmoreland v.
CBS, Inc. (1984).

The common law principles that have been considered at length in this chapter are still applied in
whole to communications that do not involve public
figures or matters of public concern, and in part to
communications which do. They are thus worthy
of continued discussion. But the very serious question posed to the Supreme Court by New York
Times Co. v. Sullivan was whether the application
of all aspects of the common law of defamation to
newspapers and other media is consistent with the
guarantees of the First Amendment. The answer
to that important question and its qualifications is
the subject of the next section of this chapter.

D. THE NEW CONSTITUTIONAL LAW OF DEFAMATION

1. New York Times Co. v. Sullivan

In New York Times Co. v. Sullivan (1962), a civil rights group bought a full page advertisement in the New York Times, entitled "Heed Their Rising Voices." The ad charged that the police of Montgomery, Alabama had improperly "ringed" a black college campus to put down a peaceful demonstration for civil rights and that certain unnamed "southern violators" had bombed Martin Luther King's home, had physically assaulted him, arrested him seven times for "speeding," "loitering" and similar "offenses;" and finally charged him with "perjury." Some of these statements were erroneous in whole or part.

While no "southern violator" was named in the ad, L. B. Sullivan, the Commissioner of Public Affairs for Montgomery, Alabama, filed suit for libel. Sullivan persuaded the jury that he had been referred to in the advertisement because he was the city commissioner in charge of the police at all times in question and thus would have been responsible for the "ringing" of the campus and the multiple arrests of Dr. King for minor infractions as part of the alleged lawless campaign of harassment and intimidation. Sullivan also contended that being identified as a "southern violator" in conjunction with the arrests had resulted in his further identification in the public mind with the other lawless acts listed. Several Montgomery residents so testified. L. B. Sullivan sought and won a jury award of $500,000 against the New York Times. The Alabama Supreme Court affirmed the judgment under ordinary common law rules of defamation, rejecting the argument that the ad was protected by the First Amendment.

No more graphic illustration of the dangers posed to a free press by the common law can be suggested than the decision of the Alabama Supreme Court in this case. That decision was, in almost all respects, in accord with accepted common law principles concerning the elements of libel, malice, compensatory and punitive damages and the recognized defenses.

The effect of that litigation in the state courts was to cause the New York Times Company to halt distribution of its newspaper in Alabama for a time and to saddle the company with a massive judgment for $500,000 damages which, if not reversed, would (along with a potential $2,500,000 more in damages claimed in other pending related suits) have caused a weakening of its financial position, with all the implications that that might have had for the Company's continued ability to adhere to its motto "all the news that's fit to print."

But the United States Supreme Court reversed a judgment for Sullivan, holding, among other things, that the identification of Sullivan with the advertisement was inadequate.

The Court acknowledged that the paid advertisement in question did contain erroneous information which, if satisfactorily identified with Sullivan, would be considered defamatory toward him at common law. However, the United States Supreme Court held that there was not adequate proof of identification of Sullivan to support liability of the defendants for defamation and reversed the state court judgment for him.

It seemed clear to the Court that, at most, the New York Times Company was guilty of negligence in publishing the advertisement without checking the facts alleged therein against its own news files to verify the accuracy of the advertisement. Money judgments against newspapers and other media for honest mistakes or negligence in publication of defamatory material concerning public officials interfered with debate on public issues. In the Court's understanding, the encouragement of such debate was part of the central meaning of the First Amendment. The court therefore laid down the rule that public officials may not recover damages for defamatory falsehoods relating to their official conduct unless they prove with "convincing clarity" that the statements are made with actual malice. "Actual malice" was defined by the Court as publication with knowledge that the statement in question is false or with "reckless disregard" for whether or not it is false.

Thus, for the first time in the long history of this country, certain false and defamatory communications were accorded constitutional protection if not maliciously made. This historic ruling represents a corollary to Barr v. Matteo (1959), discussed above, in which the Court held that government officers have an absolute privilege to make defamatory communications if specifically related to the discharge of their official duties. Critics of official conduct are given an equivalent privilege in order to encourage public oversight of these same officers.

2. Effects of the New York Times Case

The effects of the New York Times case on common law defamation have been profound. Briefly summarized they include the following:

1.   The idea of "fair comment" is broadened to include facts and to permit the communication of erroneous facts, and is raised to a constitutional privilege when the comment concerns conduct of public officials relating to their office.

2.   Strict liability for the making of defamatory communications concerning public officials is eliminated and a new fault standard of intentional or reckless conduct is substituted.

3.   The definition of actual malice to mean evil motive, spite or ill will is rejected and a new definition of knowing falsehood or reckless disregard for the truth is substituted when public officials and public figures are complaining parties. Even hard-hitting investigative reporting begun with a preconceived point of view and an "adversarial stance" does not indicate actual malice where the reporter conducts a detailed investigation and writes a story therefrom that is substantially true. Tavoulareas v. Piro Co. (1987).

4. Under common law the defense of privilege, including lack of actual malice, was for the defendant to establish; after New York Times the plaintiff public official has the burden of negating the defendant's constitutional privilege by proving that the defendant acted with actual malice (intentionally or recklessly) in publishing the false and defamatory material. Implicit in this is the shifting of the burden of proof on the issue of truth to the plaintiff. He or she must now establish falsity as part of his or her prima facie case. See Philadelphia Newspapers, Inc. v. Hepps (1986).

5. The plaintiff's proof of malice and his or her identification as the party defamed must now be made with convincing clarity; at common law the normal standard of proof for defamation is mere preponderance of the evidence.

Another important effect is somewhat more indirect. As a practical matter, plaintiff public officials have had, since the New York Times Co. case was decided, a very hard time in making out their defamation cases against media defendants because of the difficulty of establishing actual malice under the convincing clarity standard. An exception to this rule occurred in Harte–Hanks Communications, Inc. v. Connaughton (1989), discussed below, in which a public official did establish actual malice. In general, however, responsible media organizations rarely traffic in known falsehoods or act recklessly in disseminating news or information. Very often then when there is no real dispute as to the material facts, defendants are able to obtain summary judgments on the basis of preliminary papers, documents and affidavits showing insufficient proof of actual malice and thus do not have to defend themselves at trial. See Anderson v. Liberty Lobby, Inc. (1986).

3. The New York Times Progeny

As great a charter as the New York Times case is for the mass media, it raised more questions than it answered, and only the existence of three decades of subsequent court decisions permits an assessment of the true boundaries and impact of that case. One of the questions raised was the meaning of "reckless disregard." In the New York Times case itself the facts pointed so strongly to honest mistake in publication that no real clue was given as to the boundaries of the concept.

A faint ray of light is cast on this issue in St. Amant v. Thompson (1968). During a televised speech, St. Amant, a candidate for local office, repeated a union leader's charges that a deputy sheriff had taken bribes. The union leader had made his charges in an affidavit under oath, and St. Amant made no attempt to verify the charges, which turned out to be false. The state court held that St. Amant had been reckless, but the Supreme Court reversed. Justice Byron White said that "[t]here must be sufficient evidence to permit the conclusion that the defendant in fact entertained serious doubts as to the truth of his publication." See also Herbert v. Lando (1979). This came very close to requiring the public official to prove know-ing publication of falsehood and appears by implica-tion to protect those publishers who deliberately avoid discovering the truth.

But this implication was put to rest in Harte–Hanks Communications, Inc. v. Connaughton (1989). There, the Hamilton (Ohio) Journal–Bea-con was found guilty of actual malice when one of its editors not only failed to check his own news sources but also refused to listen to a tape recording which would have cast doubts on the veracity of a story the paper published about Daniel Connaugh-ton, a candidate for judge in a local election. The Supreme Court held that the editor's refusal to listen to the tape recording created evidence of actual malice. This was the first time the Court had upheld a libel judgment involving actual malice since the 1960s.

In another recent case, the Supreme Court found that knowingly misquoting a source may constitute actual malice. In Masson v. New Yorker Magazine, Inc. (1991), the Supreme Court ruled that a serious misquotation that hurts a person's reputation may be libelous if the quotation is rephrased to result in a "material change in the meaning." In this case, psychoanalyst Jeffery Masson sued the New Yorker magazine for libel when its free-lance writer Janet Malcolm quoted Masson as calling himself an "in-tellectual gigolo" who would turn the Sigmund Freud Archives into a "place of sex, women and fun" and would become "the greatest analyst who ever lived." Those exact phrases were not in the 40 hours of tape-recorded interviews Malcolm had conducted with Masson. The Supreme Court remanded the case, and a jury found free-lance writer Janet Malcolm guilty of actual malice, but could not agree on the damages, and the case ended in a mistrial with further appeals pending. Masson v. Malcolm (1993).

In addition to the definition of malice, another question expressly left open in New York Times Co. is the meaning of "official conduct." This concept now appears to parallel closely the boundaries of an executive or administrative officer's duties and responsibilities in office set forth in Barr v. Matteo, supra. As long as the defamatory material is published within the constitutional and statutory bounds of his or her office, the public official would be bound by the New York Times Co. rule. Cf. Butz v. Economou (1978). In addition, erroneous charges of criminal conduct on the part of public officials and candidates for public office, no matter how remote in time or place, are protected by the constitutional privilege because such charges are always relevant to the question of fitness to hold or seek office. Monitor Patriot Co. v. Roy (1971); Ocala Star–Banner Co. v. Damron (1971). On the other hand, even public officials are entitled to private lives and false and defamatory communications relating thereto would not be protected by the privilege established in the New York Times case. For instance, if a newspaper knowingly publishes the false accusation that a county assessor owns an extensive collection of pornographic films, the story would not be protected because possession is not a crime and is not relevant to the conduct of his or her office.

The Court in New York Times v. Sullivan also declined to provide a general definition of "public official." The cases that followed New York Times have established that "public official" includes at least those in governmental hierarchies who have or appear to have substantial responsibility for the conduct of government business, from judges to public park supervisors. The term also includes former office holders who exercised substantial responsibility while in office and who are attacked for their past official conduct. See Rosenblatt v. Baer (1966), (no finding of malice and hence no defamation on part of publisher of newspaper column critical of supervisor of public recreation facility, who qualified as public official).

While the term "public official" is thus an expansive one, it covers only a small percentage of public personages. Recognizing this, the Court subsequently extended the reach of the New York Times Co. decision to public figures and their non-official but public acts, such as famous college athletic directors and football coaches and resigned Army generals who, by their public conduct, thrust themselves into the limelight (Curtis Publishing Co. v. Butts (1967); Associated Press v. Walker (1967)); a prominent real estate developer involved in a land dispute with a local city council (Greenbelt Cooperative Publishing Association v. Bresler (1970)); and candidates for public office (Monitor Patriot Co. v. Roy (1971)).

But what of persons who are neither public officials nor public figures but who are caught up in matters of public interest? Should the media have the same constitutional privilege regarding communications about private persons who may be less able to defend themselves against false and defamatory allegations because of less access to the corrective mechanisms of the mass media? In other words, should the focus be shifted from public persons to matters of public interest, regardless of the status of the participants involved? These are extremely important questions. Affirmative answers might so alter the balance between the interest in free speech and press and the interest in individual reputation as to destroy the latter. Whomever the media deemed newsworthy might be regarded by the courts as being bound by the New York Times rule when they sought legal redress.

Initially, a plurality of the Supreme Court in Rosenbloom v. Metromedia, Inc. (1971) answered this question in the affirmative, deeming the distinction between public and private individuals to be artificial in relationship to the public's interest in a broad range of issues, including, in that case, the arrest of an obscure distributor of nudist magazines on obscenity charges and the confiscation of his magazines as pornographic.

4. The Basic Public Figure–Private Person Distinction of Gertz v. Welch

Strong dissent was registered in Rosenbloom to this extension of the constitutional privilege, and in

Gertz v. Robert Welch, Inc. (1974), a majority of the Court rejected that plurality decision, holding that the privilege recognized in New York Times Co. v. Sullivan was applicable only to cases involving defamation of public officials and public figures.

In this case Elmer Gertz, a reputable lawyer not generally known to the public and not then associated with any particular causes, was retained by the family of a youth killed by a police officer to bring a civil suit against the officer. Gertz was viciously attacked in the John Birch Society's magazine American Opinion, which accused him of being a "Leninist," a "Communist-fronter," and of arranging a frame-up of the police officer.

Gertz sued for libel, and the Supreme Court ruled that despite his prominence in the civil rights area, Gertz was not a public figure for the purposes of this lawsuit. The Court explained that private persons are more in need of judicial redress and the state has a greater interest in providing it because they have not voluntarily invited public comment, thus choosing to put their reputations at risk. Moreover, the private person will normally have less access to the channels of effective communication (the media) to correct the record than will the public person. (In later cases courts have distinguished between "pervasive" or "all-purpose public figures" who are household names, and "involuntary" or "limited purpose" public figures, meaning those who have thrust themselves into the middle of a specific public controversy or those who fall under the media limelight by chance; these distinctions are discussed in greater detail below.)

The Supreme Court stressed the fact that Gertz had not achieved any general fame in the community—the jurors had never heard of him. Moreover, the Court did not think that simply because he was counsel in the civil litigation in question that he had "thrust himself into the vortex" of public controversy.

In Gertz the Court directly modified the common law in two fundamental respects. First, they abolished strict liability for the publication of defamatory material and left to the individual states the determination of the appropriate fault standard of liability. This means that while the states may no longer impose liability on the media where there is no fault in the communication of defamatory material, they have at least three fault standards of liability to choose from (listed in ascending order of protection for the media): 1) unreasonable publication (negligence), 2) extremely unreasonable publication (gross negligence), or 3) knowingly false or reckless publication (New York Times standard).

A few jurisdictions have indicated a preference for the New York Times Company standard. See Walker v. Colorado Springs Sun, Inc. (1975); Aafco Heating and Air Conditioning Co. v. Northwest Publications, Inc. (1974); Sisler v. Gannett Co., Inc. (1986). In none of these cases, however, was the adoption of that standard of fault unanimous and subsequently the highest courts of most other states considering the question have opted for a simple negligence test. See Phillips v. Evening Star Newspaper Co. (1980) (all state holdings on this issue collected); Triangle Publications, Inc. v. Chumley (1984). But New York has chosen to impose liability for defamation only if the defendant "acted in a grossly irresponsible manner without due consideration for the standards of information gathering and dissemination ordinarily followed by responsible parties," Robart v. Post–Standard (1981), an intermediate standard between that of New York Times Company and ordinary negligence.

Second, when liability is imposed on the basis of negligence or gross negligence rather than malice, recovery is to be limited to compensation for proven actual injury caused by the defamation. But apparently in defamation actions against the media tried pursuant to the New York Times Co. standard, presumed and punitive damages might still be awarded.

This modification of the common law system of damages is clearly designed to protect the media from massive judgments based on the jury's imagination, its ideas of punishment and deterrence and its prejudices.

5. The Broad Meaning of Gertz

The case of Gertz v. Robert Welch, Inc. sets the boundaries of the constitutional privilege established in New York Times Co. v. Sullivan. From here on the privilege of the media negligently to make false and defamatory communications may be limited by the states when it is determined that the complaining party is not a public figure. But beyond this, Gertz puts an end to the expansion of the absolutist interpretation of the First Amendment which gives primacy to the societal interests in free expression.

As a result the media will have to be more concerned about what they communicate relative to the "unknowns" of our society and will have to review and strengthen verification procedures to avoid the charge of negligence in news gathering, interpretation and dissemination. The other side of the coin minted in Gertz is the greater recognition of the individual's personal worth and dignity.

6. The Public Figure—Private Person Distinction

a. Narrowing of the Public Figure Classification

In righting the perceived imbalance in constitutional protection between expression and reputation it was important for the Gertz majority to reduce the range of applicability of New York Times Co. v. Sullivan. This could be accomplished by defining narrowly who was a public figure by the stringent New York Times Company standards.

Gertz thus created the dichotomy between public figures and private persons and established the framework for distinguishing between two types of public figures: (1) the all-purpose public figure such as Johnny Carson, having such great general fame or notoriety that his or her name is a household word, or (2) limited purpose public figures, who are further distinguished as being (a) voluntary or "vortex" public figures, referring to plaintiffs' thrusting themselves voluntarily into the vortex of a specific public controversy, or (b) involuntary public figures, referring to someone who is placed in the media limelight by chance. See Dameron v. Washington Magazine, Inc. (1985) (air traffic controller on duty when a plane crashed held to be an involuntary public figure).

Within five years of the Gertz ruling, the Supreme Court agreed to hear three more cases to clarify the issue of whether plaintiffs were public figures (who had to prove actual malice) or private persons (who merely had to prove negligence). These three cases established the truly restrictive nature of the public figure category. The first case, Time, Inc. v. Firestone (1976), involved a highly publicized divorce between Mary Alice Firestone and her husband, an heir to the Firestone tire empire. After a lengthy and spicy public trial the judge granted the husband's request for a complete divorce. Time Magazine reported in its "Milestones" section that Russell Firestone was granted a divorce "on grounds of extreme cruelty and adultery." After her request for a printed retraction was rejected, Mrs. Firestone sued for libel. Time's report was false and defamatory because under Florida law an adulterous wife could not receive alimony, but the Florida court had granted her $3000 per month in alimony.

Time argued that Mrs. Firestone was a public figure, which would require her to show that Time knew the story was false or recklessly disregarded the truth. (Time was innocent of actual malice; its reporter had genuinely misunderstood the grounds for divorce).

But in rejecting Time's contention, the Supreme Court said that local social prominence is not enough to categorize a plaintiff as a public figure. Divorce is not the sort of "public controversy" referred to in Gertz; rather, it is a private matter.

The Court did not even mention Mrs. Firestone's open air press conferences or her hiring of a press agent designed to tell the public her side of the divorce story. Firestone considerably narrowed the public figure category, given Mrs. Firestone's notoriety. The category was further narrowed by two cases decided by the Supreme Court on the same day in its 1978–1979 term.

In Wolston v. Reader's Digest Association, Inc. (1979) defendant published a book about Soviet intelligence agents in the United States and listed Wolston as one of them. Sixteen years earlier Wolston had been subpoenaed to testify before a federal grand jury investigating the activity of Soviet agents in this country. Because of claimed poor health he did not comply with the subpoena and he was cited for contempt.

Wolston denied any connection to the Soviet intelligence apparatus and sued the Reader's Digest Association for libel. Although the trial court granted the Association summary judgment and the

United States Court of Appeals affirmed partly on the basis that Wolston was a public figure, the Supreme Court reversed, ruling that he was not a public figure because he had done nothing to thrust himself into a public controversy.

This holding restricts limited issue public figures to those who draw attention to themselves in order to advocate a particular view on a public matter and to affect public opinion. Thus, as in Firestone, mere involvement in a matter of public interest is not enough.

This same restrictive view of limited-issue public figures led the Court to reject the Association's other contention that any person who engages in criminal conduct automatically becomes a public figure regarding his trial and conviction. As in the Firestone case, one involved in a public trial (here a criminal one) does not necessarily become a public figure.

In the companion case of Hutchinson v. Proxmire (1979), Senator William Proxmire awarded his uncoveted "Golden Fleece of the Month" awards to NASA and the Office of Naval Research for spending almost a half-million dollars to fund Dr. Hutchinson's research on the aggressiveness of animals, particularly monkeys, for the purpose of finding ways to reduce aggressiveness in humans thrown together in close quarters for extended periods of time. In his speech making the award as well as in a related news release Proxmire described Hutchinson's research as transparently worthless and called for an end to his making "a monkey out of the

American taxpayer" and putting the "bite" on the taxpayer's resources. Dr. Hutchinson sued Senator Proxmire for libel. As in Wolston, the trial court granted summary judgment for Proxmire because the plaintiff was a public figure, and the United States Court of Appeals affirmed.

But, as in Wolston, the Supreme Court reversed on the "public figure" issue, rejecting the view that local newspaper reports regarding Hutchinson's grants and research made him a limited-issue public figure. In so ruling the Court made the point that those charged with defamation cannot create their own defense by themselves making the victim a public figure. Furthermore, the access to the media required by Gertz is a regular and continuing one and not merely that made available to rebut a specific defamatory attack.

In summary, the public figure category has been narrowed by the Gertz progeny in these important respects:

1. Simply appearing in the newspapers in connection with some newsworthy story or stories does not make one a public figure;

2. Social, professional or business prominence does not by itself make one a public figure, except in the case of those who are so famous that their names are household words such as Carol Burnett or Michael Jackson, for example.

3. Forced involvement in a public trial, either civil or criminal, does not by itself make one a public figure;

4. Those charged with defamation cannot by their own conduct in making their victims notorious thereby create their own defense;

5. Merely applying for, receiving or benefiting from public research grants does not make one a public figure;

6. In order to meet the Gertz test of thrusting oneself into the forefront of a public issue or controversy, the issue or controversy must be a real dispute, the outcome of which affects the general public or some segment of it in an appreciable way. One's conduct must be calculated or clearly be expected to invite public comment respecting that issue or controversy, as for example, the value and conduct of a federal investigation into KGB activity in the United States during the McCarthy era.

7. In order to meet the Gertz test of access to the media the access must be regular and continuing.

All in all, following the Firestone, Wolston and Proxmire decisions, the category of public figures for purposes of New York Times v. Sullivan protection is much smaller than could have been imagined when Gertz was decided.

b. *The Effect of Time Passage on Public Figure Status*

Wolston v. Reader's Digest Association was marked by an interesting concurring opinion by Justice Blackmun in which he assumed for purposes of argument that Wolston had become a public figure in 1958. But Blackmun argued that by Wolston's return to anonymity and the passage of time until the offending book was published some sixteen years later, he no longer had "significantly greater access to the channels of communication" to defend himself and had no longer knowingly chosen to run the risk of public scrutiny. Consequently, he had lost his public figure status. Justice Blackmun recognized that such analysis implies that a person may be a public figure for purposes of contemporaneous reporting of his activities but not a public figure for purposes of historical commentary on the same activities and events.

Because Justice Blackmun's approach provides less protection for the historical commentator than it does for the contemporaneous journalist, it has been rejected by at least one lower court. See Street v. National Broadcasting Co. (1981); and compare Brewer v. Memphis Publishing Co., Inc. (1980). Despite these lower court decisions the popular or scholarly historical commentator should be wary for the Supreme Court majority did not reject Justice Blackmun's analysis as a corollary means of narrowing the media's constitutional privilege. Thus, special care should be taken to achieve factual accuracy in the preparation of the "where are they now"—type features concerning formerly famous or notorious people.

7. The Fact–Opinion Dichotomy

One other major modification of the common law was effected in Gertz to the benefit of the media.

By way of dictum Mr. Justice Powell stated that "[u]nder the First Amendment there is no such thing as a false idea. However pernicious an opinion may seem, we depend for its correction not on the conscience of judges and juries but on the competition of other ideas." This dictum was restated and reaffirmed in the more recent case of Bose Corporation v. Consumers Union (1984). Justice Powell made clear in his dictum that in distinction with opinion, false statements of fact may be demonstrated to be such and are not protected when made with fault.

The difficulty is in distinguishing between fact and opinion and the dictum in Gertz provides little help with this problem. The media received some guidance from Milkovich v. Lorain Journal Co. (1990), when the Supreme Court ruled that no separate privilege exists protecting statements of opinion. Thus, statements of opinion that can be interpreted as stating or implying false facts may be actionable: in effect, Milkovich returns the media to the common law privilege of fair comment, which still provides a strong defense for those who publish pure opinions.

This case involved an Ohio sportswriter who accused wrestling coach Mike Milkovich and high school superintendent Don Scott of lying at a hearing about a brawl during a wrestling match: "Anyone who attended the meet . . . knows in his heart that Milkovich and Scott lied at the hearing after each having given his solemn oath to tell the truth. But they got away with it." Milkovich v. Lorain

Journal Co. (1990). When Milkovich sued for libel, the News–Herald claimed that the sportswriter's column was merely his opinion and was thus protected as fair comment. A lower court agreed, but the Supreme Court reversed. The Court explained that the implication that Milkovich committed perjury was factual enough to be proved true or false by simply comparing his testimony at the initial hearing with his subsequent testimony before the trial court. Thus, to say that someone told a lie is a factual allegation which the plaintiff can prove or disprove, whereas to say that someone is "ignorant" is merely an opinion. The Court thus remanded the case for further proceedings.

Since Milkovich, a number of courts have reversed summary judgments for media defendants in cases where statements of opinion were factual enough to be proven true or false. See, for example, Unelko Corp. v. Rooney (1990) (Andy Rooney's comment that Unelko's Rain–X "didn't work" not protected opinion under Milkovich, although Rooney won summary judgment on other grounds).

8. Specific Problems for the Media Created by Gertz

Aside from the pervasive specter of self censorship raised by it, Gertz presents a number of very specific problems. Distinguishing between fact and opinion or between public persons and private ones may not be easy for the media, particularly under the pressure of deadlines.

Another determination which the media may be required to make in advance of publication, depending on the standard of liability embodied in the relevant state law, is the reasonableness of their publishing procedures in every given case.

For example, if the source of a media story is a wire service, the media may avail themselves of the "wire service defense" in spite of the republication rule, which would normally hold that a newspaper which repeats a libelous story is also liable for defamation. See Appleby v. Daily Hampshire Gazette (1985).

Journalists are usually on safe ground if their source is a government official or a public document. For example, in Wilson v. Capital City Press (1975), the state police had given the newspaper access to a list of people arrested in a drug raid. The list mistakenly included the plaintiff's name, but a Louisiana court ruled that the newspaper was not negligent in relying on the state police report.

It was once an unwritten rule of journalists to have two independent sources to verify a story, but if journalists' sources are biased and they make no effort to cover an opposing view, a court may find them negligent. See Richmond Newspapers, Inc. v. Lipscomb (1987), (court ruled that jury could find reporter negligent for writing negative story about a teacher when reporter did not bother to interview anyone who had praise for teacher). Thus the "two source" rule adopted by Watergate reporters Bob

Woodward and Carl Bernstein does not always preclude a finding of negligence.

Because of the great uncertainties involved in
determining the reasonableness of the publisher's
conduct prior to trial, the media can expect less
favorable treatment on motions for summary judgment against private plaintiffs. Unless the publisher's conduct can be held by the trial judge to be
reasonable beyond question, a trial will have to be
conducted to permit the jury to decide this issue.
Thus, more protracted litigation can be expected
with increasing pressure on media defendants to
settle even nuisance claims.

Finally, the problem of large damage awards discussed previously will remain a very real concern of
the media and may add to the pressure for out of
court settlements that can only weaken the financial structure of media organizations.

9. Questions Raised by Gertz

Gertz raised important questions about the existence and operation of common law defenses. Who
now has the burden of establishing the truth or
falsity of the alleged defamatory communications?

After a number of years of uncertainty, this question was answered in Philadelphia Newspapers, Inc.
v. Hepps (1986). There, the Supreme Court ruled,
in a case involving a series of newspaper articles
linking a private figure to organized crime and his
use of those links to influence a state government's

decisions, that the *plaintiff* had the burden of establishing the falsity of the articles.

The Court also noted that placing the burden of proof on plaintiffs to establish falsity does not involve undue hardship because plaintiffs already have the burden of establishing fault on the part of the defendant and juries are more likely to find defendants in libel cases at fault if convinced that the statements complained of are false. Publication of truthful information no matter how damaging is inconsistent with concepts of negligence and gross negligence.

In Bose Corporation v. Consumers Union (1984), the Supreme Court, by a vote of 6 to 3, gave a strong endorsement to the constitutional principles enunciated in New York Times Co. and its progeny a generation before, suggesting their long-term wisdom. The central issue in Bose was a procedural one involving the scope of a federal appellate court's review of a trial court's determination of actual malice on the part of Consumer's Union, publisher of Consumer Reports magazine. The Supreme Court held that a federal appellate court could do a *de novo* review of a federal district court decision; in other words, the appellate court could make an independent determination of the mixed fact and constitutional law issue of actual malice.

In this case Consumer Reports made an erroneous and derogatory statement about the quality of the sound delivered by the public figure plaintiff's newly designed stereo speaker system. Although a panel of listeners had said that the sound moved along the wall in front of and between the two speakers, Consumer Reports engineer Arnold Seligson wrote that the sound "tended to wander about the room." At the trial, Seligson testifed that he believed the two statements meant the same thing. The district court found his testimony ludicrous and said that Seligson clearly knew he had changed the meaning of the statement. This was evidence of actual malice. The court also found the testimony of Monte Florman, Consumer Union's technical director, to be "wholly untrustworthy and . . . not credible."

But the Court explained: "The statement in this case represents the sort of inaccuracy that is commonplace in the forum of robust debate to which the *New York Times* rule applies."

10. An Attempt to "Get Around" New York Times and Its Reaffirmation a Generation Later

Because of the large burden placed upon public officials and public figures in libel cases, some enterprising plaintiffs' counsel have tried to avoid the "actual malice" standard and other requirements of defamation law by changing the designation of their claims. In Falwell v. Flynt (1986), the Reverend Jerry Falwell sued "Hustler" Magazine publisher Larry Flynt for intentional infliction of emotional distress as well as libel because of a parody of an advertising campaign in which celebrities talk about their "first time," referring, of course, to their first encounter with Campari Liqueur. In Hustler's ad parody, Falwell, in a fictitious interview, allegedly details an incestuous "first time" with his mother in an outhouse. Mother and son are portrayed in the vilest of terms. At the bottom of the "ad" is a disclaimer which states "ad parody—not to be taken seriously."

The jury ruled for Flynt on Falwell's libel claim, finding that no reasonable person would believe that the parody was describing actual facts about the minister. But on the intentional emotional distress claim, the jury returned a $200,000 verdict for Falwell, and the Fourth Circuit affirmed.

But in a unanimous decision, the Supreme Court reversed. Writing for the Court, Chief Justice Rehnquist explained that "robust political debate" will often produce sharp and caustic comments and vehement attacks. The standard for imposing liability in intentional infliction of emotional distress cases is whether or not the conduct is outrageous. But the "outrageousness" requirement is so subjective that imposition of liability would vary from jury to jury. The Court clearly feared that with a standard as subjective as "outrageousness," plaintiffs like Falwell could use the tort of intentional infliction of emotional distress to circumvent the safeguards of New York Times Co. v. Sullivan. Therefore the Court ruled that public officials and public figures who sue for intentional infliction of emotional distress must prove falsity and reckless disregard for the truth, just as in libel cases.

The Court was clearly concerned about the implications of using the intentional infliction of emotional distress tort on the satire and parody of editorial cartoons. "Despite their sometimes caustic nature, from the early cartoon portraying George Washington as an ass down to the present day, ... satirical cartoons have played a prominent role in public and political debate.... From the viewpoint of history it is clear that our political discourse would have been considerably poorer without them." Hustler Magazine, Inc. v. Falwell (1988). Although Hustler's ad parody was at best "a distant cousin of the political cartoons" of Thomas Nast and others, the Court doubted that anyone could establish "a principled standard to separate one from the other." The subjectivity of the "outrageousness" standard could permit plaintiffs like Falwell to recover damages whenever the speech in question had "an adverse emotional impact on the audience," a result which would have an immeasurable chilling effect on speech.

Given the rather transparent efforts of Falwell's attorneys to circumvent First Amendment standards by utilizing tort labels other than libel and the reaffirmation of New York Times v. Sullivan in Bose Corp. v. Consumers Union (1984), Philadelphia Newspapers, Inc. v. Hepps (1986), and Hustler Magazine, Inc. v. Falwell (1988), it is unlikely that the push to designate torts other than libel based on injurious falsehood will be successful. See also Patrick v. Los Angeles County Superior Court (1994), (legal newspaper's description of judge as a "despotic twit" and memo purportedly written by said judge declaring "court emergency" and suspending election of judge's successor held to constitute parody and not libel or intentional infliction of emotional distress, even though memo used official court seal and stationery and was distributed at courthouse).

Whereas Jerry Falwell is a public figure and the Hustler cartoon was a vulgar but distant cousin to political satire, courts may be more sympathetic to private plaintiffs who charge intentional infliction of emotional distress when no issue of public concern is involved. For example, two years after Hustler Magazine, Inc. v. Falwell, in Murray v. Schlosser (1990), a court refused to dismiss claims for both libel and intentional infliction of emotional distress. Two disc jockeys for WCCC–FM in Hartford, Connecticut broadcast a weekly program called "Berate the Brides" during which they encouraged listeners to call in their votes for the "dog of the week," chosen from pictures of brides published in the Hartford Courant. One of the disc jockeys described a bride as "too ugly to even rate," adding that she had won the "dog of the week" prize of a case of dog food and a dog collar. Although the disc jockeys moved to dismiss the bride's claims of libel and intentional infliction of emotional distress, the court denied the motions to dismiss the claims. It may be that courts are more willing to consider such claims when unsuspecting private persons are harmed as a result of frivolous malice on the part of media personae desperately seeking higher ratings or greater circulation. When the court refused to dismiss the case, however, WCCC–FM reached an out-of-court settlement with Murray; thus no precedent was set regarding this claim.

11. Non–Media Defendants and Matters of Public Concern

Over three decades have elapsed since the truly landmark decision of New York Times Company v. Sullivan. It is not surprising that during this period criticism of the decision has arisen and a desire has been expressed by some to turn back the clock to the common law way of handling media libel cases. Perhaps the most thoughtful assault on the constitutional privilege developed in New York Times and refined in Gertz was that of Justice White. In his concurring opinion in Dun & Bradstreet, Inc. v. Greenmoss Builders, Inc. (1985) Justice White said, "The New York Times rule .... countenances two evils: first, the stream of information about public officials and public affairs is polluted and often remains polluted by false information; and second, the reputation and professional life of the defeated plaintiff may be destroyed by falsehoods that might have been avoided with a reasonable effort to investigate the facts.... Gertz is subject to similar observations.... I am unreconciled to the Gertz holding and believe that it should be overruled."

Dun & Bradstreet narrowed the scope of Gertz in that it held that the requirement of showing actual malice or negligence in Gertz applies only to issues of public concern, not to libel cases involving discussions of purely private matters. This created a new distinction in the form of a "private matters" test in libel law: courts must now make a public-versus-private matter determination in libel cases. This case began when Dun & Bradstreet, a credit reporting agency, falsely informed some of its clients that the construction company Greenmoss Builders had filed for bankruptcy. The false credit report had resulted from a young worker's negligent (but nonmalicious) error in checking records. Even though Greenmoss could not show actual malice, it won a $350,000 libel judgment against Dun & Bradstreet. In upholding the judgment against Dun & Bradstreet, the Supreme Court ruled that credit rating reports are not a matter of public concern and should thus not be subject to the actual malice rule established in New York Times v. Sullivan and expanded in Gertz. The Court held that the actual malice requirement from Gertz would still apply to issues of public concern, but not in libel cases involving private matters. The Dun & Bradstreet decision suggests that the pendulum is swinging back toward the common law theory of strict liability, at least for credit reporting agencies: even if a false credit report is the result of an honest mistake, the agency will be held liable, and presumed and punitive damages may be recovered without a showing of actual malice.

Dun & Bradstreet v. Greenmoss Builders (1985) also touched on the question of whether the New York Times Co. and Gertz principles that public officials and public figures must prove actual malice applied only to media defendants or extended to non-media defendants as well. In Dun & Bradstreet the Supreme Court said that "the rights of the institutional media are no greater and no less than those enjoyed by other individuals or organizations engaged in the same activities." Dun & Bradstreet v. Greenmoss Builders (1985).

12. Miscellaneous Constitutional Privileges Claimed by Journalists in Defamation Cases

a. Nondisclosure of the Editorial Decision Making Process

In Herbert v. Lando (1979), a CBS news producer involved in the production and broadcast of "Sixty Minutes" claimed a First Amendment right not to divulge his state of mind in the preparation of a segment about Army Col. Anthony Herbert and his conduct during the Vietnam War. Col. Herbert, who did not contest his status as a public figure, claimed that the material in the segment was defamatory and was put together in a knowingly untruthful way or with reckless disregard of the truth. He attempted to establish this necessary element of malice in the course of a pretrial deposition of CBS News producer Lando. The United States District Court rejected Lando's claim of privilege and ordered him to answer Herbert's questions, but a divided United States Court of Appeals reversed. The United States Supreme Court reversed the court of appeals and ruled that no First

Amendment privilege existed to protect newspersons from testifying as to the editorial process when such testimony is material to the proof of a critical element of the plaintiff's action, here defendant's malice, i.e., knowing untruthfulness or reckless disregard of the truth.

In public figure cases, the plaintiff's inquiry into the editorial process may therefore include:

    1.   the reporter's or editor's conclusions during research and investigation regarding people or leads to be pursued or not pursued;

    2.   the reporter's or editor's conclusions about facts imparted by interviewees and his or her state of mind with respect to the veracity of the persons interviewed;

    3.   the basis for the reporter's or editor's conclusions as to the veracity of persons or information.

    4.   conversations with journalistic colleagues and others concerning the manner in which a story should be approached, handled and published, particularly discussions as to the inclusion and exclusion of material;

    5.   the reporter's or editor's intentions as manifested by his or her decisions to include or exclude particular material.

While it is now clear after the Herbert case that no privilege exists under the First Amendment for newspersons to refuse to reveal the information listed above, at least one state's reporter "shield" law has been construed as protecting newspersons from testifying as to editorial processes on the ground that forced revelations in this area would have a chilling effect on the free exchange of ideas between journalistic colleagues. Maressa v. New Jersey Monthly (1982).

b. Neutral Reportage

The concept of neutral reportage developed as a result of a case in which a New York Times reporter was covering a dispute between the Audubon Society and the chemical industry over DDT's impact on birds. Because annual bird counts were showing increasing numbers, some chemists argued that DDT was not harmful, but the Audubon Society believed that the higher numbers were due to more birdwatchers with better training. An Audubon Society publication warned members that any scientist who argued that the continued use of the pesticide DDT had not taken a serious toll on bird life was "someone who is being paid to lie about it or is parroting something he knows little about." When the New York Times reporter asked an Audubon Society official who was making these arguments, the official gave the reporter a list of five scientists whom the Society believed were being paid by the chemical industry to argue that DDT was not killing birds. The story concerning the bird count with the names of the five scientists was subsequently published by the New York Times and three of the named scientists filed libel actions against the Audubon Society, Society officials and the Times.

In reversing the jury award and judgment against the Times, the United States Court of Appeals for the Second Circuit held that the First Amendment protects the accurate and disinterested reporting of charges by a responsible and prominent person or organization, regardless of the reporter's private views regarding their accuracy. Such protection of journalists from tort liability for defamation was characterized by the Second Circuit as "neutral reportage." Edwards v. National Audubon Society. See also Medico v. Time, Inc. (1981). In a subsequent case the Second Circuit made clear that the repetition of defamatory charges in a piece of advocacy journalism espousing and concurring in such charges did not constitute neutral reportage and was not constitutionally protected. Cianci v. New York Times Publishing Co. (1980). In Dickey v. CBS, Inc. (1978), the Third Circuit rejected neutral reportage because it might permit a reporter to publish defamatory material even if he or she entertained serious doubts about whether it were true or not.

Some legal observers believe it is unlikely that the Supreme Court would deny the constitutional privilege recognized in New York Times Company to one who publishes a damaging charge he or she strongly suspects to be untrue but then substitute another constitutional privilege to protect one who, with reckless disregard for the truth, publishes the charge simply because it came from a reputable and prominent source. And if the publisher believes the story is true, he or she will be protected under the

New York Times Company privilege if the target of the charges is a public figure in relation to the controversy, without regard to "neutral reportage."

On the other hand, Justice Blackmun has commented favorably on neutral reportage in dicta: "Were this Court to adopt the neutral reportage theory, the facts of [Harte–Hanks] might fit within it." Harte–Hanks Communications v. Connaughton (1989). It is worth noting that Justice Blackmun's positive reference to neutral reportage was made in a case where the Journal News was found guilty of actual malice.

With no guidance from the Supreme Court other than Justice Blackmun's dicta in Harte–Hanks, some courts have rejected neutral reportage during the past decade, whereas other courts have adopted it. In general, however, newspersons may find the neutral reportage privilege to be a weak reed to rely on when publishing questionable charges, even if made by responsible sources.

CHAPTER III

PRIVACY AND THE
MASS MEDIA

A. INTRODUCTION

The invasion of personal privacy by government, private organizations and the mass media has reached monumental proportions by the last decade of the twentieth century. This invasion is almost inevitable given our crowded society and the development of sophisticated electronic devices such as directional microphones, powerful miniature listening devices, telephoto lenses and the all-pervasive computer with its power to store and retrieve the minutiae of our lives. The problem is exacerbated by the power of the mass media to disseminate information about individuals, including their physical images.

The difficulty that confronts the law is to control this invasion without, at the same time, crippling a free society's ability to obtain the information necessary for its proper operation. Thus far, the common law has not been very effective in harmonizing these competing private and societal interests. Perhaps this is because the competing interests are so fundamental yet so difficult to define. It has been said that the right to be let alone and to withdraw from the "madding crowd" is the essence of individualism and that privacy is the first interest to go in a totalitarian state. Nevertheless, the individual lives in a society which may, from time to time, have curiosity about him or her. And the mass media may become the instrument for satisfying that curiosity. As difficult as the task is, it is for the law to determine when public interest concerning an individual fulfills a legitimate need of a democratic society and when it does not.

B. HISTORY AND DEVELOPMENT OF THE COMMON LAW

As common law torts go, invasion of privacy is of relatively recent vintage. Its development is traceable to an article in the Harvard Law Review for December 15, 1890 by Samuel D. Warren and his then law partner Louis D. Brandeis. In it they argued that accepted tort doctrine confirmed the existence of a right to privacy, the violation of which was actionable. 4 Harv.L.Rev. 193 (1890). The article was apparently precipitated by the Boston newspapers' coverage of Warren's private social affairs. It should be remembered that this was the era of vicious circulation battles and sensational and often fraudulent press coverage to win readership—the age of "yellow journalism."

The article created great interest in the legal profession but the first test of the theory was unsuccessful. In Roberson v. Rochester Folding Box Co. (1902) a flour mill ordered a woman's portrait lithographed on its boxes without her consent. The woman, who did not relish being referred to as the "Flour of the Family," brought suit for damages for invasion of privacy. In a four-to-three ruling, the New York Court of Appeals held, contrary to Warren and Brandeis' contention, that no right of privacy existed at common law. If interests in privacy were to be protected, the legislatures would have to do it. The New York legislature did just that the following year by enacting a civil rights statute making it both a crime and a tort to appropriate the name or likeness of any person for "trade purposes" without that person's consent.

The first judicial acceptance of the existence of a right to privacy came in Pavesich v. New England Life Insurance (1905), a case very much like Roberson in which a newspaper advertisement for an insurance company contained a photograph of the plaintiff and attributed to him certain words encouraging the purchase of the company's life insurance. He had not consented to such depiction and sued the company. Contrary to the New York court the Georgia Supreme Court found a right of privacy in the common law and reversed the trial court's order dismissing Pavesich's complaint.

C. THE COMMON LAW TODAY

As of 1993 a right of privacy was recognized either by common law, statute or both, in 49 states and the District of Columbia, according to a study done by the Reporters Committee for Freedom of the Press. Four states, Nebraska, Rhode Island, Virginia and Wisconsin recognize the right only by statute. The only jurisdiction which has not recognized at least some aspect of the tort of invasion of privacy is Minnesota. See Ruzicka v. Conde Nast Publications (1993); Hendry v. Conner (1975). The right that is accorded varies to some extent in definition and scope from jurisdiction to jurisdiction, reflecting the immaturity of the tort and its imperfect development to date or conflicting legislative interests.

The imperfect development extends to the lack of any articulated theory of liability. While the tort in several of its forms is suggestive of an intentional civil wrong, it is possible that some aspects of it permit liability without a showing of fault. The uncertainty as to the theory of liability may arise from the fact that the tort has four distinct branches:

1. appropriation of another's name or likeness;
2. unreasonable intrusion upon another's seclusion;
3. publicity which unreasonably places another in a false light before the public; and
4. unreasonable publicity given to another's private life.

See Cox Broadcasting Corp. v. Cohn (1975); Restatement of Torts 2d 652A–652E; W. Prosser and W. Keeton, Handbook of the Law of Torts, 851–866 (5th ed. 1984).

1. Appropriation

We have already come across this aspect of the right of privacy in relation to the Roberson and Pavesich cases and the New York statute. What is protected here is the individual's concern for the uses to which his or her name, personality and image are put. The law gives the individual the option to prevent others from trading on his or her name or likeness or to permit such trading for a price.

a. Right of Publicity

Whereas the traditional tort of appropriation was designed to protect the right to be left alone and not to be exploited for commercial purposes, the right of publicity is designed to protect celebrities and seems to deal only with who should profit from exploitation of the celebrity's name or likeness. It is essentially a property right—in one's own personality and image—as opposed to a personal right.

The right of publicity has been defined as follows: "The distinctive aspect of the common-law right of publicity is that it recognizes the commercial value of the picture or representation of a prominent person or performer and protects his proprietary interest in the profitability of his public reputation or persona." Ali v. Playgirl, Inc. (1978), (heavyweight Muhammed Ali won injunction to stop distribution of Playgirl Magazine which included drawing of frontally nude black athlete resembling Ali and verses referring to "The Greatest").

The media are rarely sued for appropriation type invasions. It has long been settled that while the media normally disseminate news about individuals in the hope, overall, of obtaining a profit for their operations from circulation and advertising, this is not such appropriation as would justify the award of damages.

When such suits are brought they are usually in connection with a medium's self promotion in which a news or feature story involving the plaintiff is republished to illustrate the medium's self-proclaimed excellence in informing the public. For instance, in Booth v. Curtis Publishing Co. (1962), the late actress Shirley Booth (television's "Hazel" of the 1960s), whose photograph had appeared by consent in Holiday Magazine in connection with an article about a prominent resort in Jamaica where she had been a guest, sued the magazine's publisher when it reproduced her photograph in full-page promotional advertisements for the magazine published in two other periodicals. Both advertisements presented a striking photograph of Miss Booth in a large straw hat and up to her neck in water as a sample of the contents of Holiday. Beneath the photograph were the words "Shirley Booth and chapeau, from a recent issue of Holiday." But even here, the court refused to award damages under the New York privacy statute because such advertising was only "incidental" to the sale and dissemination of news. The decision turned on the court's construction of the statute and it is uncertain that a similar case would have the same resolution in jurisdictions recognizing a common law right of privacy. Prudence therefore dictates that when a medium advertises itself by use of antecedent news and feature stories and photographs it obtain the permission for republication from the individuals involved.

Although misappropriation and the right of publicity would seem to be fairly straightforward in that advertisers generally understand that they must have models' written consent to use their name or likeness, litigation has resulted from the question of whether or not the right of publicity can be passed on to one's heirs. Privacy is a personal right and normally dies with the complaining party. The only apparent qualification is that a deceased person's image or persona may be so desirable for commercial exploitation that a transferable property right in the image is created, as in the case of the actor Bela Lugosi's image as Count Dracula or the Marx Brothers' show business persona. At present, various courts have taken three different approaches: 1) One is that the right of publicity terminates upon death. Under this approach, when celebrities die, their names and likenesses are available for anyone to use without legal liability. 2) The opposite approach is that death has no effect on the right of publicity. In jurisdictions holding this view, the celebrity's heirs must consent to the use of the deceased celebrity's name or likeness. 3) Between these two extremes is a third approach holding that the right of publicity may survive death only if it was commercially exploited during the individual's lifetime. In jurisdictions where the right of publicity continues beyond death, state statutes provide for survivability of the right of publicity for periods varying from 10 years after death in Tennessee to 50 years after death in California.

In addition to the question of whether the right of publicity survives beyond a celebrity's death, the use of celebrity "look-alikes" has also resulted in litigation. The use of "look-alikes" may not only violate a person's right of publicity; it may also violate Section 43(a) of the Lanham Act, amended in 1988, which holds that anyone who falsely suggests that a celebrity endorses a particular product or service is liable if consumers or the general public will be confused by this suggestion. 15 U.S.C.A. §§ 1051; 1988 amendments 102 Stat. 3935. In recent years, Jacqueline Kennedy Onassis, Woody Allen and other celebrities have won judgments against advertisers who used models who closely resembled them. Onassis v. Christian Dior– New York, Inc. (1985); Allen v. Men's World Outlet (1988); Allen v. National Video, Inc. (1985).

In addition to allowing celebrities to recover damages against advertisers who used look-alikes, there have been cases allowing singers to recover damages for a "sound-alike" violation of their right of publicity. In this case, Ford Motor Company's ad agency Young & Rubicam approached Bette Midler, asking her to sing her hit song "Do You Want to Dance?" for a commercial. When she declined, the agency hired Midler's backup singer Ula Hedwig to sing the song and asked her to "sound as much as possible like Midler." Although the ad agency had obtained permission to use the copyrighted song, Midler sued, arguing that listeners would believe it was Midler herself singing. Midler ultimately won a jury award of $400,000. Midler v. Ford Motor Company (1988). See also Waits v. Frito–Lay, Inc. (1992), ($2.6 million verdict affirmed for singer Tom Waits for imitation of his distinctive singing voice in his song "Step Right Up;" punitive damages explicitly sustained because commercial was "calculated risk" three months after Midler decision).

In addition to protecting celebrities' right of publicity from look-alike and sound-alike imitations, courts have even protected other aspects of a celebrity's public persona. For example, a maker of portable toilets called its product "Here's Johnny," adding the phrase, "the world's foremost commodian." Comedian Johnny Carson was not amused, and sued for violation of his right of publicity. Although a trial judge dismissed the case, the appellate court held that using "Here's Johnny" as a brand name did violate Carson's right of publicity because the phrase "Here's Johnny" was associated with Carson in the minds of millions of television viewers. Carson v. Here's Johnny (1983).

Wheel of Fortune wheel spinner Vanna White relied on Carson v. Here's Johnny in her case against a company which sponsored an ad in which a female robot dressed like White is posed on a set exactly like that of Wheel of Fortune. Finding that the ad had used her "identity" even though White herself was not in it, the Ninth Circuit sustained White's common law right of publicity claim and remanded the case for a jury decision on whether the ad had violated both the Lanham Act and White's right of publicity. White v. Samsung (1992).

b. Applicability of First Amendment Theory to Appropriation Cases

It is clear after the Supreme Court's decision in Zacchini v. Scripps–Howard Broadcasting Co. (1977) that no First Amendment protection is afforded newsgathering organizations which appropriate the name, image, persona or unique presence of an individual, thus invading the individual's right of publicity. Zacchini performed a "human cannonball" act in which he was shot into a safety net 200 feet away. Over his objection his act, presented at a local county fair, was videotaped by a reporter for the defendant's television station and was shown on a news program later the same day. Zacchini sued the broadcasting company for unlawful appropriation of his professional property.

Although Zacchini was unsuccessful in the trial court, the United States Supreme Court ultimately upheld Zacchini's right to seek damages against the defendant. The Court held that the defendant's conduct invaded both Zacchini's right to earn a living as an entertainer and society's interest in encouraging creative activity. The First and Fourteenth Amendments were not designed to protect conduct of a newsgatherer that interferes with an individual's right to earn money by publicizing himself.

The rationale of the Court in refusing First Amendment protection to the newsgatherer who violates an individual's right of publicity is that news and information will not be denied the public in this type of situation because the individual will make it available to the public but for a price which he or she has a legally protected right to exact. The Court also observed that protecting Zacchini's right of publicity was analogous to enforcing copyright law: just as artists and writers need copyright laws to protect them, Zacchini's right of publicity provided the economic incentive for him to create a performance of interest to the public.

Although Zacchini makes it clear that the media may not broadcast a performer's entire act, in New Kids on the Block v. News America Publishing, Inc. (1990) the Ninth Circuit held that use of the New Kids' trademark constituted fair use and not misappropriation because the trademark was used in a newsgathering activity. In this case, USA Today and Star Magazine invited readers to participate in a survey via a 900–telephone number to determine which one of the New Kids was most popular. The New Kids charged that USA Today and Star Magazine had violated their right of publicity, but the court dismissed their claim on the basis of First Amendment protection for newsgathering.

2. Intrusion

a. *Common Law*

This tort consists of the violation of one's legally protected physical sphere of privacy without one's consent. The intrusion may or may not also constitute the tort of trespass. Often the intrusion itself is not physical but consists of eavesdropping with telephoto lenses or electronic listening devices in areas private to aggrieved individuals such as their homes or offices. When individuals are in a public zone, however, they may be photographed or otherwise recorded without fear of legal action so long as the recording is reasonable.

This particular aspect of invasion of privacy is different in nature from the other three in that no publication regarding the victim need be involved. This distinction is important when through an intrusion a news medium learns of matters of public interest and publishes them. In that situation, while the publication itself may be privileged on the basis of newsworthiness (see pp. 141–145 infra), the intrusion that made the story possible is not.

An excellent but fortunately rare example of media intrusion is Dietemann v. Time, Inc. (1971). There, a male and female employee of Life Magazine went to the home of Dietemann, a plumber who practiced healing with clay, minerals and herbs. Through misrepresentations of fact they gained entry to the plaintiff's home. Once inside, the female employee complained to Dietemann of a lump in her breast. While examining the breast with an assortment of gadgets, Dietemann was secretly photographed by Life's male employee using a hidden camera. In addition, the conversation between the woman and Dietemann was transmitted by a radio transmitter hidden in the woman's purse to a tape recorder in a parked car occupied by another Life employee and officials from the local district attorney's office and the California Department of Health. The whole affair was a cooperative venture between Life and the public officals to aid in the crackdown on quackery in Southern California and to allow the magazine to write about it. Life published its story and pictures following Dietemann's plea of nolo contendere to criminal misdemeanor charges.

Dietemann thereafter sued for invasion of privacy and won a trial court judgment for $1,000. In contending on appeal that the judgment should be reversed, Time, Inc. took the position that the First Amendment immunized it from liability for its intrusion because its employees were using the secret devices to gather news. In answer Judge Hufstedler said, "The First Amendment is not a license to trespass, to steal, or to intrude by electronic means into the precincts of another's home or office" simply because such means are used by media representatives in the course of newsgathering. Dietemann v. Time, Inc. (1971). In affirming the judgment for Dietemann, Judge Hufstedler clearly distinguished between the intrusion and the subsequent publication of the story and photographs. A privilege might exist for the publication but it does not extend to the antecedent intrusion.

Dietemann is a troubling case not so much because of its denial of any privilege to intrude in the course of bona fide newsgathering, but because it raises questions as to the extent to which newsgatherers, especially investigative reporters, may go before they are liable for intrusion. As media lawyer Floyd Abrams has said,

> "It is one thing to say that as a general matter one's home is sacrosanct from invasion by outsiders and that journalists are as responsible as the rest of us for illegal or improper eavesdropping.... It is quite another to conclude that when a person passes himself off as a doctor and uses his home as his office, journalists may not act as prospective patients and record the illegal activities that occur there." F. Abrams, "The Press, Privacy and the Constitution," N.Y. Times Magazine, Aug. 21, 1977, p. 68.

Despite the ruling in Dietemann, using concealed tape recorders is a great temptation to investigative journalists, and has resulted in continued litigation. (See McCall v. Courier–Journal and Louisville Times Co. (1981), Cassidy v. ABC (1978), Shevin v. Sunbeam Television Corp. (1977), Benford v. ABC (1980), and Boddie v. ABC (1989).

b. Federal Legislation

The use of concealed recording devices by both journalists and law enforcement officials has caused

Congress to become increasingly concerned with governmental and private intrusions upon individual privacy. In 1986 Congress had passed the Omnibus Crime Control and Safe Streets Act, 18 U.S.C.A. §§ 2510–2520. This was later amended as the "Electronic Communications Privacy Act of 1986," also known as the Federal Wiretap Statute. This prohibits under criminal penalty the interception of any conversation carried over a wire or a nonwire conversation in a setting where one expects privacy.

Therefore a journalist who uses a wiretap to record a phone conversation between two other people or "bugs" a room in which a meeting is held could be liable for violating the statute. The United States Attorney General is authorized to initiate civil actions in the United States District Court to enjoin threatened felony violations. Law enforcement personnel and other government officers authorized to engage in electronic surveillance or, as in the case of employees of the Federal Communications Commission, to monitor electronic communications, are generally exempted from the provisions of the legislation when acting within their proper authority.

The same legislation also makes unlawful many acts of intentional unauthorized accessing of information storage facilities through which electronic communications services are provided, resulting in the obtaining or altering of information contained therein or the preventing of authorized access to the information while in electronic storage. By this legislation, Congress has recognized the need to

protect privacy of communication in our high technology computer age.

But there is an important exception. The statute
expressly permits a participant in the conversation
to secretly record it, provided that the participant is
not taping it for the purpose of committing any
criminal or tortious act. 18 U.S.C. § 2511(2)(d).
This exception allows a reporter to secretly record
his or her telephone conversations with the person
being interviewed because the consent of only one
party to the conversation, in this case, the reporter
him/herself, is required. Of course, if the reporter's
purpose in taping the conversation is to commit a
tort such as libel, the reporter would be violating
the statute. The question of the reporter's motivation in such cases is generally left to a jury. Thus,
it is legal in most jurisdictions for reporters to
conceal audiotape recorders while talking to news
sources. But California, Delaware, Florida, Illinois,
Louisiana, Maryland, Massachusetts, Michigan,
Montana, New Hampshire, Oregon, Pennsylvania
and Washington have outlawed such recordings.
These states are "all-party consent" states, meaning that all parties to a wire or oral communication
must give prior consent before a conversation is
tape-recorded. The other states are "one-party
consent" states, meaning that participant recording
is permitted provided there is no intent to commit a
tort. In Maine, New Hampshire, Delaware, Georgia, Alabama, Michigan, South Dakota and Utah, it
is illegal to use a hidden video camera to record
people without their consent, but it is legal in all

other states. The right to surreptitiously audiotape a conversation is not concomitant with the right to videotape it. For example, in Massachusetts, it is illegal to conceal an audiotape recorder, but it is legal to use a hidden videocamera.

In addition to the Federal Wiretap Statute, the FCC's "Phone Rule," (47 C.F.R. § 64.501; § 73.-1206) requires that before recording a telephone conversation for broadcast, a radio or television station must tell any party to the call that it intends to broadcast the conversation, whether the conversation is being taped or broadcast live. With regard to personal interviews, the FCC states that "No person shall use ... a device ... for the purpose of overhearing or recording the private conversations of others unless such use is authorized by all of the parties engaging in the conversation." 47 C.F.R. § 2.701(a).

Anyone may be the subject of observation, photographing, recording or even questioning in a public place. The only caveat is that journalists and photographers may not hound or harass anyone. The classic example of harassment by a photographer is Galella v. Onassis (1973). Free-lance photographer Ron Galella, wanting to profit from selling pictures of Jacqueline Kennedy Onassis, followed her so closely that he endangered the safety of her and her children. For example, he nearly ran over her with his motorboat while she was swimming, and he spooked a horse her son was riding. Onassis obtained a court order requiring Galella to stay 25 feet away from her and 30 feet away from her children. Ten years later she felt compelled to sue him for intrusion again because he had ignored the original injunction; this time the court found Galella in contempt, but maintained that he still had the right to photograph Onassis in public provided that he stayed 25 feet away. Galella v. Onassis (1982).

c. Possession of Stolen Material and Intrusion by Journalists on Private Property

While Dietemann and other recent cases make clear the danger of intrusive behavior by representatives of the media, they are limited to situations in which media representatives are directly involved. In situations in which the media simply publicize the fruits of another's intrusion the courts have usually rejected the idea of liability on the part of the media. For instance in Pearson v. Dodd (1969) employees of the late Senator Dodd rifled his files, made copies of some allegedly incriminating documents and turned the copies over to defendant Jack Anderson, who was aware of the manner in which they were obtained, and who subsequently published excerpts from them. The United States Court of Appeals held that the defendants had not themselves been guilty of any intrusion. See also Liberty Lobby, Inc. v. Pearson (1967).

The position taken in the Dodd case makes considerable sense. If the media were required to consider the means by which news is obtained by independent sources out of fear for tort liability, the newsgathering process would be severely hampered. But it should be kept in mind that if media representatives actually encourage or aid and abet others in acts of intrusion, it is reasonably certain that they and their corporate employers will be held liable for such conduct under ordinary principles of tort law.

Although outright intrusion by the media into the privacy of individuals is rare, an analogous problem is becoming increasingly frequent. Property owners may refuse to cooperate with newspersons, particularly television crews, seeking news on their premises. This raises the question whether media representatives have the right under the First Amendment to go without authorization upon private property or otherwise to utilize such property in the interest of obtaining news. The issue often comes up in connection with private property which is open to the public for business purposes. For example, CBS reporters doing a story on reported health code violations at a New York restaurant entered it without permission, with cameras rolling and bright lights blazing. The restaurant, called Le Mistral, sued CBS for trespass and recovered $1200. Le Mistral, Inc. v. Columbia Broadcasting System (1978).

The basic position of media executives in this kind of situation is that their representatives ought to be able to enter privately owned places of public accommodation along with the rest of the public and that if they are not allowed to enter, the flow of news will be constricted in violation of the First Amendment.

These arguments are doubtful for reasons suggested in the analogous case of Lloyd Corp., Ltd. v. Tanner (1972), where the Supreme Court ruled that the private owner of a shopping mall could bar distributors of leaflets protesting the draft and the Vietnam War from the mall. First, the public's license to enter a private business establishment is limited to engaging in activities directly related to that business and does not normally extend to the pursuit of unrelated business such as newsgathering or propagandizing customers. And Hudgens v. N.L.R.B. (1976) permitted a shopping mall owner to bar from his premises union picketing of a particular store involved in a labor contract dispute. Second, it is generally difficult to find state action when the ordinary property owner bars media representatives from using his or her property. For example, when reporters tried to cover a demonstration by 300 members of the Sunbelt Alliance at the construction site of a nuclear power plant owned by the Public Service Company of Oklahoma, a private corporation, the reporters followed the demonstrators through fences and were arrested, convicted of trespassing and fined $25 each. Stahl v. State of Oklahoma (1983). The purpose of the First and Fourteenth Amendments is to protect freedom of expression from government encroachment only. Finally, even accepting the applicability of the First Amendment, the media's position assumes that First Amendment rights are always superior to common law property rights and statutory criminal trespass provisions. But given the current disposition of the Supreme Court and the revitalization of the balancing approach to the First Amendment this assumption is not necessarily correct.

There is thus some uncertainty as to the line between legality and intrusion regarding admission to private property. But as a result of recent cases we do know that:

(1) outright misrepresentation by newsgatherers to gain initial entry to private or even public property is a very risky business and should not be resorted to except in extremis;

(2) unauthorized entry by newsgatherers onto private or public property constitutes intrusion as to individuals present and trespass as to the property, and that goes for private places of public accommodation as well;

(3) permission of relevant public officials provides the necessary license to gather news in public buildings;

(4) permission by police or fire officials to newsgatherers to accompany the officials onto private property while they conduct official business in the absence of the owner may or may not insulate newsgatherers against tort liability in Florida. See Florida Publishing Co. v. Fletcher (1976) (no tort liability for journalists invited into private home by police), but compare Green Valley School Inc. v. Cowles Forida Broadcasting, Inc. (1976) (television journalists invited to accompany police on midnight raid of school held

liable for trespass), and Prahl v. Brosamle (1980).
See K. Middleton, Journalists, Trespass and Officials: Closing the Door of Florida Publishing Co.
v. Fletcher, 16 Pepperdine Law Review 259
(1989).

d. *Applicability of First Amendment Theory to Intrusion*

As for intrusion, since it involves no publication
in and of itself, the First Amendment is not directly
implicated. Because the wrong occurs when the
information is gathered rather than when it is
published, journalists cannot expect any protection
from the First Amendment if they are liable for
intrusion.

3. False Light

a. *Nature and Limitations*

Creating a false image for an individual or placing
him or her in a false light through publication may
be actionable as an invasion of privacy whether or
not such falsity involves defamation. One form of
this invasion is to ascribe to individuals political or
other views which they do not in fact hold or falsely
attribute to them authorship of certain writings or
remarks. Another dangerous practice is to use a
picture or videotape of someone out of context. For
example, in Leverton v. Curtis Publishing Co.
1951), a photograph of the plaintiff, a child who had
been struck down on a public street by a careless
motorist, was properly published in a local newspaper because of its newsworthiness. But the same

news photograph was published several months later in the Saturday Evening Post to illustrate an article entitled "They Ask to Be Killed," dealing with childhood carelessness. The child sued, and the defendant publisher was found liable for placing the child in the false light of being a careless pedestrian.

Similarly, a "voice-over" in a television newscast resulted in liability in Duncan v. WJLA–TV, Inc. (1984). In this case, WJLA–TV had used video footage of people walking down a crowded street in Washington, D.C. as the backdrop for a story on genital herpes. At one point, as the news anchor noted in a voice-over that there is no cure, the camera focused on Linda Duncan as she stood on a corner. Because she had been clearly identified, she sued for defamation and false light invasion of privacy, and won a small damage award from WJLA–TV.

Still another dangerous enterprise is the intentional fictionalization of activities or events involving actual identifiable persons. One book publisher discovered to its sorrow the cost of such venture when it published a fictionalized biography of the great baseball pitcher Warren Spahn. The book dramatized and fictionalized such matters as Spahn's relationship to his father, his war record, his courtship with his wife and even his thoughts while on the pitching mound. The author even invented long dialogues between Spahn and those with whom he associated. The New York trial court in Spahn v. Julian Messner, Inc. (1964) cast its decision for Spahn in terms of the New York privacy statute, specifically, appropriation of Spahn's image and personality by the defendant for commercial advantage. But the decree to enjoin further publication and distribution of the book and to award substantial damages was ultimately upheld by the New York Court of Appeals on a theory consistent with that underlying the United States Supreme Court's first decision in the area of invasion of privacy by the media. See Time, Inc. v. Hill (1967).

The importance of the element of intention in false light cases was underlined by the Supreme Court in the Hill case. There, the complaining parties, James J. Hill and his wife and five children, had become the involuntary subjects of a front page news story after being held hostage by three escaped convicts in their home for 19 hours in the late summer of 1952. The family was released unharmed and Hill stressed to newspersons at the time that the convicts had treated the family courteously and had neither molested anyone nor acted violently. After the incident Hill discouraged all media efforts to keep the family in the public spotlight. Less than a year later Joseph Hayes' novel "The Desperate Hours" was published depicting the experience of a family of four held hostage by three escaped convicts in the family's home. But, unlike the Hill family's experience, the fictional family suffered violence at the hands of the convicts; the father and son were beaten and the daughter subjected to verbal sexual harassment.

At this point a lawsuit by Hill against Hayes and his publisher for invasion of privacy would have been doubtful because of the difficulty of identifying the fictional family of four with the Hill family of seven. That difficulty was removed when, in conjunction with the production of a play based upon the book, Life magazine published an article indicating that the play "The Desperate Hours," actually mirrored the Hill family's experience. The article was accompanied by staged photographs taken in the house in which the Hill family had been held captive. The photographs dramatized supposed incidents during the family's ordeal.

Though there was no doubt that the Life article and photographs had placed Hill and his family in a false light, a closely divided Supreme Court reversed a lower court judgment awarding compensatory damages to Hill because the trial court's instructions to the jury failed to require that the plaintiff establish that the defendant either knew the facts creating the false light were untrue or that it acted in reckless disregard of the truth. Innocent mistake or negligence in creating the false light were held to be improper bases for liability under the First and Fourteenth Amendments. This ruling is obviously parallel to that in New York Times Co. v. Sullivan (1964), discussed supra, at pp. 78–79. The analogy with defamation impelled a bare majority of the Supreme Court in Time, Inc. v. Hill (1967) to limit recovery in false light cases to those situations in which the falsity was known to the defendant or the communication was made by him or her in reckless disregard for the truth. The concern of the majority was to provide a margin for error for the media in gathering and reporting the news.

b. Relationship to Defamation

As in the Hill case, not every false light case involves untruths that injure reputation, but every act of defamation will, while injuring reputation, also place the victim in a false light in the public's mind. Indeed, many actions for defamation are accompanied by actions for invasion of privacy. This raises the intriguing question whether the defamation action might not eventually fall into disuse because of the comparatively greater ease in establishing false light. The defamatory character of false communication need not be shown and many technical requirements of defamation actions may be bypassed. But unless and until defamation actions fade away, both false light and defamation should be pleaded in appropriate cases.

c. Applicability of First Amendment Theory to False Light Cases

In marked contrast to the appropriation and intrusion branches, the Constitution does place limits on the reach of the false light tort because of its potential to interfere with publication and restrict the flow of news and information to the public.

Although the Hill case was narrowly decided after oral arguments in two successive terms of the Court, its basic First Amendment thrust was confirmed by a broad majority of the Court in Cantrell

v. Forest City Publishing Co. (1974). Yet the Court in Cantrell did raise, without deciding, the question whether, parallel to Gertz v. Robert Welch, Inc. (1974), a state might constitutionally limit Hill by applying a more relaxed standard of liability, meaning negligence, for the communication of false light type statements injurious to private persons. The very act of questioning the scope of the ruling in Hill suggests that the Court may be disposed to limit the protection afforded the media in this area in much the same way it did with the protection originally afforded in the New York Times Co.– Rosenbloom line of defamation cases (see Chapter II, supra).

Without waiting for the Supreme Court to clarify its position on whether Gertz may have modified Time v. Hill so that a private person merely has to show negligence rather than actual malice to win a false light case, at least one state court, the West Virginia Supreme Court, has held that it is free to set negligence as the standard in false light cases involving private persons. Crump v. Beckley Newspapers (1983). See also Wood v. Hustler Magazine, Inc. (1984) (applying a negligence standard under supposed Texas law).

The crucial problem with the false light tort is that it covers false but non-defamatory statements. Defamatory statements raise a red flag warning editors to carefully verify, modify or delete them, but neutral or even laudatory false statements provide no such warning to editors. Editors are thus required to double check *every* asserted fact about an individual at great cost in time and resources or else risk liability. The tension between false light and First Amendment protection for the media was noted in the groundbreaking case of Renwick v. News and Observer Publishing Company (1984). In this case an associate dean at the University of North Carolina brought suit for libel and false light against two newspapers for allegedly misreporting that about 800 black students had been denied admission over a three-year period. Upon finding no defamation, the North Carolina Supreme Court considered the false light claim, but expressed concern that the false light tort would allow recovery for non-defamatory false statements. The court said it would create "a grave risk [to] ... a free press in a free society if we saddle the press with the impossible burden of verifying to a certainty the facts associated in news articles with a person's name, picture or portrait, *particularly as related to nondefamatory matter.*" Renwick v. News and Observer Publishing Company. Renwick is significant because it is the first appellate decision to wholly and specifically reject the false light tort on the basis that it is redundant of defamation.

4. Public Disclosure of Private Facts

a. Nature and Limitations

Of the four common law branches of the invasion of privacy tort the most troublesome is the unreasonable publication of private facts of an embarrassing and objectionable nature. It is not always easy for reporters and editors to determine when publicity is unreasonable or even when facts must be viewed as private. There is the further problem of determining when private facts will be viewed by a reasonable person of ordinary sensibilities as offensive and objectionable, thus making public disclosure actionable. Then, too, in contrast to false light, truth will not shield the disclosing medium since the gravamen of the tort is the publication of private *facts* which the law deems worthy of protection.

Illustrative of this type of case is Sidis v. F–R Publishing Corp. (1940). William James Sidis was a child prodigy in the field of mathematics and graduated from Harvard College at the age of sixteen amid considerable public attention. A shy and retiring person, Sidis attempted to live down his fame and succeeded quite well until the New Yorker magazine of August 14, 1937, published a brief biographical sketch of Sidis under the title "Where Are They Now?" The sketch recounted Sidis' unusual background, traced his attempts to conceal his identity through the years, described his menial employment far from the field of mathematics and detailed certain bizarre conduct such as his collecting old street car transfers. The facts stated in the article were not alleged to be untrue. Rather, Sidis sued for the destruction of the obscurity he had so laboriously constructed for himself. His suit was unsuccessful because, among other things, the facts disclosed were held not of such nature as to be offensive and objectionable to persons of ordinary sensibilities.

The Sidis case is fairly typical of the result reached in cases brought in this area of invasion of privacy. While such cases are troublesome, only a handful of plaintiffs have met with success in the years since publication of Warren and Brandeis' article. The reason for this is the recognition by the courts of a very broad defense peculiar to this branch of the tort.

b. *The Newsworthiness Privilege*

By the common law defense of newsworthiness, the media are protected in publishing truthful matters of public interest. By and large, the courts have deferred to the media in determining what is of public interest. The motto of the judiciary here might be, "If they publish it, it must news." This approach has two major virtues, according to Professors Don R. Pember and Dwight L. Teeter, Jr. First, it provides a wide range of freedom of expression and second, it is easy to administer because the judge does not have to act as a social censor, determining what is news and what is not. Pember and Teeter, "Privacy and the Press Since Time, Inc. v. Hill," 50 Wash.L.Rev. 57, 77 (1974).

Given such deference, the media would be protected in the exercise of news judgment in publishing almost anything true about individuals that has any claim to the public's interest. Certainly the content of public records, which almost by definition involve matters of public interest, may be publicized under this privilege. There are limits to judicial tolerance, however, such as the publication without consent of a photograph showing the plaintiff emerging from a fun house with her dress blown above her waist by a jet of air, as in Daily Times Democrat v. Graham (1964), publication of the intimate details of a hospitalized woman's exotic and embarrassing disease together with a picture of her in her hospital bed taken without consent as in Barber v. Time, Inc. (1942), or naming a minor father of an illegitimate child as in Hawkins v. Multimedia (1986). Another example of the limits of judicial tolerance occurred in Commonwealth v. Wiseman (1969). This case involved producer Frederick Wiseman's documentary film about patients and conditions at the Bridgewater State Hospital for the criminally insane. The film showed identifiable patients naked, being force-fed, and involved in sexual activity. Although the court permitted the film to be shown to mental health professionals, it upheld an injunction preventing the film's commercial distribution in order to protect the patients' privacy. In 1989 a judge permitted public exhibition of the film, provided that the inmates' faces were blurred, and in 1991 the same judge lifted the 1969 injunction completely, permitting public exhibition of the film provided that names and addresses of the individuals in the film remain confidential. Commonwealth v. Weissman (1991). Aside from cases such as Barber and Wiseman, however, normal judicial deference to media news judgment explains the general lack of success of plaintiffs in this area.

For example, in Virgil v. Time, Inc. (1975), the Ninth Circuit upheld a judgment for Sports Illustrated when it published an article reporting that body surfer Mike Virgil liked to put out burning cigarettes in his mouth, burn holes in his wrist with cigarettes, jump off billboards, dive headfirst down flights of stairs and eat live insects and spiders. The court accepted the defendant's argument that reporting Virgil's unusual diet was a legitimate journalistic attempt to explain his daring style of bodysurfing. Virgil v. Time, Inc.

The case of Oliver Sipple provides a second example of judicial deference to media news judgment. Sipple, an ex-Marine, saved the life of President Gerald Ford in 1975 by deflecting the shots of would-be assassin Sarah Jane Moore when he grabbed her arm as she fired. When the San Francisco Chronicle reported that Sipple was an active member of the gay community, his family broke off all communication with him. Sipple sued for invasion of privacy, but the case was ultimately dismissed on the grounds that Sipple had marched for gay rights and was a leader whose activism had often been reported in the gay press. Therefore, such personal facts were "in the public domain." Sipple v. Chronicle Publishing Company (1984).

The major exception to the newsworthiness defense is found in California, whose courts refuse to defer to the media on the issue of newsworthiness and have balanced the social value in publicity against the interests of the individual in maintaining privacy ever since Melvin v. Reid (1931), (producers of movie "The Red Kimono" held liable for invading privacy of Mrs. Melvin, a former prostitute acquitted of murder charges, who had rehabilitated herself). See also Briscoe v. Reader's Digest Association (1971) (rehabilitated ex-convict prevailed against Reader's Digest when it mentioned his crime of truck hijacking eleven years after its commission).

Obviously relevant to such judicial balancing is the social value of the information published, the lapse of time between the matter in question and its publication, the manner and context in which it is publicized and the effect on the individual of the unwanted publicity. The latter factor seems to have weighed heavily in the Melvin and Briscoe cases because of the judicial fear that publicity might seriously affect efforts at rehabilitation.

Even if authorities who take the position that the press is generally protected against liability when it publishes accounts of past news events are correct (see Pember, The Burgeoning Scope of "Access Privacy" and the Portent for a Free Press, 64 Iowa L.Rev. 1155, 1185–1186 (1979)), such republication is a fertile ground for litigation and the expenditure by the media of considerable time, energy and money.

Until First Amendment protection is accorded the media in cases like Barber, Melvin and Briscoe, journalists should approach the intimate and embarrassing facts of an individual's past or even present life with caution and exercise discretion in publishing such material. In this area good taste is the watchword.

c. Applicability of First Amendment Theory to Public Disclosure of Private Facts

The applicability of First Amendment protection to the invasion of privacy tort seems most compelling in the case of communications involving truthful matters of a private and embarrassing or harmful nature. Without broad constitutional protection here the media can be required under existing tort law to pay damages for truthfully informing the public about certain matters which individual plaintiffs consider private. As with false light the potential threat of damages could have a chilling effect on the enterprise of the media in gathering and disseminating news about individuals.

The issue here is whether the First and Fourteenth Amendments mandate the recognition of truth as an absolute defense in invasion of privacy cases. This broad issue was raised though not decided in Cox Broadcasting Corp. v. Cohn (1975). There, a reporter for an Atlanta television station learned the name of a 17–year–old gang rape and murder victim during the course of the proceedings against the rapists by examining the indictments, which had been made available by the clerk of the court. Later the same day the reporter broadcast a news report concerning the court proceedings and named the deceased victim of the crime. Shortly after the broadcast the father of the victim brought a civil action for damages against the reporter and his company, relying on a Georgia statute which prohibited the media from communicating the name of any woman who is raped and made such communication a misdemeanor.

Although the trial court entered summary judgment for the plaintiff father, who claimed his own privacy had been invaded by the broadcast, when the case reached the United States Supreme Court, the defendant broadcasters sought a broad holding that the press may not be made criminally or civilly liable for publishing information that is absolutely accurate, however damaging or embarrassing it may be to individual sensibilities. The Court reversed the lower courts' rulings in favor of the victim's father, but the broadcasters lost their bid for a sweeping privilege for the media when the Court refused to go beyond ruling that both the common law and the First and Fourteenth Amendments protected mass dissemination of truthful matters contained in public records open to public inspection, including indictments and other judicial papers.

In the decade following Cox Broadcasting, the Supreme Court decided three cases in which journalists had legally obtained and printed the names of juveniles or a judge in violation of court orders or state laws. These three cases taken together set the precedent for a second rape victim identification case to be heard by the Supreme Court.

The three cases are Oklahoma Publishing Co. v. District Court (1977) (Court held that newspaper could publish name of 11 year-old murderer because it learned the boy's name legally); Smith v. Daily Mail Publishing Company (1979) (Court held that two newspapers could publish name of a 15 year-old murderer because his name was legally obtained); and Landmark Communications, Inc. v. Virginia (1978) (Court permitted newspaper to publish name of a judge whose conduct was under investigation because information was lawfully obtained).

The Supreme Court referred to Oklahoma Publishing, Smith v. Daily Mail and Landmark Communications as "the trilogy" of cases which, taken together, established that the news media may, absent a state interest of the highest order, publish truthful information lawfully obtained. It was this trilogy which the Court cited in deciding another rape victim identification case heard by the Supreme Court, Florida Star v. B.J.F. (1989). In this case, the name of a rape victim was placed in the sheriff's press room, where a Florida Star reporter-trainee copied it verbatim. (The sheriff's department admitted they had erred by placing it in the press room.) Although it violated the newspaper's own policy to print the victim's name, the identification got past the editor and her name was published. She sued the publisher and the sheriff's department (which settled the claim for $2500) for violating a Florida statute similar to the Georgia statute in Cox v. Cohn making it a misdemeanor for anyone to publish names of sex offense victims. At trial, the victim testified that her mother had received threatening phone calls from a man who said he would rape the victim again.

Although a jury awarded the victim $100,000 in damages, the Supreme Court reversed in a 6–3 ruling. The majority cited three reasons for their decision: 1) Like the names of the minors in the Oklahoma Publishing and Daily Mail cases, the name of the rape victim in Florida Star was obtained lawfully by the newspaper; 2) The Florida statute, § 794.03, imposing liability for publication on a per se basis, meaning that liability followed automatically from publication whether the newspaper intended to publish the name or did so by mistake, swept too broadly; and 3) the statute was flawed because it applied only to instruments "of mass communication," but did not apply to a backyard gossip who might tell 50 people.

Florida Star might be viewed as a narrow ruling based on a flawed statute similar to the flawed statute in Smith v. Daily Mail which had permitted broadcasters but not newspapers to report names of juvenile criminals. Furthermore, the rape victim's name was lawfully obtained from the government.

But the irony of Florida Star is that the Court failed to address the key fact that the rapist was at large and would not have known the victim's identity if the Star had not published her name: by doing so, the Florida Star endangered her life. Similar situations arose in Tribune Publishing Co. v. Hyde and Times Mirror Co. v. San Diego Superior Court, discussed below at pp. 149–151.

In the wake of Florida Star, a number of states have proposed or passed constitutionally doubtful legislation that would prohibit and in some cases punish publication of sexual assault victims' names. See Dorman v. Aiken Communications (1990). The effect of the Florida Star decision on "private facts" cases brought under the common law is not clear. Writing for the three dissenters, Justice Byron White complained that the ruling "obliterates" this branch of the privacy tort. If the First Amendment prohibits a private person from recovering for "the publication of the fact that she was raped, I doubt that there remain any 'private facts' which persons may assume will not be published in the newspapers or broadcast on television." Florida Star v. B.J.F. (1989).

Thus the effect of the Supreme Court's decisions Cox Broadcasting Corp. and Florida Star is to leave uncertain the constitutionality of the Georgia and Florida statutes as well as similar statutes in Alaska, New York, South Carolina and Wisconsin insofar as they make punishable the identification of rape victims when such identification is not a matter of public record. Similarly, the common law rules permitting recovery of damages for the publication of truthful but embarrassing or harmful private information are left in doubt.

In addition to suing for publication of private facts, courts have upheld plaintiffs' right to sue the media for negligent infliction of emotional distress when publication of their names put their lives in jeopardy. In Tribune Publishing Co. v. Hyde

(1982), the police gave two local newspapers the name and address of a woman who had escaped from an unknown kidnapper while the assailant was still at large. The man began to terrorize the woman, whose name and address he had not known until the newspapers published them. The Missouri Court of Appeals concluded that the woman's name and address were not newsworthy compared with the high risk to the victim created by their publication. The case was eventually settled out of court when the woman accepted $6000 from the city and nothing from the newspapers.

A California court likewise held that a plaintiff could proceed on a claim for negligent infliction of emotional distress in Times Mirror Co. v. San Diego Superior Court (1988). In this case, a woman returned home just after her roommate had been raped and murdered. As she arrived, she saw the murderer leave. The Los Angeles Times printed her name and said she had discovered the body, but did not say that she had seen the fleeing murderer. She sued for publication of private facts and for negligent infliction of emotional distress, arguing that publishing her name while the murderer was at large endangered her life. Although the Los Angeles Times had taken her name from the coroner's report which was a public record, the California appellate court ruled that she could proceed on a claim for negligent infliction of emotional distress. The Los Angeles Times finally settled out of court, paying the woman an undisclosed sum of money.

The Supreme Court has never ruled on the theory of negligent infliction of emotional distress in a case such as Times Mirror Co. v. San Diego Superior Court. The Court made it clear in Hustler Magazine, Inc. v. Falwell (1988) that plaintiffs cannot use intentional infliction of emotional distress to circumvent defamation law as established in New York Times v. Sullivan (1964). But can one substitute charges of negligent infliction of emotional distress for charges of public disclosure of private facts? If B.J.F. had tried to recover for emotional distress rather than publication of private facts in Florida Star, would she have succeeded? In Tribune Publishing Co. v. Hyde and Times Mirror Co. v. San Diego Superior Court, courts refused to grant summary judgments for the defendant newspapers when they published the victims' names while the kidnapper and murderer were at large, just as B.J.F.'s name was published when the rapist was still at large. The facts of Florida Star bear enough similarity to Tribune Publishing and Times Mirror to raise the question of whether negligent infliction of emotional distress may circumvent the charge of publication of private facts, but it is a question unanswered by the Supreme Court thus far.

Obviously, the issue of whether or not the Constitution mandates truth to be a complete defense in these cases will have to be faced by the Supreme Court eventually. In Florida Star the Court implied that truth might not be a complete defense if there is a state interest of the highest order; however, it did not elaborate on what might constitute such an interest.

It is worth noting that in contrast with the United States, Great Britain has never had a tort of invasion of privacy in any form, despite the Royal Family's wishes to the contrary. Some legal scholars argue that the tort of public disclosure of private facts creates too great a burden for the news media; along with false light, courts should reject this tort in the coming century.

5. Common Characteristics of the Four Types of Invasion of Privacy

Although it is useful to an understanding of the tort of invasion of privacy to recognize the existence of its four branches, it must also be recognized that these branches often overlap each other or are bound up together. For instance, the same act of appropriating a woman's name and photograph for an advertisement endorsing a particular brand of whiskey may also place her in a false light as a serious drinker of alcoholic beverages. And an act of intrusion such as in the Dietemann case may be followed by publication of private information.

Whatever the invasion, the damages recoverable to the plaintiff are the same: (1) general damages; (2) special damages, though in contrast to slander or libel per quod they are not required; and (3) punitive damages, upon a showing of malice in the form of ill will, spite or improper motive.

Finally, there are certain defenses common to all four branches. The most obvious is consent. If the plaintiff can be found to have consented to the alleged invasion, the defendant's conduct is not actionable. Rarely in these cases will the plaintiff's alleged consent be express and unequivocal. With this defense the question for the trier of fact is normally whether the plaintiff's words or deeds implied consent to the defendant's appropriation, intrusion, false characterization or publication of private information.

The other common defense is that of privilege. It is generally accepted that the privileges recognized in the law of defamation are included in the law of privacy. If the circumstances would protect the publication of false and defamatory material, then the publication of truthful material is also protected.

In addition to the Federal Wiretap Statute and FCC Phone Rule discussed above, the other important federal legislation in this field is the "Privacy Act of 1974," 5 U.S.C.A. § 552a. Because the purpose of this legislation is to curb abuses by the federal government in the handling and dissemination of information about individuals, it is discussed in the chapter on newsgathering and access to information by the media. See Chapter VII, pp. 242–243, infra.

CHAPTER IV

RESTRAINT OF OBSCENE EXPRESSION

A. GENERAL THEORY

1. The Definitional Problem

Western societies generally seem to have a preoccupation with suppression of explicit public discussion or depiction of sexual matters. And English speaking societies are no exception. Censorship and confiscation of sexually obscene materials and even prison sentences may be the lot of the professional or amateur pornographer. There are those in positions of authority who would characterize all public expression concerning sex as obscene and suppress or punish it, but the prevailing view in this country is to the contrary and clearly not all sexual expression is condemned.

This view has within it the seeds of confusion because it requires a definition of what is obscene. And because obscenity, like beauty, is in the mind of the beholder, a precise definition seems beyond the reach of the law. Even the 1986 report of the United States Attorney General's commission on pornography fails to define it. It may be that the only honest test for obscenity is the one authored by the late Supreme Court Justice Stewart, "I know it when I see it." Jacobellis v. Ohio (1964). Because the First Amendment requires more than instinctual reaction to suppress and punish obscene expression, the Supreme Court has spent the last thirty or more years attempting to separate the chaff of obscenity from the wheat of protected sexual expression.

2. Background

Attempts at suppressing the dissemination of obscenity were sporadic in both England and the United States until shortly after the end of the American Civil War. At that time the English judiciary crystallized a standard for suppression which was by and large accepted in the United States. Contemporaneously, the Congress enacted certain statutes advocated by the notorious blue-nose Anthony Comstock prohibiting, with criminal penalties, the importation or mailing of materials characterized as obscene (now 18 United States Code, Sections 1461–1463). Many of the states followed suit with their own criminal obscenity statutes.

The standard set down in the English case of Regina v. Hicklin (1868) was a very broad one: suspect material was to be judged by the effect of isolated passages upon persons particularly susceptible to prurient appeal or lustful thoughts. The combination of the Comstock laws and the Hicklin test provided much work for the censors and the prosecutors. Occasionally, lower federal courts inveighed against the Hicklin test but it remained influential well into the twentieth century.

3. Modern Doctrinal Development

Until 1957 the Supreme Court, while assuming the constitutionality of attempts to suppress obscene expression in Near v. Minnesota (1931), had never definitively held that obscenity was beyond the pale of First and Fourteenth Amendment protection. In that year in Roth v. United States (1957) the Court so ruled, over the strong dissent of Justices Black and Douglas. The Court then considered the appropriate standard for separating protected expression from unprotected obscene expression. In affirming the conviction of Roth for sending obscene matter through the mails, the Court rejected the Hicklin standard because its concern for isolated passages and particularly susceptible individuals would result in the condemnation of much material legitimately and seriously dealing with sexual matters that ought to be protected by the First and Fourteenth Amendments. In its place the Court adopted the test whether to the *average* person, applying contemporary community standards, the dominant theme of the material taken as a *whole* appealed to prurient interest.

Although this test or definition of obscenity is clearly narrower than Hicklin and has had some liberating influence regarding serious expression concerning sex, it still permits censorship and criminal punishment for mere incitation to impure sexual thoughts not shown to be related to overt antisocial conduct. In the years since the decision in Roth, shifting majorities and pluralities of the Court have had difficulty and shown dissatisfaction with the test laid down there because of the uncertainty in (1) gauging the psychic effect of specific material on mythical "average" persons; (2) measuring the dominance of particular obscene themes in large unified works such as books or motion pictures or collections of materials such as in magazines; (3) determining the relevant community to be referred to in judging the suspect material, i.e., local, state or national; and (4) protecting against the danger of condemnation of serious expression.

New tests were formulated and coupled with the Roth standard in an effort to meet these problems until in the celebrated "Fanny Hill" case, A Book Named "John Cleland's Memoirs of a Woman of Pleasure" v. Attorney General of Commonwealth of Massachusetts (1966), a plurality of the Court announced a basic three-fold formulation to isolate obscenity: (1) a restatement of the Roth standard; (2) a test that the material be patently offensive because it affronts contemporary community standards relating to the description or representation of sexual matters; and (3) a test that the material be utterly without redeeming social value. Because the tests were stated in the conjunctive a censor or prosecutor was required to establish that the expression in question met all three. This would be extremely difficult to do.

The question inevitably arises in a free society whether almost unrestricted publication, distribution and exhibition of obscenity is too high a price to pay for the protection of serious expression concerning sex. This is a political question as well as a legal one and a large portion of the electorate appeared to answer the question in the affirmative in the election of 1968 when they elected as President Richard M. Nixon, a man who had publicly pledged to clean up the spreading pornography traffic. But his pledge could only be redeemed by changing the direction of the Supreme Court and this in turn would require new faces on the Court.

4. The Last Word on Obscenity: Miller v. California

Finally, in Miller v. California (1973) and Paris Adult Theatre I v. Slaton (1973) a five-person majority made up of the Nixon appointees, Chief Justice Burger and Justices Blackmun, Powell and Rehnquist together with Justice White, a Kennedy appointee, laid down new and tougher legal standards for dealing with the problem of obscenity and made clear that even "consenting adults" might not be exposed to "hard core" pornography. The following term the same five-person majority elaborated on these rulings in the important case of Jenkins v. Georgia (1974). For a fuller understanding of the Court's new position these three decisions are considered together.

In Miller, the petitioner had been convicted of mailing unsolicited sexually explicit material to persons in Orange County, California in violation of a California statute that approximately incorporated the tests for obscenity formulated in the Fanny Hill decision. The trial judge gave these tests to the jury and instructed them to evaluate the materials in light of the contemporary community standards of the state of California. The new Supreme Court majority affirmed Miller's conviction and did the following:

1. reaffirmed the holding in Roth that obscenity is not protected by the First and Fourteenth Amendments;

2. rejected important aspects of the tests set out in Fanny Hill, especially the "utterly without redeeming social value" standard and substituted its own conjunctive three-fold test to guide the trier of fact (normally the jury):

(a) whether the average person, applying contemporary community standards, would find the material taken as a whole, appeals to prurient interest (a restatement of the Roth test);

(b) whether the work depicts or describes, in a patently offensive way, sexual conduct specifically defined by the applicable state law; and

(c) whether the work, taken as a whole, lacks serious literary, artistic, political or scientific value;

3. indicated that only "hard core" pornography might be condemned under these tests and included in that classification for the guidance of legislative draftspersons patently offensive repre-

sentations or descriptions of ultimate sexual acts, normal or perverted, actual or simulated and patently offensive representations or descriptions of masturbation, excretory functions and lewd exhibition of the genitals; and

4. held that hard core pornography is to be determined by reference to local or state community standards and not national standards.

In the companion case of Paris Adult Theatre, decided the same day, the Court upheld the right of states to enjoin the exhibition of motion pictures which are hardcore pornography under the Miller standards even when the exhibitor makes every effort to limit the audience to consenting adults. In so ruling, the majority recognized that the states, and, by necessary extension, the United States, have a legitimate interest in shielding from the obscene not only the young and the unwilling but the consenting adult as well. This legitimate interest encompasses the elevation of the quality of life and the environment in the community, the tone of commerce in the cities and, arguably, the public safety itself. In this connection the majority refused to extend the individual constitutional right of privacy in personal heterosexual intimacies of the home (see Griswold v. Connecticut (1965)) to the viewing of pornography in a place of public adult accommodation. By this refusal, the Court avoided the necessity of balancing the state's recognized interest in preventing the exhibition of pornographic films against any individual privacy interest in viewing them.

In Miller, the Chief Justice said all he could, given the limitations of the English language, to prevent local suppression of serious expressions concerning sex. This did not inhibit the State of Georgia from convicting Billy Jenkins, the manager of a movie theater in Albany, Georgia for exhibiting the film "Carnal Knowledge," produced by a recognized group of serious movie makers, including director Mike Nichols and actor Jack Nicholson. Jenkins' conviction was affirmed by a divided Georgia Supreme Court which concluded that the judgment accorded with the standards laid down in Miller.

The Supreme Court, in holding "Carnal Knowledge" not obscene and reversing the conviction, was forced to confront the paradox of differing community standards delimiting the protection afforded by a national constitution. The Court first made clear its commitment to local community standards though indicating its willingness to accept statewide community standards if the states should decide to use them instead.

The Court then turned to the state's contention that under Miller, the obscenity of the film was a question for the jury and that the jury having resolved the question against Jenkins under the evidence and pursuant to local community standards, the conviction should be affirmed. In other words, the state was arguing that appellate review of the constitutionality of the conviction was precluded so long as the jury was properly instructed pursuant to the three-fold test laid down in Miller. Here the Court simply held that the scope of protection afforded by the First and Fourteenth Amendments was ultimately for it to decide and substituted its own judgment regarding the nature of the film for that of the local jury.

But the paradox remained troublesome and in Pope v. Illinois (1987), the Court acknowledged that one aspect of an obscenity prosecution under the three-fold test of Miller v. California could not be made the subject of local community standards but had to be governed by an objective national standard if the First Amendment were to be complied with. There, over objection of defendants charged with selling obscene magazines in violation of Illinois law, the state trial courts instructed the respective juries that in determining whether the magazines, taken as a whole, lacked serious literary, artistic, political or scientific value (the third prong of Miller), they were to judge the materials by the standard of "ordinary adults in the whole state." The defendants were convicted and their convictions were upheld on appeal.

The United States Supreme Court vacated the convictions and remanded the cases for further proceedings, ruling that while the first two prongs of Miller should be decided with reference to contemporary community standards, the third or "value" prong is to be judged by whether a reasonable person would or would not find such value in the materials, taken as a whole. The Court reasoned that "just as the ideas a work represents need not obtain majority approval to merit protection, neither, insofar as the First Amendment is concerned, does the value of the work vary from community to community based on the degree of local acceptance it has won." The jury instructions therefore violated the First and Fourteenth Amendments.

In retrospect, it appears that the Court, in a very indirect way, was suggesting in Jenkins v. Georgia the solution to the national standard-community standard paradox which it finally articulated clearly in Pope.

5. Effects of Miller, Paris Adult Theatre and Jenkins

The Miller, Paris Adult Theatre and Jenkins decisions have had considerable effect on the administration of state and federal obscenity statutes and free expression. The most important effect is to encourage prosecutors and censors to renew the fight against obscenity. In the Atlanta, Georgia area, for instance, one zealous prosecutor managed to close down all of the "adult" movie houses.

The very fact that convictions were affirmed in two of the three cases should hearten the anti-obscenity forces. Moreover, the Court in Paris Adult Theatre relaxed the evidentiary burden on the public officials charged with suppressing obscene expression. The material is now allowed to speak for itself and expert testimony as to its obscene nature is not required. In addition, proof that the material is utterly devoid of redeeming social value is no longer necessary. Now the prosecutor need only show that it is patently offensive and lacks serious literary, artistic, political or scientific value.

Conversely, the burden on the defendant to rebut the claim of obscenity is increased because evidence that the material in question is acceptable by national standards is relevant only to the "value" prong of the three-fold Miller test. As to the first two aspects of the test, the defendant must make out his or her case with expert testimony that it is acceptable locally or, as in Miller, statewide. The sanctioning of local standards also encourages the anti-obscenity forces to shop for the most unsophisticated and intolerant localities within which to seek criminal or civil suppression of material. Of course, the Supreme Court, as it demonstrated in Jenkins and Pope, stands ready to correct the worst abuses arising out of the application of local standards. But not all abuses are likely to be corrected.

Another effect is to narrow the theoretical boundaries of unprotected expression set by the majority in Roth. After Roth, even serious material could be condemned if, taken as a whole, it appealed to the prurient interest of the average person. After Miller, this is theoretically impossible because one of the three tests laid down there requires the prosecutor or censor to establish that the material taken as a whole lacks serious literary, artistic, political or scientific value. Of course, more practically, the Court has now made it easier than it once was to prove lack of serious value.

The other test in Miller which could have the effect of narrowing the area of unprotected expression is that of patent offensiveness. The Court equates this to hard core pornography and gives some reasonably explicit examples of what it means by hard core expression. If the state legislatures and the Congress were to amend existing general obscenity statutes in conformity with Miller by including concrete statements of sexual conduct which could not be publicly expressed, the target area for the anti-obscenity forces ought to be constricted.

The Paris Adult Theatre decision has the effect of limiting the area of the consenting adult's constitutional right of privacy to view pornographic material to one's own home. It seems clear that the majority did this to insure the primacy of the state's interest in maintaining and elevating the quality and tone of life and environment particularly in the large urban centers where commercial pornography often flourishes.

Finally, the Court's encouragement of local efforts at suppression will almost surely result in the disruption of the national distribution of sexual films, books, magazines and other materials. Rather than risk confiscation or prosecution in localities like Albany, Georgia, film makers and publishers may pass up these markets and distribute their wares only in more sophisticated urban population centers, if that is economically feasible. If it is not, the film maker or publisher's work may not see the light of day.

6. Difficulties With the New Approach

The Court's new approach perpetuates certain myths regarding obscenity control. The majority assert that beyond "knowing it when they see it," they can define obscenity with sufficient precision to give fair advance warning as to what is forbidden. But clearly the "serious value" test is highly subjective and in the final analysis only a majority of five justices can say, after the fact of publication, what is serious expression and what is not. And even the patent offensiveness-hard core pornography test will allow for subjectivity unless the legislatures are willing to define in obscene detail the sexual conduct to be suppressed. So far there has been no great trend in that direction.

The other major myth fostered by the Court is that obscenity can be constitutionally controlled at the local level using local standards. But as the Court was forced to admit in Jenkins and Pope, First and Fourteenth Amendment rights and protections are uniform and do not vary depending on the nature of the jurisdiction in which the attempt is made to suppress allegedly obscene expression. Try as it might, the Supreme Court, under the present approach, cannot escape the need to impose national standards to measure national rights and protections and, in the end, to act as a national censorship board.

7. Supplemental Obscenity Standards

Certain other standards have been developed by the Supreme Court to permit suppression and punishment of expression which does not meet the basic obscenity test directed to the average adult laid down in Miller and earlier in Roth and Fanny Hill. These supplemental tests are designed to prevent pandering of borderline material as the real thing, to suppress expression directed to the prurient interest of sexually deviant adults and to shield minors from "adult" materials such as "girlie" magazines and from exploitation and abuse in the production of sexually explicit material. The most important of these supplemental standards are those protective of minor children.

In Ginzburg v. United States (1966), the defendant publisher of a purported sexual autobiography, a hard-cover sex magazine and a sex newsletter, was convicted of sending obscene matter through the mail. His conviction for violation of Title 18, Section 1461 of the United States Code was affirmed at least in part because of his open advertising representations and other suggestions that the materials would appeal to the recipient's prurient interest. A majority of the Court ruled that where the purveyor's sole emphasis is on the sexually provocative aspects of his or her publications, that fact may be decisive in determining whether the material is obscene. Otherwise stated, in a close case, one who panders material as obscene will be taken at his or her word.

Because audiences vary as to age and sexual preferences, the Court has also held that the standards for suppression may also vary as to these audiences. In Mishkin v. State of New York (1966), the Court rejected the argument of a publisher and seller of sex books for sadists, masochists, fetishists and homosexuals that his materials were not obscene because they would not appeal to the prurient interest of average persons but rather would disgust and sicken them. The Court held that where material is designed for and primarily disseminated to a clearly defined deviant group, the prurient appeal test of Roth is satisfied if the dominant theme of the material taken as a whole appeals to the prurient interest in sex of members of that group. And in Ginsberg v. State of New York (1968) the defendant, an operator of a stationery store and luncheonette, was convicted of violating a New York penal statute which prohibited the knowing sale to minors under the age of 17 of any picture which depicts nudity. Ginsberg sold two "girlie" magazines to a sixteen-year-old male. While conceding that the magazines were not obscene for adults, the Court affirmed the conviction because of its belief that obscenity varies with the age of the audience and that the state has the constitutional power more greatly to restrict minors in their access to sex materials. And finally in New York v. Ferber (1982), the so-called "Kiddie porn" case, the court held that states may, consistent with the First Amendment, utilize more relaxed standards than those in Miller v. California, supra, to obtain criminal convictions in order to protect minors from exploitation and abuse in the production of sexual materials.

To combat the rising tide of sexual exploitation and abuse of minors exemplified by cases such as Ferber, Congress enacted the "Protection of Children Against Sexual Exploitation Act of 1977," P.L. 95–225, 18 U.S.C.A. §§ 2251–2253. This legislation imposes severe fines and penalties upon those convicted of encouraging or coercing minors to engage in sexually explicit conduct for still and motion picture cameras of any kind.

Congress has substantially strengthened the anti-child pornography law through amendments passed in 1984 (P.L. 98–292, 98 Stat. 204 (1984), codified at 18 U.S.C.A. §§ 2251–2255 (Supp. 1989)), 1986 (P.L. 99–628, 100 Stat. 3510 (1986), codified at 18 U.S.C.A. §§ 2251(c), 2256(5) (Supp. 1989)) and 1988 (P.L. 100–690, 102 Stat. 4485 (1988), codified at 18 U.S.C.A. §§ 2251(c), 2251A, 2252(a), 2257 (Supp. 1989)). The net effect of these amendments has been to dramatically increase the number of child pornography convictions.

8. Feminist Proposals for Statutory Civil Actions to Counter Pornographic Depictions of Women

In recent years feminists have become concerned that pornography may serve as a "catalyst" to incite real-life violence against women. Social scientists have also gathered evidence that pornography has either incited or legitimized actual violence against women. There is also a growing body of laboratory and field research supporting the theory that pornography instigates or legitimizes actual

violence against women. Citing such studies, the
Attorney General's Commission on Pornography:
Final Report, July 1986 (U.S. GPO 0–158–315) concluded that "the available evidence strongly sup-
ports the hypothesis that substantial exposure to
sexually violent materials ... bears a causal relationship to antisocial acts of sexual violence and, for
some subgroups, possibly to unlawful acts of sexual
violence" (p. 326). The Commission cites research
suggesting that male subjects are more likely to
accept "the legitimacy of sexual violence against
women" when women are portrayed as enjoying
rape or other abuse, a theme which pervades pornography.

One of the Commission's formal recommenda-
tions was that "[l]egislatures should conduct hearings and consider legislation recognizing a civil remedy for harm attributable to pornography." This
recommendation was a direct reflection of a model
anti-pornography ordinance drafted by feminists
Andrea Dworkin and Catherine MacKinnon, citing
pornography as a violation of women's civil rights.
The legislation has been introduced in several city
councils including Los Angeles, Minneapolis, Indianapolis and Cambridge, Massachusetts, but has not
become law thus far. The legislation identified
pornography as a form of discrimination on the
basis of sex and defined it as "graphic sexually
explicit subordination of women," meaning, for example, women "presented as sexual objects enjoying
rape, pain or humiliation, being penetrated by objects or animals, ... or in scenarios of degradation

or torture in a context that makes these conditions sexual" (Indianapolis–Marion County, Ind., Ordinance 35, ch. 16 (1984)). Civil claims for damages are created for 1) coercion into pornography, 2) forcing pornography on a person, 3) assault incited by specific pornography, and 4) trafficking in pornography, i.e. production, sale, exhibition or distribution (Indianapolis–Marion County, Ind., Ordinance 35, S16–3(g)(4)–(7), (1984)). The Commission supported this because "the civil rights approach, although controversial, is the only legal tool suggested ... which is specifically designed to provide direct relief to the victims of the injuries so exhaustively documented in our hearings throughout the country" (Report p. 749). The legislation was actually enacted in Minneapolis and Indianapolis. In Minneapolis the Mayor vetoed the ordinance. In Indianapolis its constitutionality was challenged in American Booksellers Association v. Hudnut (1985). The Seventh Circuit accepted the premise of the legislation, agreeing that "depictions of [female] subordination tend to perpetuate [it]" and that the "subordinate status of women in turn leads to affront and lower pay at work, insult and injury at home, battery and rape on the streets," but upheld the district court decision overturning the ordinance because it was "vague and overbroad" and established "a prior restraint of speech." The appeals court pointed out that the definition "graphic sexually explicit subordination of women ..." did not refer to prurient interests, to offensiveness, or to the standards of the community required by Miller v. California (1973). The U.S. Supreme Court summarily affirmed the Seventh Circuit decision in Hudnut v. American Booksellers Association, Inc. (1986). Thus proponents of the anti-pornography ordinances will have to find a definition of pornography that courts will view as "constitutional" or accept defeat of their cause.

B. IMPORTANT SPECIAL AREAS OF RESTRAINT OF SEXUAL EXPRESSION

1. Motion Pictures

A medium of expression which has felt the hand of the censor acutely over the years is the motion picture. Movies have been and are still being censored locally for obscenity prior to exhibition and more often are simply seized in police raids. Some of the leading prior restraint cases have involved motion pictures and a distinct area of obscenity law has been carved out.

a. Background and Modern Doctrine

Until 1952 the motion picture was not considered a medium of expression protected by the Constitution and the censors were free to control film exhibition in any way they saw fit. In that year the Supreme Court in Joseph Burstyn, Inc. v. Wilson (1952) rejected earlier doctrine and held that expression by means of motion picture film is protected by the First and Fourteenth Amendments even though it be assumed that motion pictures have a greater impact on the mind than other modes of expression. Thereafter, attempts at censorship for obscenity have generally been measured by prevailing constitutional standards. But since obscenity can be constitutionally suppressed under Roth and Miller, prior licensing and confiscation of films as well as subsequent punishment for their exhibition are permissible under certain circumstances and a general constitutional attack on a local ordinance or state statute requiring submission of motion pictures for prior censorship will fail. See Times Film Corp. v. City of Chicago (1961).

One indirect approach to controlling "adult" motion pictures and thereby avoiding the constitutional standards of Roth and Miller and necessary procedural safeguards that accompany those standards is the control of land use in order to concentrate adult movie houses in so-called "combat zones" or, conversely, to prevent concentrations, which have the tendency to destroy commercial and residential neighborhoods. Either way, non-proliferation of such establishments is the goal. This indirect approach relying on time, place and manner limitations on the exhibition of "adult" films was approved by the Supreme Court in Young v. American Mini Theatres, Inc. (1976) and City of Renton v. Playtime Theatres, Inc. (1986) because neither complete suppression of adult movies nor criminal sanctions were involved.

A slightly different use of time, place and manner restrictions was involved in Barnes v. Glen Theatre, Inc. (1991). The Court upheld the application of an

Indiana public indecency statute to nude dancers in an adult entertainment establishment. Conceding that nude dancing is expressive conduct protected by the First Amendment, the Court, in a plurality opinion, found that requiring nude dancers to wear pasties and a G-string furthered a substantial government interest in protecting societal order and morality, that this interest was unrelated to the suppression of free expression, and that the restriction was no broader than necessary to further that interest.

b. Procedural Safeguards for Film

After the Times Film Corp. case, supra, it was clear that there could be constitutional as well as unconstitutional prior restraint on motion pictures, and the Supreme Court began to evolve the rules under which the censors might operate. Freedman v. Maryland (1965) involved a challenge by a film exhibitor to a state statute authorizing certain procedures of the now defunct Maryland Board of Censors, including a lengthy appeal process. The Supreme Court struck down the statute as unduly restrictive of protected expression and set out certain procedural safeguards for regulating the censor's business. Prior restraint statutes and ordinances are now required to:

(a) place the burden of proving that the film in question meets constitutional standards for obscenity (i.e., Roth and Miller) on the censor;

(b) provide that the censor will, within a specified very brief period, either issue a license for exhibition or go into court to seek to restrain exhibition and;

(c) assure a prompt final judicial decision in order to minimize the deterrent effect of an interim refusal to license.

In addition, prior restraint legislation whether it involves outright censorship or merely mandatory film classification for the protection of minors, as in Interstate Circuit, Inc. v. City of Dallas (1968), must be narrowly drawn, detailed, and precise as to the standards to be employed by the classifier. Anything less will inhibit protected expression and run afoul of the First and Fourteenth Amendments.

Similarly, procedural safeguards have been established for the seizure of films by law enforcement officials. A judicial warrant issued consistent with Fourth and Fourteenth Amendment standards must be obtained before any seizure. The fact that First Amendment interests may be affected by such search warrants does not require a higher probable cause standard for issuing the warrants. New York v. P. J. Video, Inc. (1986). Failure to obtain such warrant will result in the suppression of the film as evidence of obscenity law violations at subsequent judicial proceedings. Roaden v. Kentucky (1973); Lee Art Theatre, Inc. v. Virginia (1968). And it is not sufficient justification for the issuance of the warrant that the prospective seizing officer made conclusory assertions of the film's obscene nature. Rather, the magistrate must concern himself or herself deeply with the question of the film's probable nature before issuing the warrant. Ibid. But an adversary proceeding at this stage is not required. Heller v. New York (1973). The seizure of a copy of the film pursuant to a constitutionally valid warrant must be for the limited purpose of preserving it as evidence in a subsequent adversary proceeding and must not prevent continued exhibition of the film until a prompt determination of its nature is made in that proceeding. If there is only one copy at hand, the film seized must be made available to the exhibitor for copying so that he or she may continue its exhibition. Ibid.

These procedural safeguards may not be avoided by legislation providing for indirect prior restraints such as statutes (1) which permit enjoining the operation of adult movie houses as public nuisances because of past exhibition of obscene films; (2) which prohibit the unapproved future exhibition of motion pictures that have not yet been found to be obscene; and (3) which require the judiciary to place its imprimatur on such future exhibitions before the films may be shown to the public without penalty. See Vance v. Universal Amusement Co. (1980).

Although the focus here has been on the constitutional limitations on prior restraint of motion pictures because this is where most of the legal battles have been fought, parallel safeguards have been developed to protect other modes of expression from overzealous censors. See, e.g., Kingsley Books, Inc. v. Brown (1957) (booklets); Marcus v. Search Warrant (1961) (books and magazines). But cf. New York v. P.J. Video, Inc. (1986).

2. Mail and Customs Censorship

Until recent times the United States Post Office Department carried on a largely futile campaign of administrative censorship of the mails in addition to referring certain cases to the Justice Department for criminal prosecution. Unsuccessful administrative devices have included removal of material from the mail, revocation of the publishers' second class mailing privilege and refusal to deliver mail to alleged commercial pornographers.

Recently a more indirect approach to the problem of obscenity in the mail has proved both workable and less threatening to First Amendment interests. Pursuant to present section 3008 of title 39 of the United States Code, individual addressees who have received "pandering advertisements" which offer for sale matter which the addressee believes to be erotically arousing or sexually provocative may request the Postmaster General to issue an order directing the sender and his or her agents to refrain from further mailings to the named addressee. If after notice and hearing it should be determined by the Postmaster General that the order has been violated, the Postmaster General may request the Attorney General to seek a federal court order directing compliance with the Postmaster's order. Violation of the court order will, of course, subject the sender to sanctions for contempt of court. The constitutionality of this statute was upheld in Rowan v. United States Post Office Department (1970).

Customs censorship through seizure and confiscation of incoming materials has had a long history and continues to the present within obscenity standards laid down in Roth and Miller, supra, and pursuant to procedural safeguards required by Freedman v. Maryland, supra.

C. SUBSEQUENT CRIMINAL SANCTIONS

The threat of criminal prosecution can have a restraining influence on sexual expression almost as profound as prior censorship. While criminal prosecutions for obscene expression are in general outline much like other criminal prosecutions and the rights accorded defendants are the same, certain special aspects of criminal obscenity proceedings are particularly significant to the eventual outcome.

Before one can be convicted of violating any criminal statute, the statute must give reasonable notice of the conduct that is prohibited. This has presented substantial difficulties for the drafters of criminal obscenity legislation in the past because of the definitional problem; convictions have sometimes been reversed because the statute alleged to have been violated was held "void for vagueness." See, e.g., Winters v. New York (1948); cf. Interstate Circuit, Inc. v. City of Dallas (1968). This drafting problem may be alleviated by legislatures utilizing the definition of unprotected obscenity set forth in Miller.

As noted earlier in connection with the discussion of the effects of Miller, Paris, Jenkins and Pope, *where* an obscenity prosecution is brought is of the greatest importance because of the Supreme Court's sanctioning of the application of local standards. Because a prosecution for violation of the Comstock Law may be brought in any district from, through or into which the mail in question is carried, federal prosecutors will usually have an advantageous choice as to venue. Reed Enterprises v. Clark (1967), affirmed (1968). Similar options as to venue between counties are often available to state prosecutors. Thus a defendant in an obscenity prosecution may be tried far from his or her residence or base of operations.

The burden of proof is always upon the state or federal government and the standard is the same as in all criminal cases: guilt beyond a reasonable doubt. The burden has been eased somewhat by the Supreme Court's holding in Paris Adult Theatre that the material complained of "speaks for itself" and thus expert testimony as to its obscene nature is no longer required.

An important element of the prosecutor's burden is scienter or guilty knowledge. It may be difficult in certain cases to establish beyond a reasonable doubt that a book seller, magazine dealer or movie exhibitor knew of the obscene nature and contents of the material he or she was purveying. But neither the states nor the federal government may constitutionally eliminate this mental element in their criminal obscenity statutes.   Smith v. California (1959).

The chief defense in most obscenity prosecutions is that the material is protected expression under the prevailing Supreme Court tests.   The defense will normally call expert witnesses to testify that the material has serious literary, artistic, political or scientific value and perhaps local psychologists or psychiatrists to testify that the material does not appeal to the prurient interest of the average person in the particular locality.   Defense counsel may attempt to establish "tolerant" community standards through expert testimony and the introduction of comparable materials freely available in the local area.   This latter defense is meeting with only mixed success before the courts.

CHAPTER V

RESTRAINT OF THE PRESS FOR PURPOSES OF NATIONAL SECURITY

A. THE CONFLICT

Since the founding of the Republic the federal and state governments have laid claim to the right to keep secrets on the ground that disclosures of certain matters would be harmful to the public interest. Obvious examples are troop deployments and diplomatic judgments concerning foreign governments. The working assumption of government officials is that the people would not want to know about sensitive matters if such knowledge would be harmful to their best interest.

While this assumption may have validity, official judgments as to precisely what knowledge would be harmful to the public interest are coming under increasing challenge. The common theme of the advocates of a freer flow of information is "the people's right to know" or "freedom of information."

The conflict has grown sharper with the growth of governmental activity since the New Deal and the increasing distrust of "big government" engendered in part by an unpopular war in Indochina and the Watergate scandal. Representative of the heightened conflict is the willingness of the media, particularly a once deferential press, to publish material which the government wishes to keep secret and a readiness on the part of governmental officials to retaliate against the media and to seek injunctions against publication of those secrets.

B. LEGAL BACKGROUND

There is no question but that the federal government has an inherent right to keep certain matters secret, especially information relating to national security and diplomatic affairs and that it may invoke executive privilege and establish a classification system to prevent disclosure. See United States v. Nixon (1974) (the Nixon Tapes case); United States v. Reynolds (1953). Furthermore, there is little doubt that those individuals privy to secret government information or those who come across it accidentally might be enjoined from disclosing what they have learned or, in certain cases, be criminally punished for actually making disclosures to others. And in the process of protecting government secrets the executive's judgment concerning the need for secrecy for the specific material involved will not be reviewed by the judiciary because of the separation of powers doctrine.

The problem becomes considerably more complex, however, when disclosure is made or threatened by the media. In this situation, of course, First Amendment considerations first raised in Near v.

Minnesota (1931) intervene. While in Near prior restraint of the press was generally disapproved as violative of the First and Fourteenth Amendments, the Supreme Court did recognize that such restraint might be permissible in extraordinary situations including the threatened publication of military secrets in time of war. This left the door open for the federal government forty years later to attempt to stop the presses from printing the so-called "Pentagon Papers."

C. NEW YORK TIMES CO.
v. UNITED STATES

Disillusioned with the war in Vietnam he had once supported, Daniel Ellsberg, a former Department of Defense official, arranged for the photocopying, without authorization, of a "top secret" multi-volume Department of Defense study of American involvement in the war between 1945 and 1967 entitled "History of U.S. Decision Making Process on Vietnam Policy" and a one-volume "Command and Control Study of the Tonkin Gulf Incident" and made them available to selected newspapers throughout the United States. On June 12, 13 and 14, 1971 the New York Times became the first paper to publish summaries and portions of the text of the two studies popularly known as "The Pentagon Papers." The United States Justice Department sought and obtained a temporary restraining order from the United States District Court to prevent the Times from continuing publication of the classified material. This restraining order remained in effect until the Supreme Court decided the case, thereby preventing further publication of the material for 15 days. At approximately the same time the Washington Post began publishing excerpts from the two studies and the government likewise sought to restrain the Post and for a short time succeeded. But the temporary restraining order binding the Post expired prior to the Supreme Court's resolution of the case and the anomalous situation was then presented of the Post being free to publish while the New York Times was not.

The issue presented to the Supreme Court in the historic case of New York Times Co. v. United States (1971) was very simply whether publication by the press of secret matters relating to the history and past conduct of an ongoing war could be enjoined consistent with the First Amendment. The Court by its judgment freed the Times to continue publication along with the Post. But its per curiam opinion is not, as some at first suggested, a ringing endorsement of a free press. The Court stated, " 'Any system of prior restraints of expression comes to this Court bearing a heavy presumption against its constitutional validity.' ... The Government 'thus carries a heavy burden of showing justification for the imposition of such a restraint.' ... The District Court for the Southern District of New York in the New York Times case and the District Court for the District of Columbia and the Court of Appeals for the District of Columbia Circuit in the

Washington Post case held that the Government had not met that burden. We agree."

The Court thus implied that if the government had sufficient proof of some serious effect on the war effort or national security, the government could enjoin the media from publishing truthful matters of public interest. What saved the press from being permanently gagged by court order for the first time in our history was the government's inability to prove to the Court's satisfaction that publication of the Papers would clearly result in direct, immediate and irreparable damage to the nation or its people.

In addition to the per curiam opinion, the Pentagon Papers case is marked by six concurring and three dissenting opinions. A close analysis of these opinions must be considered generally discouraging to those favoring a free press. A majority of the Court did not rule that such prior restraint was unconstitutional—only that the government had not met the heavy burden of proving that such restraint was necessary in this particular case.

Thus, what appeared at first blush to be a great victory for the press was, at best, a pyrrhic one. The Court gave notice that there are limits to the media's right to publish and the people's right to learn government secrets relating to national security. As a result of this case, the media may have become more wary of publishing classified material obtained without authorization. At best, the Pentagon Papers case encourages self-censorship by the news media. At worst, it forms the predicate for successful government censorship and prosecutions in the future.

Indeed, in the three reported cases following the Pentagon Papers case, the government was successful in enjoining disclosure of certain CIA secrets in a book by a former agency official (United States v. Marchetti (1972); Alfred A. Knopf, Inc. v. Colby (1975)) and information on the workings of the hydrogen bomb contained in a magazine article (United States v. Progressive, Inc. (1979)).

United States v. Marchetti began when former CIA agent Victor Marchetti submitted to Esquire magazine and six other publishers an article in which he reported some of his experiences as a CIA agent. Marchetti had spent 14 years with the CIA, rising to the position of special assistant to the executive director, but left because he had become disillusioned with the CIA's covert actions to destabilize governments considered unfriendly to the U.S. The government charged that Marchetti's article contained classified information concerning intelligence sources, methods and operations. The government won a broad injunction from the U.S. District Court for the Eastern District of Virginia to enjoin publication of the article. On appeal, Marchetti argued that the injunction should be barred by the Supreme Court decision in the Pentagon Papers case because the government had failed to meet the heavy burden against prior restraint of expression. But the court of appeals rejected Marchetti's argument and held that the secrecy agreement Marchetti had signed when he was first hired by the CIA in 1955 should be enforced. The agreement required Marchetti (and all CIA agents) to submit material to the CIA for approval before it was published. If the material was classified and published without prior review, the CIA could enjoin disclosure. Given this agreement, the court of appeals for the Fourth Circuit affirmed the district court's injunction, except to rule that the CIA could delete only classified information. Marchetti was the first writer in the United States to be subjected to such a censorship order.

Marchetti and a co-author John Marks, a former State Department employee who had also signed an agreement not to disclose classified information learned during his employment, later wrote a book, "The CIA and the Cult of Intelligence," which they submitted to the CIA for prepublication review. The CIA demanded that they delete 339 passages, comprising 15 to 20 percent of the entire manuscript. Heavy deletions were made in chapters concerning the Bay of Pigs operation against Fidel Castro, the Vietnam War and the CIA's attempt to prevent Salvador Allende's election as president of Chile. With their publisher Alfred A. Knopf, Inc. the authors sued. By the time of the trial, the CIA had reduced the number of deletions from 339 to 168. The U.S. District Court for the Eastern District of Virginia permitted publication of all but 26 of the 168 passages, at which point all parties appealed.

The court of appeals ruled that if the government could prove that each item deleted disclosed classified information, then it could require deletion of those items solely on that basis. Alfred A. Knopf, Inc. v. Colby (1975). Furthermore, the court said that Marchetti and Marks effectively relinquished their First Amendment rights regarding disclosure of classified information when they signed the secrecy agreements. The First Amendment is no bar to an injunction forbidding such disclosure when the classified information was obtained during employment with the CIA. The court of appeals remanded the case to the district court, ruling that the authors could disclose only information which they had obtained after leaving the CIA and State Department. Ultimately the CIA permitted 25 of the 26 missing passages to be printed in whole or in part, leaving one to wonder why they had been deleted in the first place.

Four years after Knopf v. Colby, the Justice Department obtained an injunction to prohibit The Progressive magazine from publishing an article by free-lancer Howard Morland entitled "The H–Bomb Secret: How We Got It, Why We're Telling It." United States v. The Progressive, Inc. (1979). The U.S. District Court for the Western District of Wisconsin issued a preliminary injunction against publication after concluding that some of the information would probably violate the Atomic Energy Act of 1954. The Justice Department contended that the Morland article contained "Restricted Data," defined by the Atomic Energy Act of 1954 as "all data concerning the design, manufacture or utilization of atomic weapons." 42 U.S.C.A. § 2104(y). This law specifically forbids anyone possessing "restricted data" about nuclear weaponry from disseminating it in a way that might be utilized "to injure the U.S." or "secure an advantage to any foreign nation." 42 U.S.C.A. § 2274. It also authorizes the attorney general to request a court order to enjoin communication of such restricted data. 42 U.S.C.A. § 2280.

The injunction was appealed, but three days after the court of appeals heard oral arguments and before it had made a decision, a small Wisconsin newspaper, the Madison Press Connection, published a letter, written by a California computer programmer, which contained essentially the same information as The Progressive article. When the Press Connection learned that the government had just won a temporary restraining order preventing another newspaper, the Daily Californian, a student newspaper at the University of California, Berkeley, from printing the letter, it rushed the letter into print.

When the Press Connection published the letter, the court of appeals dismissed the case against The Progressive. Many journalists expressed relief because numerous legal scholars had speculated that the injunction against The Progressive would have been sustained by the Supreme Court.

D. OTHER INHIBITIONS
ON PUBLICATION

1. Withholding Passports

Aside from direct injunctive restraints on the release of national security information attempted in the New York Times Co., Marchetti, Colby and Progressive cases, the federal government has successfully employed other techniques to discourage disclosure of sensitive diplomatic, military and intelligence information.

The denial or revocation of a passport because of expression which the Government perceives as potentially damaging to national security or foreign policy is one technique for inhibiting the release of undesired information or comment. This technique was upheld by the Supreme Court in Haig v. Agee (1981). Haig involved former CIA agent Philip Agee's attempt to expose existing CIA agents in foreign countries and have them driven out by anti-CIA groups in those countries.

2. Legislative Prohibitions

Perhaps in response to Haig v. Agee, the Reagan Administration persuaded Congress in 1982 to make it a federal crime for anyone to publish anything they have reason to know will disclose the identity of United States intelligence agents, even if their source is public or unclassified information. Intelligence Identities Protection Act, P.L. 97–200, 50 U.S.C.A. §§ 421–426. A survey of news stories written before the act was passed in 1982 turned up more than 80 major books and news articles, the authors of which could arguably have been indicted under the law. (A representative sample would include The New York Times' investigation of ex-CIA agents Wilson and Terpil; revelations that former CIA agents were involved in the Watergate break-in; accounts of illegal domestic spying by the CIA; and disclosures that a CIA employee tried to infiltrate the House and Senate intelligence committees in 1980 at the direction of the KGB. Jay Peterzell, "The Government Shuts Up," Columbia Journalism Review, pp. 31–37 (July–August 1982).

3. Contractual Prohibitions

In Snepp v. United States (1980) the government, relying on its claimed contractual rights, got the courts to seize the profits from a book published without CIA prepublication review, causing financial disaster for the author. Frank Snepp, a former CIA agent, published a book, "Decent Interval," about certain CIA activities in South Vietnam without submitting it for prepublication review as expressly required by his employment agreement with the CIA. Even though the CIA conceded that "Decent Interval," did not reveal one item of classified information, the Government brought suit to enforce the agreement by, among other things, capturing all profits that Snepp might earn from publishing the book in violation of the agreement. The district court entered a judgment for the Government, giving it the relief it sought, but the United States Court of Appeals refused to approve the turning over of the profits from the book to the Government. The Supreme Court summarily and without benefit of briefs or oral argument on the subject, upheld the Government's right to capture all profits from the publication—over $125,000. Thus, the financial burden placed on Snepp to pay off the Government was substantial and should give pause to other government employees considering writing about sensitive official matters.

Perhaps the most chilling aspect of the Marchetti, Colby and Snepp cases is the subordination of First Amendment interests to "boilerplate" contract clauses in CIA employment agreements. In Snepp, the Supreme Court majority relegated First Amendment considerations to a footnote in rigorously enforcing the CIA employment contract against Snepp.

The Snepp opinion also contained broad language that could be interpreted to permit the same prepublication review procedure to be applied to the thousands of non-CIA employees who also have access to classified information. The Government had not sought that degree of power in the Snepp case, and it is not clear that the Court intended that result. But, citing the Snepp decision, in 1983 President Ronald Reagan issued National Security Decision Directive 84, "Safeguarding National Security Information." 9 Med.L.Rptr. 1759, July 5, 1983. This directive would have required thousands of federal employees to submit to lie detector tests if asked; an employee who refused to take such a test could be subject to "adverse consequences." Previously federal employees, except for those in the CIA and certain sections of the Justice and Defense Departments and the National Security Agency—had the right to refuse to submit to such tests without their refusal being held against them or included in their personnel files. The directive also would have required any federal employee with access to classified information to submit for prepublication review any manuscripts containing intelligence information. It would have covered about 128,000 employees who would be bound by the contract for the rest of their lives.

In response to the President's directive, Congress attached a rider to a State Department appropriations bill ordering the administration to delay enforcement of the directive on prepublication review till 1984. The President signed the bill and agreed not to enforce the directive. But despite this promise, the General Accounting Office (GAO) reported in 1984 that aspects of the directive had been in effect since 1982. The GAO found that 156,000 employees of the Defense Department had signed the secrecy agreements and that there had been a sharp increase in the number of articles and books being reviewed by the Reagan administration. See FOI Digest, p. 1 (May–June 1984). Furthermore, thousands of government officials were being required to acknowledge in writing that they would face criminal and civil penalties for unauthorized disclosures for the rest of their lives. See Washington Post, p. A16, May 7, 1986. National Security Decision Directive 84, implemented by Reagan's

Executive Order 12356, is still in effect, but is under review by the Clinton administration.

4. News Blackouts

The Reagan Administration exercised an even more controversial form of prior censorship when it ordered an unprecedented 48–hour news blackout of the invasion of Grenada by American troops in 1983. About 400 journalists were denied transportation to Grenada, and the military stopped and threatened to shoot a few reporters who tried to reach Grenada by boat from nearby islands. Pentagon officials argued that they had banned journalists for 48 hours because they needed absolute secrecy to launch the invasion, and they were also concerned for the journalists' safety. The press scoffed at both reasons. Journalists had accompanied American military forces in every war since at least the Mexican–American War of 1848. Although reporters did accede to censorship in both world wars and the Korean War, they had always been allowed on the scene to cover the fighting. Journalists even accompanied Allied forces when they invaded Europe in 1944 on D–Day, one of the most secret military operations of all time. There was little censorship, however, during the Vietnam War, and many in the military had apparently developed an intense distrust of the press, blaming the press in part for the United States having lost the war in Vietnam.

Following severe criticism of the administration and the military for its exclusion of the press from the early aspects of the Grenada operation, Defense Secretary Caspar Weinberger asked retired army Major General Winant Sidle to form a panel on press-military relations. The Sidle panel recommended that a small pool of reporters should accompany the military on all future missions, secret or not, and should share the information obtained with others in the press. The pool, formed in 1984, was activated for the U.S. bombing of certain targets in Libya in 1986. Eight reporters and photographers boarded a U.S. aircraft carrier in the Mediterranean and got first-hand reports of the bombing from the pilots and others.

Subsequent uses of this pool arrangement have been heavily criticized. During the U.S. invasion of Panama, the media complained that reporters were not allowed where the real action was taking place. See "Panning the Pentagon," Editor & Publisher, March 31, 1990 at 11. The Gulf War also led to extensive criticism. Media pools were not even called until U.S. troops had been in Saudi Arabia for almost a week. Once there the media complained that the pools were often taken to unnewsworthy locations and that the military sometimes picked the soldiers to be interviewed. Other complaints concerned the required "security review" of press stories.

In January 1991, several publications sought an injunction prohibiting implementation of many of these press policies. Several months later, after the hostilities had ceased, a federal district court held that the issue was moot even though the situation was capable of repetition. Because the restrictions on press access had been lifted at the end of the war, the court held that there was "no longer any presently operative practice" for the court to enjoin. The Nation Magazine v. Department of Defense (1991).

Under guidelines issued by the Pentagon and approved by the American Newspaper Publishers Association and the American Society of Newspaper Editors, only Pentagon-accredited journalists may report on military operations and they may report only "releasable information," with releasable information defined by the Pentagon. Accreditation is lost if the groundrules are violated. The releasable information list does not include estimates of enemy strength (the issue in Westmoreland v. CBS, Inc.) and the "information not releasable" list prohibits such things as "cancelled operations," as in the Carter Administration's failed Iranian hostage rescue mission.

5. Criminal Prosecutions and Threats Thereof

In addition to barring reporters from Grenada initially, the Reagan Administration began a campaign to stem unauthorized leaks of sensitive government information. In 1985 the Justice Department successfully prosecuted former naval intelligence analyst Samuel Morison for furnishing three secret U.S. spy satellite photos to a British magazine. Morison was sentenced to two years for espionage and theft. He was the first person ever convicted of the crime of leaking national security information to the press, and was found guilty under an interpretation of the law that could subject news organizations, as well as their sources, to criminal prosecution. United States v. Morison (1988).

The interpretation under which Morison was convicted may have paved the way for threats of prosecution of members of the press by the late CIA Director William Casey against NBC News, The Washington Post, The New York Times, Time, Newsweek and The Washington Times for alleged violation of the 1950 "COMINT" (Communications Intelligence) statute that prohibits publishing classified information about codes, ciphers or "communication intelligence activities of the United States. . . ." It also forbids "the divulging of any information" gleaned from code-breaking activities in order "to prevent the indication to a foreign nation that we may have broken their code system." 18 U.S.C.A. § 798 (1953). The stories that triggered the CIA Director's threats of prosecution dealt with our interception of messages between Tripoli and the Libyan People's Bureau in East Berlin, and the government's prosecution of Ronald Pelton, a former intelligence specialist with the National Security Agency who later received a life sentence for selling secrets to the Soviets. When Time Magazine's attorney asked the CIA which of its articles had violated the law, the CIA refused to identify the article. Washington Post, p. A3, May 8, 1986.

The CIA Director also tried to persuade Department of Justice officials to obtain an injunction to restrain The Washington Post from publishing an article describing the technology used by American submarines in intercepting Soviet communications before this information-gathering technique was compromised by Pelton. But the Justice Department turned down Casey's request, citing New York Times Co. v. United States, supra. Casey then threatened the Washington Post with prosecution under the COMINT statute, which had never before been used against a news organization. The Post finally published a less informative version of the story, deleting three paragraphs describing the interception device. See Washington Post, p. A38, May 21, 1986.

E. KEEPING OUT THREATENING PERSONS AND MATERIALS FROM ABROAD

The Reagan Administration also intensified use of the Immigration and Naturalization Act provision known as the McCarran–Walter Act (S 212(a), 8 U.S.C.A. § 1182). It was adopted over President Harry Truman's veto in 1952, and provides that foreigners may be denied visas to visit the U.S. if a consular officer or the Attorney General "has reason to believe" the prospective visitor seeks "to engage in activities which would be prejudicial to the public interest," or who "advocate the economic, international ... doctrines of world communism...." (§ 212(a)(28)(D).

The Supreme Court upheld the Attorney General's right to deny a visa in Kleindienst v. Mandel (1972). In that case, Ernest Mandel, a journalist and writer of a two-volume work, Marxist Economic Theory, was invited to speak at a Stanford University conference on Technology and the Third World in 1969. He had been in the United States in 1962 and 1968, but the Immigration and Naturalization Service denied his 1969 visa application on the grounds that his 1968 activities in the U.S. went beyond the stated purposes of his trip, although these activities were merely that he spoke at more universities than his visa application indicated. Furthermore, no one had given Mandel prior notice that he was required to adhere to a stated itinerary in 1968. Mandel and eight university professors challenged the decision, arguing that the Immigration and Naturalization Act § 212(a)(28) denied them equal protection by permitting entry of "rightists" but not "leftists." The district court observed that although Mandel had no personal right to enter the United States, U.S. citizens did have a First Amendment right to hear him explain his views, and it held that the Attorney General could not deny Mandel a visa.

On appeal, the U.S. Supreme Court acknowledged the idea that the First Amendment protects the public's right to hear differing viewpoints. But the Court concluded that it would not address or decide the First Amendment issue. It held instead that the Attorney General "had validly exercised plenary power delegated to the Executive and the courts would not look behind his decision or weigh it against the First Amendment interests of those seeking entry of [Mandel] to personally communicate with him or engage in academic exchange."

In 1986, Colombian journalist Patricia Lara met the same fate as Ernest Mandel. She was detained for five days in New York and then expelled. She had come to the United States with a valid visa to attend a Columbia University awards ceremony, but the State Department detained her at a maximum-security federal prison, said that her visa had been issued in error, revoked it, and then deported her to Colombia without giving her specific reasons for her deportation. After she left, Elliot Abrams, assistant secretary of state for inter-American affairs, claimed that Lara was a liaison with Cuba and a member of M19, a leftist Colombian guerilla movement. She denied the charge, and the Colombian foreign minister said he had no evidence that she was a member of M19 or an agent of the Cuban government. Immigration authorities have invoked the McCarran–Walter act against other foreign journalists as well. The News Media and the Law, Winter 1987, pp. 4–5.

CHAPTER VI

THE FREE PRESS—FAIR TRIAL CONFLICT

A. THE PROBLEM

1. Introduction

The Sixth Amendment guarantees that in criminal prosecutions the accused shall be entitled to a speedy and public trial "by an impartial jury." A necessary implication of this constitutional mandate is that jurors must not be influenced in their determination of the guilt or innocence of the accused by forces outside the courtroom or by information or material not admitted into evidence at the trial.

But news stories concerning a criminal case published before or during trial, particularly those containing information adverse to the accused not presented to the jury at trial such as a past criminal record or some incriminating statement or confession may influence individual jurors and destroy their impartiality. Because accused persons are entitled only to "impartial" juries and not favorably biased ones, the constitutional requirement binding on the states through the Fourteenth Amendment may also be violated by publicity adverse to the prosecution.

In addition, the criminally accused may not be deprived of life, liberty or property without due process of law, as guaranteed by the Fifth Amendment. Due process may be affected by the media and their representatives by both the generation of pressures on the trial judge through editorial content and by disruption of the repose of the courtroom, making fair procedure and calm deliberation difficult if not impossible.

The problem for the courts in attempting to safeguard an accused's Fifth and Sixth Amendment rights arises out of the potentially conflicting guaranty of the First Amendment that Congress shall make no law abridging freedom of the press. This guaranty is interpreted to include court orders. Therefore, orders designed to assure fair and impartial trials and which directly or indirectly restrict the newsgathering and news disseminating functions of the press may run afoul of the First Amendment. Some restrictive orders, particularly those that bar newspersons from the courtroom, may also violate the "public trial" requirement of the Sixth Amendment itself.

While most of the potential conflicts between fair trial and free press might be avoided by the exercise of restraint and common sense by the media, judiciary, trial participants and law enforcement officials, these qualities are sometimes in short supply in relation to criminal cases of great public interest. Then the conflict becomes real and troublesome. One example will suffice to illustrate the extreme bounds of the problem.

2. A Case Study: Sheppard v. Maxwell

The classic case of excessive and abusive pretrial and trial publicity and improper courtroom behavior by the media is Sheppard v. Maxwell (1966). Correlatively, it is a classic case of abdication of responsibility by a member of the judiciary to safeguard the rights of an accused.

Dr. Samuel Sheppard's pregnant wife Marilyn was brutally bludgeoned to death in an upstairs bedroom of their home in a suburb of Cleveland. Sheppard was charged with her murder although he steadfastly maintained his innocence. Before and during his trial there were many outrageous instances of highly prejudicial publicity. Repetition of only a few of them will suggest the environment in which the jurors decided Sheppard's fate.

During the trial, a Cleveland police officer gave testimony that tended to contradict portions of Sheppard's written statement made to the police. Two days later, in a broadcast again over WHK, Robert Considine, Hearst feature writer and radio personality, likened Sheppard to a perjurer and compared the episode to Alger Hiss' confrontation with Whittaker Chambers. Defense counsel asked the judge to question the jury to determine how many had heard the broadcast and, again, the judge refused and overruled a motion for a continuance based on the same incident. Later a story dealing with the defendant's temper appeared under an eight column headline reading "Sam Called A 'Jekyll–Hyde' By Marilyn, Cousin To Testify." No such testimony was ever produced at trial. Similarly, two weeks later a police captain not at the trial and never called as a witness denied certain trial testimony given by Sheppard under the headline "'Bare–Faced Liar,' Kerr says of Sam."

Only after the case was submitted to the jurors were they sequestered. However, after the guilty verdict was returned, defense counsel discovered that jurors had been allowed to make telephone calls every day and no record was kept of the calls. The trial judge had failed to instruct the bailiffs to prevent such calls. Defense counsel moved for a new trial. The motion was overruled. Sheppard's initial state appeals were unsuccessful and review by the United States Supreme Court was denied. He served ten years in the Ohio penitentiary before obtaining a review of his conviction in the federal courts under a habeas corpus application. In those ten years the Supreme Court's attitude toward trial and pretrial publicity had been changing. In Marshall v. United States (1959), the Supreme Court, exercising its supervisory authority over the lower federal courts, reversed a conviction for unlawfully dispensing drugs because jurors had seen newspaper stories indicating that the defendant had two prior convictions, one of which was for practicing medicine without a license. The Court ordered a new trial despite assurances from the jurors that they would not be influenced by these stories. Then in Irvin v. Dowd (1961), the Supreme Court held for the first time that the exposure of jurors to massive and highly inflammatory pretrial publicity (including news stories that the accused had confessed to six murders) violated the accused's right to a fair trial guaranteed by the due process clause of the Fourteenth Amendment. Again, in Rideau v. Louisiana (1963), a conviction was reversed because of pretrial publicity undermining a fair trial, this time in the form of a televised "interview" of the accused by the local sheriff during which the accused admitted to bank robbery, kidnapping and murder. Finally, in Estes v. Texas (1965), a conviction for large scale fraud was reversed because pretrial and trial proceedings were televised and filmed. The Court held that such coverage denied to the accused a fair trial because of the psychological impact on and the distraction of the jurors, judge, witnesses and the accused himself.

In requiring a new trial in Sheppard's case, the Supreme Court signalled its determination to end free-wheeling media coverage of important criminal cases. Its decision intensified the conflict between the judiciary and the media. While noting that a responsible press is regarded as an indispensible handmaiden of fair and effective judicial administration, the Court in Sheppard recognized that in cases involving probable jury exposure to massive publicity relating to information not introduced in evidence at trial, jurors might be improperly influenced in their deliberations and decisions. The Court then ruled, relying on almost a decade of precedent, that in cases involving a high probability of prejudice to one or the other of the parties

stemming from pretrial and trial publicity, such
prejudice could be presumed to exist and actual
evidence of the exposure to and the effect on individual jurors of such publicity need not be presented. Sheppard's case was held to be one of those in
which the presumption would apply.

The Court further stated that the trial judge
compounded the problem of undue publicity in the
case by acting as if he lacked the power to control it
in any way. The Supreme Court catalogued a number of approaches and tactics that the judge might
have utilized to guarantee Sheppard a fair trial
without imposing restrictions or sanctions *directly*
against the press. These will be discussed shortly.

Courts do not automatically assume that massive
trial and pretrial publicity always results in the
denial of a fair trial. Otherwise the more notorious
the crime, the less the likelihood of obtaining a
valid conviction in this age of mass communications. It has often been suggested that had Lee
Harvey Oswald lived he could not have been convicted for the assassination of President Kennedy
because a fair trial would have been impossible
anywhere. But the judicial system will not allow
itself to be paralyzed. If the presumed prejudice is
clearly rebutted on voir dire examination of the
prospective jurors and the atmosphere in the local
community and the circumstances surrounding the
trial do not betray inflamed community sentiment,
there is no denial of a fair trial merely because of

the publicity. In Irvin v. Dowd, 268 of the 430 veniremen were excused, as compared with only 20 of the 78 potential jurors questioned in Murphy v. Florida (1975). In Murphy, unlike the Sheppard, Rideau and Estes cases, the conduct of the trial and atmosphere in and around the courthouse was proper. In such circumstances, the Supreme Court held that the defendant had not been deprived of his constitutional right to a fair trial. The importance of the Murphy case lies in its necessary implication that claims of prejudicial publicity will be considered on a case-by-case basis, with careful scrutiny by the courts of the circumstances surrounding the trials. Convictions will not be reversed automatically because of the presence of substantial publicity. See also Patton v. Yount (1984), and Mu' Min v. Virginia (1991).

Even so there is still a serious free press-fair trial problem created by media coverage of criminal and other proceedings. The blame for the existence of the problem can be widely apportioned among prosecutors and defense counsel who violate their code of professional responsibility by trying their cases in the news media, law enforcement officials seeking glory for their agencies, judges who cannot resist the limelight, prominent uninvolved parties such as Presidents of the United States who pass judgment on accused in advance of trial and, of course, media representatives who aid, abet and encourage these sources.

B.   APPROACHES TO THE PROBLEM

1.   Resort to Judicial Procedural Devices

It is the judge's responsibility to maintain strict control over the courtroom and courthouse environment to ensure that neither the media nor the public interfere with a defendant's fair trial.   There are a number of procedural devices available to judges to neutralize the possible prejudicial effect of publicity and behavior of media representatives without *direct* limitation on them.   These include 1) postponing the case until the danger of prejudice abates (granting a continuance), 2) transferring it to another county if the publicity has not saturated the entire state (granting a change of venue), or importing jurors from another county instead of exporting the trial, a rarely used but legal alternative (granting a change of venire), 3) supervising the voir dire to ensure that veniremen with pre-conceived opinions on the defendant's guilt or innocence do not become jurors, 4) sequestering the witnesses or at least admonishing them not to follow the proceedings in the media until they have testified, 5) sealing off or sequestering the jury as soon as it is empaneled to shield the jurors from trial publicity, 6) ordering a new trial (an extreme measure not to the judiciary's liking), and 7) issuing a restrictive order prohibiting all parties involved in a case from making prejudicial statements to the media (a gag order).   The latter two devices are last resorts; issuing a restrictive order constitutes a prior restraint which is presumed to be unconstitutional except in the most extreme of circumstances, as is discussed below. But the other measures may not, in given circumstances, be fully effective in insuring a fair trial. For instance, postponements and venue changes will have little effect if the publicity is dramatic and pervasive, and sequestration does not shield the jurors from prejudicial publicity before they are selected.

2. Limiting Access of the Media to Information About Pending Legal Matters

a. Institutional Reactions Favoring Restrictions on News Flow to the Media

The Judicial Conference of the United States, the agency responsible for formulating policy for the federal courts, has recommended that the United States District Courts firmly regulate both the physical courtroom environs and the release of information by members of their bars and by federal court personnel, but it has rejected the use of the contempt power to prevent unwanted publicity. See Judicial Conference Fair Trial—Free Press Guidelines, 6 Med.L.Rptr. 1897 (1980).

The ABA's Code of Professional Responsibility establishes standards for all attorneys. Consistent with the Reardon Report, Code disciplinary rule DR 7–107 provides guidelines for prosecutors and defense counsel alike regarding the release of information concerning pending criminal cases roughly parallel to the Katzenbach Rules. Guidelines are also provided for professional disciplinary proceedings, juvenile justice proceedings, civil cases and administrative proceedings. In those states that have adopted DR 7–107 by statute or court rule, attorneys may be disciplined for violating its precepts. Although the ultimate sanction of disbarment has yet to be invoked for violation of DR 7–107, harsher disciplinary penalties can be expected in the future. See Gentile v. State Bar of Nevada (1991).

b. Exclusion of Camera Operators and Equipment From the Courtroom and Environs

Although the American Bar Association vigorously opposed cameras in the courtroom for decades through its ABA Canon of Judicial Conduct No. 3A(7), the Supreme Court held in Chandler v. Florida (1981) that states could permit cameras in the courtroom, even in criminal cases and even if the defendants objected. By 1993, only three states, Mississippi, Indiana and South Dakota, still prohibited cameras in all courts in accordance with the original ABA Canon. See 17 News Media & the Law 32 (Winter 1993).

As a result of this change of judicial attitude toward the use of cameras in the courtroom, the American Bar Association, bowing to the inevitable, revoked Canon 3A(7) in 1982 and in its place adopted a guideline stating that judges should be able to authorize unobtrusive camera use under carefully devised local court rules. Although cameras had long been barred from federal courts, the Judicial Conference of the United States voted to permit an experimental program of television coverage of certain civil proceedings in two circuit courts of appeal and six district courts for three years beginning in July 1991. Report of the Judicial Conference Ad Hoc Committee on Cameras in the Courtroom, Agenda E–22 at 8 (Sept. 1990).

Although courts have traditionally been concerned with effects of television coverage of their proceedings, in the 1990s courts will have to confront the obverse problem resulting from the proliferation of camcorders and amateur videotapes introduced as evidence as, for example, in the first Rodney King case, which involved the original criminal prosecution and subsequent acquittal of four police officers accused of using excessive force on Rodney King. There will also be the concomitant problem of whether the repeated broadcast of such "home videos" over national television will interfere with a defendant's right to a fair trial: few criminal prosecutions in American history have generated more pervasive media coverage and commentary than that of the Rodney King beating. Powell v. Superior Court (People) (1991). Will programs such as Eyewitness Video which show actual scenes of alleged crimes on network television interfere with the defendant's right to a fair trial? The growing popularity of Court TV on cable television also raises questions about its effects: will Court TV educate people about the court system or will it acculturate the public to watch trials as merely another form of entertainment like made-for-television movies? These are questions which remain to be answered.

c. Sealing Arrest and Other Public Records

Another increasingly popular tactic of the judiciary in restricting access of the news media to information potentially affecting criminal prosecutions is the sealing of arrest and other public records, either pursuant to statute or under the inherent power of the court. The premier example of this latter approach is the trial of the Watergate defendants in which Judge Sirica sealed many of the documents and tapes in the case from public view. When officials of the Reporters Committee for Freedom of the Press wrote the Judge a letter requesting that the material be unsealed and made available for inspection by the news media as representatives of the public, the letter itself was ordered sealed.

But while secrecy in judicial proceedings is increasing, the press is beginning to attack the practice of sealing public records and removing them from public inspection, and the media are now recognized as having legal standing to assert the public's right to be informed about judicial proceedings when individual judges (or statutes) would otherwise shield those proceedings.

d. Closing the Courtroom

Parallel to the sealing of public records is the exclusion of the public and the news media from the courtroom during trial and pretrial proceedings, usually in sensational criminal cases. This device, though once rarely if ever resorted to by American courts (see In re Oliver (1948)), became increasingly popular following the Supreme Court's imposition of strict limits on trial courts' power to issue injunctive orders preventing publication of news concerning pending criminal trials in Nebraska Press Association v. Stuart (1976), discussed infra, pp. 216–220. The problems engendered by judicial resort to the court-closing device are considered in detail in Chapter VII at pp. 249–256, infra.

3. Prior Restraint of the News Media

The devices previously discussed are employed to prevent the news media from obtaining information about judicial proceedings which the judiciary believes would prejudice such proceedings. An even more difficult legal question than restricting access to news is posed by the judiciary restraining the media from publishing news that they have already obtained. The media's pejorative term for such judicial conduct is "gag order" and, indeed, the effect of judicial restrictive orders is prior restraint of the press.

a. *Problems Engendered*

Once the news media obtain information about pending judicial proceedings which, if published, might seriously affect their conduct and outcome, the courts must choose between previously discussed procedural devices designed to minimize or eliminate the impact of publication and the issuance of restrictive or "gag" orders directly against the news media. In some cases journalists have refused to obey constitutionally invalid orders enjoining publication of the news. For example, in United

States v. Dickinson (1972), a black civil rights worker in Louisiana became the subject of an allegedly
baseless prosecution for conspiracy in a murder.
Two reporters were assigned by their news service
to cover a federal hearing challenging the legality of
prosecuting the civil rights worker on the grounds
that law enforcement officials were trying to har-
rass or frame him. When the reporters defied the
judge's order not to report details of evidence given
in open court, they were each fined $300 for crimi-
nal contempt. On appeal of the contempt convictions the restrictive order was held to violate the
First Amendment, but the United States Court of
Appeals further held that even constitutionally invalid injunctive orders must be obeyed until they
are successfully challenged on appeal. This means
that reporters, editors and publishers may properly
be prosecuted for ignoring restrictive orders violative of the First Amendment while such orders are
in effect. The Dickinson case thus held that journalists must, under threat of criminal penalties,
obey unconstitutional judicial orders until they are
dissolved. This principle has generally been recognized in the state courts as well. See Annot., 12
A.L.R.2d 1059, 1107–16 (1950). But see State ex
rel. Superior Court of Snohomish County v. Sperry
(1971) (criminal contempt convictions of two reporters for violation of patently unconstitutional restrictive order vacated on appeal). See also Note, "Defi-
ance of Unlawful Authority," 83 Harv.L.Rev. 626,
633–638 (1970).

But a more recent case suggests that the force of Dickinson may be weakening. In United States v. Providence Journal (1986), the Providence Journal sought to publish a story based on FOIA material about a deceased alleged organized crime boss, but the district court had granted a temporary restraining order in an action brought by the dead man's heirs. The newspaper appealed the temporary injunction but also published the story before the appellate court could decide the appeal, and the district court found its executive editor guilty of contempt.

The First Circuit reversed his conviction, specifically distinguishing the Dickinson principle. The crime boss' "privacy" rights were not sufficient to lay the basis for a prior restraint and, even if they could, the district court had not demonstrated that less extreme measures were unavailable.

But then the appeals court, in an en banc modification of its opinion (820 F.2d 1354 (1987)), made clear that news organizations covered by what they believe to be transparently invalid restraining orders must exhibit good faith when they publish restrained material by seeking emergency relief from the appropriate appellate court first. If timely access to the appellate court is not available or if timely decision is not forthcoming, the publisher may then proceed to publish and challenge the constitutionality of the order in the subsequent contempt proceeding.

Dickinson and Providence Journal can, of course, be reconciled by noting that in Dickinson the prior restraint was not "transparently" invalid, while the Providence Journal restraint was held to be so. But it is by no means self-evident that an asserted right of privacy can never be the basis for some type of prior restraint. All a news organization can do to reduce the risk of contempt sanctions is build a record of good faith action if it decides to publish.

b. *Nebraska Press Association v. Stuart*

Fortunately for the news media the indiscriminate issuance of restrictive orders directly binding their representatives was finally halted by the United States Supreme Court in Nebraska Press Association v. Stuart (1976). There the Court unanimously reversed restrictive orders of Nebraska courts barring newspersons from (1) reporting testimony and evidence presented in an open preliminary hearing concerning a ghastly multiple murder case; (2) reporting the existence and nature of any confessions or admissions made by the accused to law enforcement officers or others; and (3) reporting any other facts "strongly implicative" of the accused. This was the first time the Court had considered the question of judicial restrictive orders aimed directly at the press. It took the opportunity to make clear that its distaste for prior restraints on the press first expressed in Near v. Minnesota (1931) had not abated.

Terming prior restraints on expression "the most serious and the least tolerable infringement on

First Amendment rights" (Nebraska Press Association v. Stuart), the Court reaffirmed the idea expressed in the "Pentagon Papers" case (pp. 183–186, supra) that every form of prior restraint comes to the Court with a strong presumption of its unconstitutionality. But a majority of the justices explicitly rejected the idea that the First Amendment (at least at this time) absolutely bars all prior restraints of the press when First and Sixth Amendment interests are in competition. Instead the majority set out certain considerations to aid trial courts in determining whether in a given and obviously rare case the proponents of a judicial restrictive order might meet their heavy burden of justifying prior restraint of the media on Sixth Amendment grounds.

First, the courts must determine whether there is "a clear and present danger" that pretrial publicity will impinge upon the defendant's right to a fair trial.

Second, the courts must seriously examine the alternatives to prior restraint of publication that may be available to them such as change of venue and postponement of the trial and make findings supported by probative evidence that alternatives short of prior restraint orders will not be effective.

Third, even where the courts believe that they can establish the ineffectiveness of less drastic alternatives, they must also assess the probable effectiveness of prior restraint on publication as a method of safeguarding the accused's right to a fair trial.

If, as a practical matter, a prior restraint order will not safeguard the accused's rights it should not be entered. In the Nebraska Press Association case the facts militated against entry of such orders. Among other things, the issuing courts could not obtain jurisdiction over all news media organizations and persons reporting on the murder case, and thus might not be able to enforce their orders uniformly and effectively. Furthermore, because the murders took place in a small community of 850 persons, mouth-to-mouth rumors would saturate the community anyway and might be more prejudicial to a fair trial than reasonably accurate news accounts.

Fourth, trial courts must consider whether proposed restrictive orders would prevent the reporting of events transpiring in open court. To the extent they have this effect, such orders are constitutionally invalid.

Finally, the courts must consider carefully the terms of such orders. The prohibitions on the media must be precise and not overbroad. In the Nebraska Press Association case one restriction on the news media was that they not disseminate information "strongly implicative of the accused as the perpetrator of the slayings." This language was held too vague and too broad to avoid abridgment of the First Amendment.

Regarding this last consideration, a restrictive order to be valid must be appropriately narrow and precise and yet must also be effective in safeguarding the accused's Sixth Amendment rights. Walking this constitutional tightrope will not be easy. It is safe to say that the matters which must be considered before a prior restraint order may be entered will severely curtail resort to such orders in the future. For this reason and because of the Supreme Court's unanimous reaffirmation of its attitude of hostility toward prior restraints, Nebraska Press Association v. Stuart was an important victory for the press, but not the last word on the subject.

The relative security provided by Nebraska Press Association was called into question in Cable News Network, Inc. v. Manuel Noriega (1990). After the U.S. invasion of Panama, the Panamanian dictator Manuel Noriega was captured and brought to Miami to stand trial for drug trafficking. Several of Noriega's telephone calls to his attorneys were apparently recorded by federal prison officials in violation of their own policy against monitoring attorney-client conversations. The Cable News Network (CNN) obtained seven of these tapes from an unidentified source and broadcast one of the tapes. The United States district court judge ordered CNN to turn over all the Noriega tapes so that he could determine whether anything in the tapes presented an immediate and irreparable danger to Noriega's right to a fair trial. The judge also enjoined CNN from further broadcasting privileged communications in the tapes. The Eleventh Circuit denied CNN relief from the restraining order and directed

CNN to turn over the tapes, and the Supreme Court denied certiorari a week later.

5. Subsequent Criminal Punishment of the News Media

Subsequent criminal punishment of the news media may be just as dangerous to the media's ability to inform the public about judicial matters as prior restraints or "gag orders." In Landmark Communications, Inc. v. Virginia (1978) the Supreme Court struck down as unduly restrictive of press freedom a Virginia statute making it a crime to divulge information regarding proceedings before a state judicial review commission hearing complaints alleging the disability or misconduct of sitting judges. In this case the Virginian Pilot was convicted of violating the statute by accurately reporting on a pending commission inquiry and identifying the judge involved.

In reversing the conviction the Court made it clear that subsequent punishment of the press for the publication of accurate information of interest to the public can be just as dangerous a violation of the First and Fourteenth Amendments as judicial and legislative attempts to prevent publication in the first instance. Compare the media contempt cases of Bridges v. California (1941); Pennekamp v. Florida (1946); Craig v. Harney (1947); Wood v. Georgia (1962).

A case similar in effect to the Landmark decision is Smith v. Daily Mail Publishing Co. (1979). In this case, a 15 year-old shot and killed a 14 year-old classmate, and two newspapers published his name, violating West Virginia statutes (W.Va. Code § 49–7-3, 20 (1976)) making it a misdemeanor for a *newspaper* (but not a radio or television station) to publish, without the written approval of the juvenile court, the name of any youth charged as a juvenile offender. (See pp. 147–148 in chapter III for a discussion of Landmark and Smith with regard to invasion of privacy.) The West Virginia Supreme Court of Appeals ruled that the statute under which the newspapers were indicted violated the First and Fourteenth Amendments, and the United States Supreme Court affirmed.

Both Landmark and Smith require a balancing of the media's interests in free dissemination of information against the state's interests in confidential judicial proceedings. In Landmark, the Supreme Court held that the state's interests in confidentiality of investigations of members of the judiciary simply did not outweigh First Amendment interests. In Smith the Court held that whatever the weight of the state's interest in confidentiality of juvenile proceedings, it would not be furthered by a criminal statute which permitted broadcast media but not newspapers to disclose the names of alleged juvenile offenders.

CHAPTER VII

FREEDOM TO GATHER NEWS AND INFORMATION

A. INTRODUCTION

The freedom of expression guaranteed by the First Amendment would have little meaning if there were nothing to express. The First Amendment assumes that the citizenry will have access to information, particularly concerning their governance, as the grist for meaningful expression in a democratic society. As James Madison wrote, "A popular Government, without popular information, or the means of acquiring it, is but a Prologue to a Farce or a Tragedy; or, perhaps both. Knowledge will forever govern ignorance: And a people who mean to be their own Governors, must arm themselves with the power which knowledge gives." Letter to W.T. Barry, August 4, 1822, quoted in Environmental Protection Agency v. Mink (1973) (dissenting opinion of Douglas, J.).

Nevertheless, since the time of George Washington, the federal and state governments have claimed the right to withhold information about their activities and operations in the "public interest" and to restrict the access of individuals and the media to certain sources of information. But it is clear that not all governmental secrecy and restrictions on the gathering of information are justified.

In the 1950s the media began a movement to reverse the trend toward secret government. And by the late 1970s they had won some notable successes in the fight for open government, such as the federal Freedom of Information Act (FOIA) and federal and state open meetings legislation. Unfortunately the 1980s saw a pendulum swing in the opposite direction with the introduction of a comprehensive package of amendments to FOIA which could only be described as constricting the flow of information from the government to the press and public. But the pendulum may be swinging back toward an open government again: Clinton administration Attorney General Janet Reno rescinded a Reagan-era memorandum calling for federal agencies to withhold information whenever they found a "substantial legal basis" for doing so; in contrast, Reno's memorandum calls for "maximum responsible disclosure," an approach which will be a welcome relief to journalists and the public. Memorandum for Heads of Departments and Agencies from Attorney General Janet Reno, Oct. 4, 1993.

It is clear, then, that ease of access to government data cannot be taken for granted but depends to a large extent on the good will and grace of the legislative and executive branches of government.

B. THE FEDERAL FREEDOM OF INFORMATION ACT (FOIA)

1. Historical Background

In 1966 Congress passed the Freedom of Information Act (FOIA), 5 U.S.C.A. § 552, which requires federal executive and independent regulatory agencies to publish indexes in the Federal Register and make documents and records available to anyone who requests them if they are not specifically exempted from disclosure by the Act itself. The language of the Act is affirmative in requiring disclosure; nowhere does it require nondisclosure. Documents generated by Congress and the Office of the President are not subject to FOIA, but those of federal agencies are. An agency may, if it chooses, refuse to release information under a claim that the information is covered by one or more of the nine enumerated exemptions discussed below, but then it may be required to defend its refusal in federal court where the burden of justification is on the withholding agency, not on the person or organization seeking disclosure. With Congress' bestowal of jurisdiction upon the federal courts to hear complaints of alleged FOIA violations, agency officials are no longer the sole judges of what information should and should not be made available to the public.

2. Operation of the Original Act

a. In the Courts

Results of litigation under the original FOIA were mixed. Although the courts placed the burden on the agencies to justify withholding information and exercised the injunctive jurisdiction to force disclosure when deemed appropriate, they also construed certain of the exemptions broadly.

b. At the Administrative Level

Although litigation or the threat of it is very important to the operation of FOIA, the proof of the legislation is in its day-to-day administration by the agencies themselves. Litigation is costly and time consuming. Information is needed by the media quickly and at reasonable cost. At the administrative level, too, the results have been mixed. Some agencies such as the Department of Justice (excluding the FBI) and the Department of Defense have promulgated fair and reasonable regulations for the expeditious release of information and are generally following them. Some agencies have not been as conscientious. Charges for searches and copying have too often been exorbitant and extensive delays in releasing information have been frequent. Nevertheless, vast amounts of information have been made routinely available to the public and the media which prior to the Act would have been kept from view.

3. Amendments to FOIA

After experience with the operation of FOIA over several years, Congress amended it in 1974 and again in 1986 to increase and expedite governmental disclosure. The amendments were both substantive and procedural. One substantive amendment defined a federal agency to encompass any executive or military department, including the Executive Office of the President itself, government corporations, and any independent regulatory agency. These amendments were needed because in the past some administrative units had tried to avoid responding to FOIA requests by claiming they were not "agencies."

The procedural amendments were designed to speed the release of information and reduce the costs to those who request it. The amendments required the agencies to establish uniform fee schedules and limit fees to reasonable charges for document searches and duplication. Agencies must respond to FOIA requests within 10 working days, for example, and are given 20 working days to process an appeal of a denial of a request. If the agency fails to comply with the time limits, the requester is given immediate access to the appropriate U.S. District Court for a hearing with the agency. The 1986 amendments provided for limited fee waivers for the news media, educational and scientific institutions.

4. Litigation Involving the FOIA's Nine Exemptions

The discussion below covers the nine exemptions which may be invoked to avoid disclosure, as well as examples of litigation and judicial construction of the exemptions.

(1)(a) specifically authorized under criteria established by an executive order to be kept secret in the interest of national defense or foreign policy and (b) are in fact properly classified pursuant to such executive order.

In Environmental Protection Agency v. Mink (1973), the Supreme Court held in effect that the executive branch had some authority to determine under Executive Order 10501 (setting up the present government classification system) what information was to be kept secret in the interest of national defense or foreign policy. The Court ruled that Exemption (1) as originally adopted in 1966 permitted no challenge whatsoever to the classification of a document. It would not allow a United States District Court to study in closed chambers classified documents concerning an underground nuclear test on Amchitka Island in order to isolate non-secret portions and order their release. A classified stamp on a file meant that nothing in that file could be disclosed. The Mink case became the catalyst for Congress to amend FOIA in 1974 to give courts the power to inspect classified documents in closed chambers to determine whether they are properly classified, and order their release if they are not. P.L. 93–502, 88 Stat. 1561.

(2) related solely to the internal personnel rules and practices of an agency.

The only real controversy regarding Exemption 2 is whether it applies to agency staff manuals. When a citizen sought access to a Bureau of Alcohol, Tobacco and Firearms staff manual titled "Surveillance of Premises, Vehicles and Persons," the

United States Court of Appeals upheld the Bureau's decision to release all but 20 pages, which described its internal practices. Crooker v. Bureau of Alcohol, Tobacco & Firearms (1981).

(3) Matters specifically exempted from disclosure by statute (other than [the Privacy Act]), provided that such statute (a) requires that the matters be withheld from the public in such a manner as to leave no discretion on the issue, or (b) establishes particular criteria for withholding or refers to particular types of matters to be withheld.

This exemption is designed to prevent disclosure of information required or permitted to be kept secret by numerous other federal laws. An example of a statute which would exempt information from disclosure is the National Security Act of 1947, which Congress amended in 1984, exempting entire systems of CIA files from search and review. The law provides for judicial review of whether the files are classified, but judicial review has not been effective because judges are reluctant to second-guess the executive branch on classification of national security materials.

The courts' willingness to defer to Exemption 3 in the interests of national security is illustrated by the case of CIA v. Sims (1985). From 1953 to 1966, the CIA financed a research project code-named MKULTRA in which 185 researchers at over 80 universities received funding to study the effects of mind-altering substances on people. Several MKULTRA subprojects involved experiments in which researchers surreptitiously administered dangerous drugs such as LSD to unwitting human subjects. At least two people died as a result of MKULTRA experiments, and others may have suffered impaired health. In 1963 the CIA's inspector general investigated the project and reported that people were being used as guinea pigs without their knowledge. CIA files on MKULTRA were declassified in 1970. The Public Citizen Health Research Group and a private attorney filed a FOIA request, asking for the names of universities and individuals who had conducted the experiments. The CIA refused to disclose names of the researchers and 21 of the institutions involved, saying that they had been promised confidentiality. The CIA argued that their names were exempt from disclosure under the National Security Act of 1947 which states that "the Director of Central Intelligence shall be responsible for protecting intelligence sources ... from unauthorized disclosure." The Supreme Court agreed with the CIA that Exemption 3 of FOIA, providing that an agency need not disclose matters specifically exempted from disclosure by statute, was applicable, and the CIA could withhold the information. The Court added that the CIA Director's decisions, because he "must of course be familiar with the whole picture, as judges are not, are worthy of great deference given the magnitude of the national security interests and potential risks at stake." CIA v. Sims (1985). The Court has thus given the CIA an indeterminate degree of latitude in making disclosure decisions within the context of

intelligence-gathering. The Court's "great deference" standard may encourage the CIA to assert
national security justification in an effort to hide
improvident behavior. In effect, CIA v. Sims ex-
pands permissible Exemption 3 nondisclosure in a
manner that may virtually exempt the CIA from
FOIA coverage. L. Good and D. Williams, "Developments under the Freedom of Information Act—
1985," 1986 Duke L.J. 384, at 433.

(4) in the nature of trade secrets and commercial
or financial information obtained from a person
and privileged or confidential.

The so-called "reverse FOIA case," Chrysler
Corp. v. Brown (1979), gives an expansive interpretation to FOIA to permit federal agencies to release
certain classes of information required to be submitted to these agencies by private businesses, including their trade secrets and confidential statisti-
cal data. In so ruling the Court repeated the idea
that FOIA is exclusively a disclosure statute and
that the exemptions in it, particularly the one dealing with trade secrets, permit agencies to withhold
records but do not require them to do so. This
ruling has created problems for the government in
collecting privately held confidential business information; it has resulted in calls from the business
community for amendment of the Act to require
agencies to withhold certain records in order to
prevent harm to businesses which make disclosures
of information to the government.

In 1982 two agencies did release information that hurt some companies. The EPA mistakenly disclosed the formula for one of Monsanto's most profitable products, an herbicide, to one of its major competitors in response to the latter's FOIA request. Washington Post, Sept. 18, 1982, p. A1. The Food and Drug Administration (FDA) released "the ingredients and molecular structure of a new drug about to be marketed by a major pharmaceutical company" to that company's competitor. 4 Gov. Disclosure Rep. Bull. No. 2, Prgrph. 2.2 (Feb. 8, 1983). These two incidents contributed to corporations' long-standing fears that the commercially sensitive data that they are compelled to disclose would inadvertently be made available to competitors through FOIA.

Possibly in response to these incidents and Chrysler v. Brown, Congress passed the National Cooperative Research Act of 1984, P.L. 98–462, 15 U.S.C.A. § 4305(d), which limits antitrust liability for companies embarking on joint research projects if they notify the Federal Trade Commission (FTC) and the Attorney General about their joint projects. The Research Act qualifies as an Exemption 3 statute of the FOIA by mandating nondisclosure by the FTC. Because it permits no agency discretion regarding disclosure, the Research Act limits the effect of the pro-disclosure interpretation in Chrysler v. Brown.

(5) in the nature of inter-agency or intra-agency memoranda or letters which would not be avail-

able by law to a party other than an agency in litigation with the agency.

This exemption is designed to protect working papers, studies and reports prepared within an agency or circulated among government personnel as the basis of an agency's final decision. Communications between an agency and its legal counsel are also shielded from disclosure.

This exemption is also called the executive privilege exemption. Executive privilege is a common law privilege which presidents beginning with George Washington have invoked to keep records and documents of the executive branch and the administrative agencies secret. In United States v. Nixon (1974), Richard Nixon argued that his White House tapes were protected by executive privilege when the special prosecutor subpoenaed them. But the Supreme Court ruled that the president has an absolute executive privilege only when the material in question consists of military or diplomatic secrets. Because the White House tapes did not contain such secrets, there was only a limited privilege, and Nixon was ordered to surrender the tapes. When Nixon tried to take his White House papers with him upon leaving office, the public outcry was so great that in 1974 Congress passed the Presidential Records and Materials Preservation Act, 44 U.S.C. § 210 (1989), to prohibit destruction of records related to the Watergate scandal or otherwise of historical significance. Insisting that the papers were his personal property, Nixon sued for compensation. In 1992 United States Court of Appeals ruled that the papers had indeed been Nixon's private property, and directed the federal district court to determine how much money Nixon should receive as compensation. Nixon v. United States (1992).

More recently, officials of the Reagan and Bush administrations attempted to erase all electronically stored information when they left office. Director of the National Security Archive Scott Armstrong obtained a temporary injunction to prevent the Reagan administration from destruction of its electronic files, and then asked the court to extend the order to prevent the Bush administration from destroying its computer tapes four years later. Armstrong v. Bush (1992). On appeal, the United States Court of Appeals ruled that the Bush administration could not destroy the electronic records created by the Executive Office of the President and by the National Security Council during the Bush and Reagan administrations; electronic mail memos are also records under the Federal Records Act (44 U.S.C.A. § 2100). Armstrong v. Executive Office of the President (1993).

A United States Court of Appeals recently expanded Exemption 5 in a case dealing with the Department of Justice's Office of Special Investigations' report on former United Nation's Secretary–General Kurt Waldheim. The court held that the report, which detailed Waldheim's involvement in Nazi massacres of Yugoslav partisans and Jews and deportation of 60,000 Jews from Greece, was exempt from disclosure as an internal memorandum in the form of an "attorney work product" because former Attorney General Edwin Meese used the report to place Waldheim on a list of aliens to be barred from the United States. Mapother v. Department of Justice (1993).

> (6) in the nature of personnel and medical files and similar files the disclosure of which would constitute a clearly unwarranted invasion of personal privacy.

An example of litigation involving Exemption 6 occurred when NBC legal correspondent Carl Stern requested information about three FBI officials who had been censured for their involvement in the FBI's domestic surveillance operations (COINTELPRO) in the 1970s. Stern obtained copies of the letters of censure, but the names were deleted. The U.S. Court of Appeals for the District of Columbia Circuit ordered the FBI to release the names, rejecting the FBI's claim of invasion of privacy and ruling that such privileges do not exist "when relatively high-placed officials entrusted with the performance of important public business actually jeopardize an agency's integrity by covering up a government wrong doing." Stern v. FBI (1984).

But the reported cases in which the balance has been struck against release of information are more numerous. For example, the St. Louis Post–Dispatch, a newspaper on Nixon's "Enemies List," was unable to obtain a CIA document on some its reporters. St. Louis Post–Dispatch v. FBI (1977). More recently, the D.C. Circuit held that Exemption

Six applied to the tape recording of the astronauts' voices just before the space shuttle Challenger exploded because it was a "similar file;" releasing a tape recording of the astronauts' last words would constitute an unwarranted invasion of privacy. New York Times Co. v. NASA (1990) (en banc).

The following year the Supreme Court reversed an Eleventh Circuit ruling in favor of disclosure of the names of Haitian nationals who had been returned to Haiti; the purpose of the disclosure was to verify reports that the Haitian government was persecuting those who were returned. But the Supreme Court reversed in a unanimous decision, holding that because the government had promised confidentiality, the State Department could, under Exemption 6, refuse to release names of Haitian nationals who had been returned to Haiti. Ray v. Department of Justice (1990).

(7) in the nature of investigatory records compiled for law enforcement purposes, but only to the extent that the production of such records would (a) interfere with enforcement proceedings, (b) deprive a person of a right to a fair trial or an impartial adjudication, (c) could reasonably be expected to constitute an unwarranted invasion of personal privacy, (d) disclose the identity of a confidential source and, in the case of records compiled by a criminal law enforcement authority in the course of criminal investigation, or by an agency conducting a lawful national security intelligence investigation, confidential information furnished only by the confidential source, (e) dis-

close investigative techniques and procedures, or (f) endanger the life or physical safety of law enforcement personnel.

Congress tightened disclosure under this exemption in 1986. Under the 1986 amendments, informant files are no longer disclosable under FOIA. The 1986 amendments also changed the wording in Exemption 7 from "will interfere with [law] enforcement" to "could reasonably be expected to interfere with [law] enforcement. In addition, the FBI need no longer confirm or deny the existence of documents in counter-intelligence and terrorism files if the files are classified. P.L. 99–570, amending 5 U.S.C.A. § 552. The FBI had argued that those who were targets of its investigations were being tipped off by utilizing the FOIA to determine whether files had been compiled on them.

The threshold test of Exemption 7 is whether the requested documents are "compiled for law enforcement purposes." 5 U.S.C.A. § 552(b)(7)(1988). The Supreme Court ruled in John Doe Agency v. John Doe Corporation (1989), that the term "compiled" covers materials put together at different times and without regard to the original purpose of the collection. The effect of this decision is that routine records that were available at one point will become unavailable when put into an investigative file. Thus, the Court expanded Exemption 7 to shield from public scrutiny any information collected for a law enforcement purpose.

In the same year, the Supreme Court expanded Exemption 7(C) in U.S. Department of Justice v. Reporters Committee for Freedom of the Press (1989). In this case, CBS news correspondent Robert Schnake and the Reporters Committee for Freedom of the Press asked the FBI to disclose its rap sheets on Charles Medico and three other members of his family. The FBI's rap sheets contain information indicating arrests, indictments, acquittals, convictions and sentences on about 24 million people in the United States. These computerized files are compilations of what are usually public records held by law enforcement agencies across the country. The Justice Department has simply compiled all the information about an individual from various police agencies into a single computerized file. Medico, a defense contractor, was allegedly connected to organized crime. His company, Medico Industries, had allegedly obtained a number of defense contracts through an improper arrangement with a corrupt congressman. Schnake argued that a record of financial crimes by Medico would be a matter of public interest; furthermore, Medico could not assert a privacy claim because the criminal process is public. But the Department of Justice denied Schnake's request, citing the personal privacy factor in Exemption 7(C).

When the case reached the Supreme Court, it upheld the Department of Justice's denial in a unanimous decision, ruling that rap sheets in the FBI's computerized database of criminal history information were protected by Exemption 7(C).

The Court held that individuals' privacy interests in their rap sheets outweighed the public interest in disclosure, even though a diligent search of public records throughout the country could uncover the same information held in the rap sheets. But the Court explained that rap sheets do not shed any light on government activities, and are therefore protected by Exemption 7(C). It is worth noting the difference in phrasing between Exemption 6, referring to "a clearly unwarranted invasion of person privacy," and Exemption 7(C), referring to information which "could reasonably be expected to constitute an unwarranted invasion of personal privacy." Because Exemption 7(C) permits withholding of information if there is merely a reasonable expectation rather than a certainty that privacy would be invaded as in Exemption 6, it provides a more relaxed standard by which the Court found that Medico's privacy outweighed public interest in disclosure of the rap sheets.

The Reporters Committee standard substantially broadens the protection of personal privacy interests under FOIA. Although the Supreme Court's decision protects individual privacy, its narrow interpretation of the public interest fails to ensure the FOIA will continue to serve its main purpose of providing open access to government-held information. S.E. Wilborn, "Developments under the Freedom of Information Act—1989," 1990 Duke L.J. 1113, at 1125.

(8) contained in or related to examination, operating or condition reports prepared by, on behalf

of, or for the use of any agency responsible for the regulation or supervision of financial institutions.

This exemption is designed to prevent disclosure of sensitive financial reports or audits that if made public could undermine public confidence in banks and other financial institutions. It has seldom been litigated, even when the savings and loan industry collapsed in the 1980s. Despite widespread allegations of wrongdoing and misfeasance by government officials and owners of savings and loans, Exemption 8 remains a serious obstacle to any attempts by journalists and the public to fully understand why American taxpayers have been left to pay nearly half a trillion dollars to cover the losses resulting from the theft, corruption and irresponsibility of those in power. Even historians may be unable to write an intelligible history of the fiasco. Only if the supervisory and regulatory agencies involved in oversight of failed savings and loans decide to release financial reports will they become available to the public. And in deciding whether to release such information, agencies will consider the embarrassment such release may cause their past and present officials. See Gregory v. Federal Deposit Insurance Corporation (1980).

(9) in the nature of geological and geophysical information and data, including maps, concerning wells.

This exemption protects the valuable proprietary information of oil companies and mining companies from disclosure.

5. Assessment of FOIA

There is some criticism regarding the uses to which FOIA is put. But journalists have used the FOIA to expose the following abuses:

— disclosures about nuclear bomb testing and danger of the radiation to Utah residents

— the litany of FBI and CIA excesses during the 1960s and 1970s, such as illegal spying on Americans

— organized crime's infiltration of the coal industry

— Navy admirals with $14,000 sofas and $41,000 carpets on their destroyers

— the Pentagon permitting military contractors to charge the Department of Defense for the costs incurred in lobbying Congress for appropriations for their weapons systems. See New Statesman, Jan. 10, 1986, pp. 12–13.

In short, despite its problems and limitations, FOIA provides the American people and the media which serve them with a significant instrument for holding their government accountable.

6. Applicability of FOIA to Computer Files

Although the FOIA does not distinguish between information stored in computers from paper files, some agencies have contended that the Act does not apply to electronic records. Despite the growing use of computers, federal agencies have not established policies on access to computerized records and do not uniformly recognize reporters' rights to receive such data under FOIA.

Applying FOIA to computer files raises numerous questions affecting access: How much effort must an agency expend to cull discloseable data from a database which contains exempt information? Does culling information from a database create a new record? Would a government agency be obligated to translate data into another software program if a journalist does not have a proprietary software program used by the agency? If an agency provides a computer file which would fill a boxcar in hard copy form, does the computer file have to be in a readable form? Under the current FOIA, written with paper files in mind, agencies are required to permit access to existing records but are not required to create new records. The Justice Department, which advises all federal agencies on FOIA, contends that agencies are not required to program their computers to respond to information requests.

Congress has not amended FOIA to keep pace with technology, although at this writing journalists have asked President Clinton to support bills such as Senator Patrick Leahy's Electronic Freedom of Information Act and the Government Printing Office Electronic Information Access Enhancement Act, which would require the GPO to publish electronic versions of the Federal Register and the Congressional Record, as well as computerized databases of government information.

Despite disagreement among federal agencies over policies regarding access to electronic data, several courts have ruled that electronic records are public under FOIA. See Long v. IRS (1979), and Petroleum Information Corporation v. Department of Interior (1992).

C. LEGISLATION LIMITING ACCESS IN THE NAME OF PERSONAL PRIVACY

In contrast to the movement toward disclosure embodied in FOIA, more and more legislation is being passed to prevent public scrutiny of government-assembled information about individuals. In 1974, Congress passed the Privacy Act, 5 U.S.C.A. § 552a, to curb abuses by the federal government in its handling of personal information about individual citizens. The idea behind the federal statute has spread to the states and by 1992, 29 states had enacted some kind of privacy act covering, for example, information about an individual's criminal history and whether it may be released to the press and the public. At least 39 states have legislation providing for expungement of nonconviction arrest records. See U.S. Department of Justice, Bureau of Justice Statistics, Criminal History Record Information: Compendium of State Privacy and Security Legislation, 1992: Current Status of the Law and Summary of State Statutes. Because of privacy claims, the press has less access to government records, especially arrest records.

When the Privacy Act was passed, Congress attempted to avoid confusion about whether Exemption 3 of FOIA (matters exempt from disclosure by statute) referred to the Privacy Act. Congress thus tried to clarify in the 1974 amendments to FOIA that Exemption 3 was not applicable to the Privacy Act; in other words, FOIA should take preference over the Privacy Act if there is a question about whether to release information or not. But a government official who refuses to disclose information merely faces a vague threat of disciplinary action under FOIA, whereas if the same official discloses too much information about an individual, he or she faces monetary penalties under the Privacy Act. This in itself creates a subtle pressure on government agencies to defer to the Privacy Act over FOIA, even though this was not the intent of Congress.

After various conflicting lower court decisions, Congress tried partially to resolve the conflict between FOIA and the Privacy Act (5 U.S.C.A. § 552a(q)(1) with a 1984 amendment to the National Security Act of 1947 (50 U.S.C.A. § 431) which declared that the Privacy Act is not an Exemption 3 statute. If the Privacy Act had been declared an Exemption 3 statute, it would have protected all information within its scope from disclosure under FOIA; entire systems of records could have been withheld. The Privacy Act clearly states that "no agency shall disclose any record ... unless disclosure of the record would be required [under FOIA]."

D. OPEN MEETINGS—OPEN RECORDS LEGISLATION

1. The Federal Government in the "Sunshine"

Parallel to the Federal Freedom of Information Act are federal and state "government in the sunshine" statutes which require federal, state and local governmental units to conduct their business in the open. In 1976 Congress passed the Government in the Sunshine Act, the federal open meetings law. P.L. 94–409, 5 U.S.C.A. § 552b. This statute affects about 50 federal boards, commissions and agencies which are required to conduct their business meetings in public. The law also prohibits informal communication between officials of an agency and representatives of companies with whom the agency does business unless this communication is recorded as part of the public record.

2. State Open Meetings Laws

Statutes similar to the federal Government in the Sunshine Act are now in force in a large majority of states, but vary considerably, and journalists and lawyers must acquaint themselves with the provisions in their particular jurisdiction if the legislation is to be effectively utilized.

Some states limit their "sunshine" legislation to the final stages in the decision-making process such as meetings at which final votes are taken. The spirit of open government may be easily avoided by agencies making the real decisions behind closed doors and then ratifying their decisions in the "sunshine."

The "sunshine" statutes of most states provide specific exemptions from the public meeting requirement to ameliorate unwarranted disclosure. These exemptions are generally similar to those in the federal Sunshine Act.

E. MEDIA ACCESS TO GOVERNMENTALLY RESTRICTED PLACES AND INSTITUTIONS

A field in which the freedom to gather news and information has not expanded in recent years is that of access to governmentally restricted institutions such as military bases and penitentiaries and geographic areas such as unfriendly foreign countries. While the Supreme Court recognized in the abstract in Branzburg v. Hayes (1972), that "without some protection for seeking out the news, freedom of the press could be eviscerated," the Court in that very case appears to have restricted First Amendment protection for newsgathering to those areas accessible to the general public.

Such an approach to access assures that the media will not be discriminated against in the gathering of information. But no guarantee is given that public access and, hence, media access, to sources of information will not be further curtailed by a security conscious government.

Initially it was thought that because Branzburg involved a claim of indirect restriction on newsgathering (see pp. 264–266, infra for a discussion of the case), the limitation on protection for newsgathering might not be applicable to direct governmental restrictions on media access. This has not proven to be the case. In Pell v. Procunier (1974) and Saxbe v. Washington Post Co. (1974) the California Department of Corrections and the Federal Bureau of Prisons had by regulation barred representatives of the media from interviewing specifically designated penitentiary inmates.

This view of the Constitution was reaffirmed by the High Court in Houchins v. KQED, Inc. (1978), although Houchins is significant because of Justice Stewart's concurring opinion in which he emphasized that, although journalists had no more right of access to prisons than the general public, they should be allowed to use their "tools of the trade," including videocameras and tape recorders.

The Department of Justice now prohibits videotaping executions in federal cases and limits access to inmates during the week before the death sentence is carried out. Implementation of Death Sentences in Federal Cases, 58 Fed. Reg. 4898 (1993), to be codified at 28 C.F.R. § 26.

The principle that journalists are not accorded special access to news sources by the First Amendment is a broad one and would seemingly apply to any situation in which the state or federal government limits public access reasonably and in a nondiscriminatory way. A common situation is the setting up of police lines to seal off a geographic area in the interest of public safety. By definition police lines are designed to keep the public out of even public areas for limited periods of time and if there exists a reasonable basis for the lines it would seem to follow that the media could also be excluded. In practice, accredited journalists are often permitted by police authorities to cross the lines. If such permission is given, however, it must be extended on a nondiscriminatory basis to all journalists with proper credentials and the credentials must be issued in a fair and nondiscriminatory manner.

But if police officers order everyone except rescue workers to leave the scene of an accident, courts are usually unsympathetic to journalists who defy such orders. For example, in State v. Lashinsky (1979), a news photographer refused to leave the scene of an accident after a policeman had ordered him to do so. The photographer wanted to take pictures of a car that had run off the Garden State Parkway, crashed down an embankment and overturned. A badly injured girl was trapped inside the car under her mother, who had been killed. Because of the car might catch fire, the police officer ordered everyone not involved in rescue efforts to leave the scene. The photographer was convicted for violating the policeman's order and the New Jersey Supreme Court affirmed his conviction. The photographer argued that the policeman's order should not apply to him because he was a member of the press, but the court held that the needs of journalists must yield in some circumstances so that police can take care of those who are their immediate responsibility.

Similarly, in City of Oak Creek v. King (1989), a television cameraman defied a police officer's order not to enter the closed off site of a plane crash. A four-member crew from a Milwaukee television station drove through a police roadblock to get to the scene of the crash. Although three of them left when a detective advised them to, cameraman Ah King refused and was charged with disorderly conduct. The Wisconsin Supreme Court affirmed his conviction, ruling that he did not have a First Amendment right of access to the scene of the plane crash when the public had been reasonably excluded.

While the prevailing judicial view refuses to mandate constitutional protection for the media in their newsgathering function beyond that afforded the general public, special consideration may still be accorded the media by legislative or administrative grace. For example, under California Penal Code § 409(d), a police officer may permit access to a closed off disaster scene to a "duly authorized representative of any news service," meaning anyone with a press card. In addition to such examples of credentialed newspersons being permitted to cross police lines, there are Department of State regulations giving professional journalists special authorization for travel to restricted foreign areas if the purpose of the travel is to make information available to the public concerning these areas. But, of course, what is given at the government's discretion may also be withdrawn at its discretion.

F. MEDIA ACCESS TO COURTS AND JUDICIAL RECORDS

1. Access to Trial Proceedings

Another major source of concern about media access to governmentally generated information has recently developed, this time in relation to the courthouse. (See Chapter VI for more in-depth coverage of the free press–fair trial issue.) While it had long been our history that the doors of American courtrooms were open to the public and press (see Justice Black's opinion in In re Oliver (1948)), a trend toward closing the courtroom developed in the 1970s as a judicial response to the threat to fair trials allegedly posed by publicity surrounding those trials. By the end of that decade the Reporters Committee for Freedom of Press had documented several dozen cases in which pretrial and trial proceedings across the country had been closed to the public and press by judicial order. This movement to deny access of the media to judicial information and news reached its zenith with the decision in Gannett Co. v. DePasquale (1979). In a 5–4 decision, the Supreme Court ruled in Gannett that judges may close pretrial hearings.

The four dissenters in Gannett warned that secret judicial proceedings would be a menace to liberty. More than 75 percent of federal criminal prosecutions never reach a full trial. Serious plea bargaining often takes place, perhaps because a prosecutor realizes that the case is not as strong as desired. When such plea-bargaining takes place, there are no public proceedings after the pretrial hearing, which then is the last point for the public to learn what happens to the defendant. An example of abuse during plea-bargaining in a closed pretrial hearing occurred in Chico, California in 1979. When three white hunters were unable to find deer to shoot, they went looking for "dark meat," as they put it. They maliciously shot and killed a deaf and mentally handicapped black man. The judge closed the preliminary hearings. He allowed the three hunters to plead guilty in return for lesser sentences and placed a gag order on the press for a year. Detroit Free Press, Feb. 24, 1980, pp. 1B, 4B. The local media assumed that the black man's death was a random hunting accident, and did not learn that the murder was premeditated and racially motivated. Thus, they did not bother to challenge the gag order. Such abuses of plea-bargaining during closed pretrial hearings were a source of concern to the four dissenters in the Gannett decision.

Fortuitously, a case was already in the judicial system of the State of Virginia which squarely raised these questions and would quickly give the Supreme Court an opportunity to clarify what it had decided in Gannett. In Richmond Newspapers, Inc. v. Virginia (1980), a murder trial was closed to the public and the press on the motion of the defendant, who had already gone through three

previous mistrials of the same case. Neither the
prosecutor nor the reporters covering the trial for
Richmond Newspapers objected to the closure at the
time the trial judge granted the motion. But later
that same day, Richmond Newspapers and their
reporters sought a hearing on their motion to vacate the closure order. A hearing was held the next
day at which time constitutional objections were
raised by Richmond Newspapers and the reporters.
The court denied the motion to vacate and ordered
the trial to proceed "with the press and public
excluded." The media corporation and its employees then appealed to the Virginia Supreme Court
which denied the petition for appeal. The United
States Supreme Court then granted a petition for
certiorari to review the case.

In his opinion reversing the judgment of the
Virginia Supreme Court, Chief Justice Burger noted
at the outset that the Richmond Newspapers case
involved exclusion from a trial and not from a
pretrial proceeding. The Chief Justice explained
that while the Sixth Amendment provided the press
with no right of access to trials, the First Amendment, as applied to the states through the Fourteenth Amendment, did: "We hold that the right to
attend criminal trials is implicit in the guarantees
of the First Amendment; without the freedom to
attend such trials, which people have exercised for
centuries, important aspects of freedom of speech
and 'of the press could be eviscerated.'" Chief
Justice Burger relied on both an historical and a
functional analysis of public access to trials. He

found an historical presumption of openness, noting that criminal trials had been open to the public dating back to thirteenth century England. Justice Brennan concurred and expanded on the "structural" or functional view of the First Amendment, referring to the importance of informed debate in a democracy and the need for the media to function as surrogates for the public.

But Chief Justice Burger made clear that the First Amendment right of access to trials was not absolute. If the trial court could find, as the Virginia trial court did not, that there was a specific overriding interest in closing a trial, then an occasional courtroom closure might pass constitutional muster.

However, he did not state the precise constitutional standards that litigants would have to meet to obtain such closures or whether different standards might be applied to the closing of pretrial proceedings permitted by Gannett. The Court avoided reversing Gannett. Pretrial proceedings pose greater risks of generating publicity prejudicial to a fair trial because prospective jurors may be influenced by the news stories arising out of such proceedings before they are even chosen, and the judicial devices to prevent potential prejudice in such cases are limited.

There has been, however, a clear trend toward upholding access to courtrooms for press and public in nearly all situations since the Richmond Newspapers decision. In Globe Newspaper Co. v. Superior

Court (1982), the state of Massachusetts closed a rape trial involving minor victims because of a state law requiring that trials be closed without exception when juvenile victims of a sexual assault testified. The Supreme Court struck down the statute, holding that it violated the First Amendment right of access to court proceedings. Even the compelling interest of the state to protect minor victims of sex crimes from further trauma and embarrassment was held insufficient to justify indiscriminate exclusion of the press and public from those portions of criminal trials during which the victims testify. The qualified right of access to attend criminal trials outlined in Richmond and upheld in Globe was extended to civil trials by the United States Court of Appeals for the Third Circuit in Publicker Industries, Inc. v. Cohen (1984).

But because the Supreme Court did not clearly resolve the question of access to pretrial hearings in Gannett Co. v. DePasquale, supra, some confusion remained in the lower courts during the five years following Gannett concerning the openness of these often significant civil proceedings.

2. Access to Pretrial Proceedings

Then in 1984 the Supreme Court issued the first of three decisions that helped resolve the issue. The Press–Enterprise in Riverside, California protested the exclusion of reporters from nearly six weeks of jury questioning (voir dire) at the trial of Albert Greenwood Brown, who was later convicted and sentenced to death for the rape and murder of a

13 year-old girl. In a unanimous opinion, the Supreme Court ruled that voir dire proceedings should be open to press and public unless those wishing to close the proceedings can demonstrate that 1) there is an overriding interest that would be prejudiced by open proceedings, 2) the closure is no broader than necessary to protect that interest, 3) reasonable alternatives to closure have been considered, and 4) the trial court made findings adequate to support closure. Press–Enterprise Co. v. Superior Court (1984).

In the second case signalling a trend toward increased access to pretrial proceedings, Waller v. Georgia (1984), the state of Georgia tried to close the pretrial hearing in one case so that they might use the same wiretap evidence against other people not yet charged. But Waller, the defendant, wanted the hearing to be open. The Supreme Court unanimously upheld his position, ruling that hearings are presumptively open and cannot be closed against the defendant's wishes unless there are compelling reasons to do so. The Court held that the defendant's Sixth Amendment right to a public trial extends to pretrial hearings except where the party seeking to close the hearing meets the four-part test outlined above in Press–Enterprise.

Finally, in Press–Enterprise Co. v. Superior Court (II) (1986), the same newspaper that had won access to the voir dire two years before won a Supreme Court ruling that the public and media have a qualified First Amendment right to attend pretrial proceedings in criminal cases. The case began when a California court closed a pretrial hearing at the request of a nurse accused of murdering 12 elderly patients at a nursing home by injecting them with lethal doses of the heart drug lidocaine. The Press–Enterprise protested the closure.

When the case reached the Supreme Court, the first question to be addressed was whether there was a presumption of openness attached to the jury selection. To answer this question, the court applied a two-part test involving 1) an historical analysis (referring to a tradition of public access), and 2) a functional analysis (referring to whether openness serves a positive function such as enhancing both the fairness of a criminal trial and the appearance of fairness essential to public confidence in the judicial system). Having determined that a presumption of access to jury selection existed, the Court then applied the same analysis as in Press–Enterprise I: "The presumption [of openness] may be overcome only by an overriding interest based on findings that closure is essential to preserve higher values and is narrowly tailored to serve that interest." Press–Enterprise Co. v. Superior Court (II).

Thus the Supreme Court ruled that a pretrial hearing may be closed only if 1) there is a substantial probability that the defendant's right to a fair trial will be prejudiced by publicity, and 2) a judge cannot find reasonable alternatives to closure to protect the defendant's fair trial rights. Mere risk of prejudice does not automatically justify refusing public access to pretrial hearings. If judges find a "substantial probability" of prejudice, they may order closure only in the narrowest manner which will be effective. For instance, if three hours of testimony during a four-day pretrial hearing might cause prejudice, the hearing may be closed only during those three hours. The Supreme Court has thus made it extremely difficult for those wishing to close pretrial hearings.

Although the Court's opinion in Press–Enterprise II is directed to pretrial hearings in California, the question arises whether the 7–2 decision tacitly overrules the Court's earlier decision in Gannett Co. v. DePasquale that criminal pretrial hearings may be closed to press and public. But the majority opinion relies heavily on historical analysis, arguing that if pretrial hearings have generally been open in the past, there is a presumptive First Amendment right of access. In any case, the Court avoided a blanket ruling that pretrial proceedings must be open to the public and press.

3. Access to Evidence Introduced in Judicial Proceedings

In Seattle Times Co. v. Rhinehart (1984), the Supreme Court ruled that the news media do not have a First Amendment right of access to discovery materials, although subsequent lower court decisions suggest that discovery materials are available to the public once they have been filed with the trial court. For example, in Public Citizen v. Liggett

Group, Inc. (1988), Public Citizen and the Wall Street Journal won access to a tobacco company's discovery documents in a lawsuit by survivors of a smoker. See also In re Agent Orange Litigation, (1987).

CHAPTER VIII

NEWSPERSONS' PRIVILEGE, SUBPOENAS, CONTEMPT CITATIONS AND SEARCHES AND SEIZURES

A. SUBPOENAS VS. CLAIMS OF PRIVILEGE

1. The Contemporary Problem

Until the late 1960s the subpoenaing of newspersons by various branches and agencies of federal, state and local governments to testify about their sources and other information did not pose much of a problem for the media. Through the 1950's, there were only a handful of cases involving attempts by the government to force disclosure from unwilling members of the press. And as late as the advent of the Nixon Administration the problem was not one of major concern.

But then a number of social and political forces combined to embolden prosecutors, judges, legislators and other government officials to seek unpublished information of interest to them in the hands and heads of newspersons. Mutual distrust and even enmity between public officials and reporters began to grow, particularly in the large urban areas, fueled at least in part by the Vietnam war, a troubled economy, widespread graft and corruption at all levels of government, leaks of secret government information, doubtful media coverage of government and its personnel and what some might characterize as anti-establishmentarianism by some elements of the media. Then too, stories about the drug and sex subcultures and violence-prone anti-government organizations became of greater interest to the press. As a result, reporters were made privy to information concerning violations of law that prosecutors wanted and could not obtain through traditional means. In addition, "law and order" concerns began to grip the land in the wake of an ever-increasing crime rate. The 1970s engendered a widespread attitude among government officials that if reporters had unpublished information concerning crimes and anti-establishment conduct, they had the same legal duty as anyone else to disclose it.

This attitude has persisted into the 1990s, and poses special problems for newspersons. First, the ethics of their profession require that they not divulge information obtained in confidence. Second, any disclosure or appearance of disclosure of sources or other information obtained in confidence will mark reporters as "unreliable" in the view of those from whom they are obtaining information and will have an inhibiting effect on their ability to gather and disseminate news. Third, reporters think of themselves as "professionals" like lawyers or doctors. This gives them a basis for claiming protection from disclosure of their non-published work product. News media personnel thus insist that the law must accord them a privilege not to testify or produce materials under compulsion of subpoena when their testimony would run counter to their ethical obligations or have an adverse effect on their ability to gather the news. But the question of the professional status of newsgatherers is in doubt.

Not having professional status might be an advantage to journalists with regard to making them eligible for collective bargaining, but it is disadvantageous to the extent that courts do not accord them an absolute privilege against being compelled to testify, in contrast, for example, with physicians and attorneys. Whether the courts consider them professionals or not, in many cases today, newspersons are refusing to obey subpoenas and choosing to face jail for contempt when the claimed privilege is denied.

There is now a serious and growing confrontation between those who would gather the news and those who would use these newsgatherers to provide information for governmental purposes. What makes the problem especially difficult is that both sides to the dispute may say with some justification that by their actions they are serving the public interest.

2. Legal Background

a. Common Law Privilege

The common law, while recognizing testimonial privileges for the attorney-client, doctor-patient and

marital relationships, has never accorded a like
privilege to the newsperson-news source relationship or any other aspect of the newsgathering process. A strong policy argument can be made that a
newsperson's privilege is at least as necessary to the
public welfare as the recognized privileges are because of its societal benefit in encouraging a freer
flow of news and information to the public. But
the law has accepted the strong opposing policy that
the public, in the words of Dean Wigmore, "has a
right to every man's evidence." The more testimonial privileges that are recognized, the less evidence
will be available to those who must attempt to
reconstruct the truth in a judicial proceeding or
establish public policy in the halls of a legislature or
in an executive office. Not surprisingly, then, the
common law courts have consistently refused to
expand the number of recognized privileges in order
to cover newspersons.

b. Newspersons' Shield Statutes

An alternative to persuading the courts to fashion
a newsperson's privilege is to convince legislatures
to enact statutes embodying such a privilege. The
first so-called newspersons' shield law was enacted
in Maryland in 1898 to protect the confidentiality of
news sources. It remained unique for more than
three decades before New Jersey adopted a similar
statute. Thereafter, lobbying campaigns by the
newspaper industry have resulted in the enactment
of shield statutes of one type or another in just over

half the states. These acts are analyzed below at pp. 276–279.

Though such legislation is now widespread, the statutes at best provide uncertain protection for the newsperson because they are subject to interpretation and application by the state courts, which have generally been hostile to their aim. They are, with few exceptions, narrowly construed and sharply limited as to the protection they afford.

The first federal shield statute was proposed in 1929, but though numerous bills have been introduced in Congress since then, no federal statute extending a testimonial privilege to newspersons has been enacted. Perhaps this is because no consensus has ever developed within the media regarding either the necessity for such legislation or its proper scope. See pp. 266–275.

c. Claims of Privilege Under the First Amendment

A relatively recent claim of newspersons to immunity from testimonial compulsion is based on the Constitution. The argument is that compelling reporters to testify in judicial and other proceedings will have a detrimental effect on their access to sensitive and confidential news sources and will consequently restrict the flow of news to the public in violation of the First Amendment.

The argument was first made in Garland v. Torre (1958). Judy Garland had brought an action against the Columbia Broadcasting System alleging, inter alia, that the network had fostered the publi-

cation of false and defamatory statements about her
to the effect that she was refusing to rehearse a
show for CBS. Some of the allegedly defamatory
statements appeared in a radio-TV column in the
New York Herald Tribune written by Marie Torre
and were attributed by her to an unnamed CBS
executive. When Garland's attorney deposed Torre
she refused to disclose the name of the executive,
asserting that to do so would violate a journalistic
confidence. Court proceedings were initiated to
compel her to disclose the name. Again Torre
refused to make disclosure. She was held in criminal contempt and sentenced to ten days imprisonment. On appeal she raised the constitutional issue. Judge (later Justice) Potter Stewart affirmed
her conviction, and Ms. Torre was forced to leave
her newborn child and her toddler and serve the
10–day sentence. Judge Stewart, while recognizing
that compulsory disclosure of a journalist's confidential sources might entail an abridgment of press
freedom, held that such abridgment had to be balanced against the obvious need in the judicial process for testimonial compulsion. And where, as
here, the need for the testimony sought went to the
heart of the plaintiff's claim, the Constitution conferred no right on Torre to refuse to answer.

In his opinion Judge Stewart had noted that the
judicial process was not being used to force whole-
sale disclosure of a news source or to discover the
identity of a source of doubtful relevance or materiality. He thereby implied that there might be situations in which the First Amendment would provide

the newsperson with a qualified privilege not to testify under compulsion of legal process.

Yet state court decisions after Garland and prior to 1972 held that the First Amendment provided no testimonial privilege of any kind. See In re Taylor (1963); State v. Buchanan (1968). Thus, the existence of even a limited First Amendment testimonial privilege for the newsgatherer was in doubt and the issue could only be decided by the Supreme Court.

3. The Branzburg–Pappas–Caldwell Trilogy

The issue was finally presented in three different contexts and eventually decided by the Supreme Court in Branzburg v. Hayes, In re Pappas and United States v. Caldwell (1972). The Court not only held that "the First Amendment does not guarantee the press a constitutional right of special access to information not available to the public generally," discussed at pp. 245–249, supra, it denied to newsgatherers a testimonial privilege to refuse to appear before grand juries and testify about possible criminal activities they may have witnessed in the course of their professional responsibilities and the identity of those who engaged in such activities.

a. What the Supreme Court Decided

What the Court decided in the trilogy of newsperson privilege cases is not entirely clear because of the failure of Justice White, the author of the majority opinion, to relate his lengthy reasoning to the three cases at hand and to make distinctions

among them. The issue is further confused by the
presence of what appears to be a conflicting concurring opinion of Justice Powell, a member of the five-
person majority. The confusion results in part because Justice Powell seems to suggest that confer-
ring the reporter's privilege should be determined
on a case-by-case basis; in this call for ad hoc
balancing, Justice Powell seems to agree with the
dissent.

It is clear that the majority recognized no basis
for a newsperson to refuse to appear and answer
some questions when summoned by a grand jury.
And it is also clear that the majority held that
members of the news media may be compelled to
provide information if they witness criminal activity. It also seems to follow from these holdings that
the appearance and testimony of newspersons
would be compelled in criminal and civil trials. If
immunity against compelled testimony is denied in
a closed and freewheeling grand jury proceeding, it
would be difficult to justify allowing such immunity
in open public trials controlled by strict evidentiary
rules. The Court clearly rejected the idea that the
First Amendment confers an absolute privilege
upon newspersons not to appear and testify in judicial proceedings.

In contrast, dissenters Stewart, Brennan and
Marshall would have required ad hoc balancing
before the reporter was required to appear before a
grand jury. Under their approach the government,
in a proceeding to quash the subpoena, would have
to: (1) show that there is probable cause to believe

that the newsperson has information that is clearly
relevant to a specific probable violation of law; (2)
demonstrate that the information sought cannot be
obtained by alternative means less destructive of
First Amendment rights; and (3) demonstrate a
compelling and overriding interest in the information. In the years following Branzburg, many federal and state courts have applied Justice Stewart's
three-part test in deciding whether to compel journalists to testify or not. The strength and clarity of
the dissenters' three-part test may explain the continued interest of these courts in determining the
scope of a qualified constitutional privilege for
newspersons.

b. The Legal Situation After Branzburg

(1) In Detail

Most lower federal and state courts have limited
the application of Branzburg. In the leading civil
case of Baker v. F & F Investment (1972), plaintiffs,
alleging racial discrimination in the sale of houses
to blacks in Chicago, sued certain local real estate
organizations and sought prior to trial to depose
Alfred Balk, a writer and editor, as to the true
identity of the fictitiously named "Norris Vitchek,"
a real estate agent and the main source for Balk's
article published in the Saturday Evening Post on
"blockbusting" in Chicago. Balk and his publisher
had previously promised Vitchek that they would
not reveal his true identity. Consequently Balk,

while highly sympathetic to the plaintiffs' cause, refused to provide Vitchek's true identity, claiming First Amendment protection. The plaintiffs sought an order from the United States District Court directing Balk to provide the information. The order was denied and the Second Circuit handed down a decision after Branzburg affirming that denial. Recognizing that to compel disclosure of newspersons' confidential sources has a "chilling effect" on the flow of news to the public, the court of appeals balanced the competing interests along the lines suggested by Justice Stewart in his dissent in Branzburg, thereby de facto recognizing a qualified constitutional privilege in civil cases. See Silkwood v. Kerr–McGee Corp. (1977) (documentary film-maker treated as a reporter when making film about mysterious death of Karen Silkwood after she found she had been contaminated by plutonium radiation at processing plant run by Kerr–McGee); Loadholtz v. Fields (1975) (disclosure of unpublished background materials sought and refused); Democratic National Committee v. McCord (1973) (disclosure of unpublished background materials sought and refused); Apicella v. McNeil Laboratories, Inc. (1975) (disclosure of identity of anonymous author sought and refused); Los Angeles Memorial Coliseum Commission v. National Football League (1981). But see Dow Jones and Co., Inc. v. Superior Court (1973); Caldero v. Tribune Publishing Co. (1977) (reporter refused to reveal name of source of libelous story; court inferred that no source existed); Matter of Farber (1978) (reporter

found to be in criminal contempt for refusing to
give up his notes).

Of course, the balance may, on occasion, be
struck in favor of compelling the newsperson to
reveal confidential sources and to provide unpublished background materials and work product.
See Winegard v. Oxberger (1977). With the exception of Matter of Farber, which was a criminal case,
the cases cited above involved only the claim of the
reporter's privilege at the pretrial discovery or motion stage in civil proceedings. At that stage the
relevance and materiality of the journalist's information may not be as clear, and the person suing
the reporter will probably not have thoroughly ex-
plored alternative sources for the same information.

It is not yet clear whether the newsperson will be
protected as regularly and to the same degree at the
trial of a civil case when a litigant seeks confidential
information from a journalist which will likely make
or break his or her case. In such situations the
interests of the individual litigant and the public in
fair and peaceable settlement of private disputes
comes into direct confrontation with the First
Amendment interest of the public in the free flow of
news and information.

The courts are not likely to be very sympathetic
to a reporter defendant sued for libel or invasion of
privacy who asserts the qualified privilege to prevent an allegedly wronged plaintiff from proving his
or her case. In this context Garland v. Torre
(1958) discussed earlier, states the applicable princi-

ple: the balance is to be struck in favor of disclosure if the information sought goes to "the heart of the plaintiff's claim."

This principle has taken on increased importance with the advent of the New York Times v. Sullivan line of defamation cases requiring the plaintiff, if a public official or public figure, to establish knowing falsity or reckless disregard for the truth on the part of the defendant. This may be impossible to prove unless the plaintiff can see the defendant's notes and background materials and examine his or her sources for the defamatory message. The Supreme Court expressed such a concern in Herbert v. Lando (1979), discussed in detail in Chapter II, supra. In that case, Lando, an editor-producer for CBS' "Sixty Minutes," was sued by Army Col. Anthony Herbert, an admitted public figure. Lando claimed a privilege under the First Amendment not to divulge his thought processes or the state of mind he possessed when he was editing and producing the program segment complained of. The Supreme Court, in rejecting the claimed privilege, ruled that to give Lando the privilege would make it far more difficult for Herbert to establish actual malice as required by New York Times Co. v. Sullivan. It would appear then that if a newsperson has evidence relevant to the actual malice issue in a libel suit brought by a public figure, and if the evidence cannot be otherwise obtained and goes to the "heart of the case," the courts will not grant a qualified privilege.

Turning from civil to criminal proceedings, the lower federal and state courts generally follow the narrow holding of Branzburg and deny the privilege when newspersons assert it before grand juries to protect (1) the identity of sources who may have engaged in criminal activity and (2) reporters' unpublished notes, information and background materials which might lead to the discovery of the criminals. See Lewis v. United States (1974) (claim of privilege by radio station manager to withhold original document of Weather Underground and tape recording of Symbionese Liberation Army from federal grand jury rejected). Because the grand jury has evolved by and large into a prosecutorial device, prosecutors have been quite successful both before and after Branzburg in having claims of constitutional privilege rejected during the preliminary stages of criminal investigations.

Thus, the availability of qualified protection from the reporter's privilege is not great if the case involves testimony before a grand jury. But in cases not involving grand jury testimony, nine of the twelve United States Courts of Appeal have accepted the idea of a qualified privilege which protects reporters when they are subpoenaed to testify about confidential matters.

Reporters, however, cannot successfully claim the privilege in every case involving a criminal defendant, however, especially if disclosure of an informer's identity is relevant to the defense of an accused. In Matter of Farber (1978), the court rejected New York Times reporter Myron Farber's claim of privilege not to disclose sources and documents he used in his articles leading to prosecution of Dr. Mario Jascalevich for poisoning five patients. And in Kansas v. Sandstrom (1978), in which a woman was charged with killing her husband, reporter Joe Pennington testified at the trial that a confidential source had told him that one of the state's witnesses had threatened to kill the husband shortly before the murder. Pennington said the informant had heard about the threat from someone who had attended a party at which the state's witness made the threat, but Pennington refused to identify the informant, claiming a privilege. Noting that after Branzburg, courts had generally tried to balance the need of the defendant for a fair trial against the reporter's need for confidentiality, the Kansas Supreme Court ruled that the constitutional privilege did not apply in this case because the informant's identity was critical to the defense and there was no other way to get the information.

(2) In Summary

While generalization in the field of reportorial privilege is risky, the following principles and rules are suggested in summary:

(1) There is no absolute First Amendment newspersons' privilege.

(2) The recognition by the courts of a qualified newspersons' privilege depends to a great extent on the legal context in which the claim of privilege is made.

(3) The courts will not honor the claim of privilege made before grand juries and trial courts when it would protect sources and others who have been seen by the reporter engaging in the suspected criminal activity under investigation.

(4) The courts will not honor such claim made before grand juries when the reporter is asked to produce physical evidence in his or her possession of suspected criminal activity under investigation such as tape recordings and documents.

(5) The courts will not honor such claim at a criminal trial or collateral hearing when the information or evidence is sought by the prosecutor and it is relevant and material to his or her case.

(6) The courts will honor such claim at a criminal trial or collateral hearing when the confidential information or evidence is sought by the accused and it is not critical to his or her defense.

(7) The courts will generally honor such claim in civil pretrial proceedings and trials unless the information or evidence sought by the litigant goes to the heart of his or her case and there is no alternative source for that information.

(8) When the newsperson is a defendant in civil litigation (usually defamation or invasion of privacy actions), the courts are more likely to find that the information or material sought to be protected under the privilege goes to the heart of the plaintiff's case and cannot be obtained from alternative sources.

Ch. 8 NEWSPERSONS' PRIVILEGE 273

(9) When the newsperson is a plaintiff in civil litigation and claims the qualified privilege to prevent the defendant from obtaining information relevant to his or her defense, the claim of privilege will be denied. See Anderson v. Nixon (1978).

(10) If the newsperson's claim to a qualified privilege in the particular context is not accepted, he or she will have to choose between revealing confidential information or material and accepting the consequences of disobedience of a lawful court order.

c. *The Practical Effect of Branzburg on Newsgatherers*

Despite the well-meaning efforts of lower federal and state courts to carve out a qualified privilege, particularly in civil cases, the holding in Branzburg has had a serious effect on newsgatherers. The majority's rejection of an absolute privilege has left the newsperson to guess whether and to what extent the courts will protect promises of confidentiality which journalists make to their sources. At the time assurances of secrecy are given to sources, reporters will often be unable to determine in what legal context they will be asked to breach such confidences. Thus, even assuming the rules of the game to be clearly established after Branzburg, reporters cannot always be sure which rule or rules will be applicable when their testimony is sought to be compelled. It should be clear, however, that journalists cannot have it both ways, either claiming the privilege or disclosing a source's identity depending on whichever suits them. See Cohen v. Cowles Media Co. (1991), infra.

(1) Confrontations With Congress

Journalists have occasionally been served with subpoenas to testify or provide outtakes to Congress and have likewise asserted the reporter's privilege. In 1848 reporter John Nugent of the New York Herald sent his editor a confidential draft of a proposed treaty to end the Mexican–American War. The U.S. Senate, which had been debating the treaty in secret, subpoenaed Nugent and demanded to know his source. When Nugent refused to answer, he was held in contempt of Congress and jailed. Ex parte Nugent (1848).

Over a century later, in 1971, a House subcommittee subpoenaed Frank Stanton, then president of CBS, and demanded that he turn over all outtakes and other materials CBS had used in producing the documentary The Selling of the Pentagon, which dealt with Defense Department expenditures for public relations and propaganda during the Vietnam era. Stanton refused, taking the risk of being held in contempt of Congress. But in a rare disavowal of one of its own committees, the House voted 226–181 to return the contempt resolution back to committee, thus ending the attempt to punish CBS for its award-winning documentary. In 1976 then-CBS reporter Daniel Schorr refused to tell Congress his source for the Pike Committee's report on CIA activities; Schorr narrowly avoided a contempt citation from the House Ethics Committee. Daniel Schorr, Clearing the Air, 1977.

More recently, the Senate voted in October 1991 to appoint special counsel Peter Fleming to investigate news leaks regarding influence-buying by savings and loan owner Charles Keating, and leaks of an FBI report revealing that law professor Anita Hill had accused Supreme Court nominee Clarence Thomas of sexual harassment. Fleming subpoenaed four reporters to testify about their sources and two news organization officials for company records, notes and outtakes. Fleming argued that the press has no right to resist subpoenas in criminal investigations and added that the leaks probably violated 18 U.S.C.A. § 641, which outlaws the theft of government property. In other words, Fleming tried to argue that information is property, just like a desk or a paperclip. None of the reporters or news organization personnel would disclose their sources or any materials. Fleming then asked for subpoenas for the records of the reporters' long-distance phone calls. The House Rules Committee refused to issue the subpoenas, and after six months of interviews of nearly 400 people and the expenditure of $200,000 of taxpayers' money, Fleming concluded that he would not be able to identify the sources of the leaks. See 16 News Media & the Law 3–5 (Spring 1992).

B. NEWSPERSONS' SHIELD LAWS

In Branzburg Justice White wrote that Congress and the state legislatures were free to write laws extending to journalists a privilege against being forced to testify so long as such "shield" legislation did not run afoul of the First Amendment. Since Branzburg, a number of states have added shield statutes and numerous bills have been introduced in Congress to provide some kind of protection for newsgatherers.

1. State Shield Laws

a. *Statutory Analysis*

More than half the states have enacted some form of shield legislation, and one state—California—has adopted a constitutional provision protecting newspersons. Although they vary somewhat in their language and provisions, these statutes usually address the following essential questions: (1) who should be protected against testimonial compulsion (reporters only or others communicating to the public and those aiding and abetting in such communication); (2) which kinds of media should be covered (newspapers only or radio, television, motion pictures); (3) what information should be protected (the identity of confidential sources or other unpublished matter as well); (4) at what types of government proceedings and at what stages in these proceedings is the privilege against testimonial compulsion available (judicial proceedings alone or legislative, executive and administrative proceedings); (5)

whether there are any exceptions or conditions to
the availability of the privilege (such as the need for
regular publication and general circulation, thereby
excepting many nonestablishment publications);
and (6) whether the privilege may be waived by the
protected individual (by disclosing the identity of a
source to third persons). In analyzing one's local
shield legislation, these are the issues that determine the availability and scope of the privilege
afforded.

State shield statutes are divided into three main
groups, according to a study of the Freedom of
Information Center of the University of Missouri
School of Journalism. 1) The first group of statutes
provides for the unqualified protection of reporters
against having to divulge the source of information
obtained in the course of their employment, but
most statutes in this group only refer to sources
and do not expressly cover the reporter's work
product or unpublished information and materials.
Given the propensity of the courts to construe
shield statutes narrowly, it is not safe for reporters
to assume that these matters are also protected by
such statutes. 2) The second group of shield laws
provides a privilege against disclosure of the source
of information actually published or broadcast.
While absolute in their terms, statutes in this group
are very weak in protecting sources because neither
the source nor the reporter can be certain at the
time the information is given that the information
will actually be published or broadcast. Moreover,
like the statutes in the first group, these statutes do

not protect the information itself. 3) The third group includes statutes which are conditional in their grant of privilege to newspersons or which provide a basis for the waiver of the privilege. The statutes in this category are also narrow in scope, protecting only sources and often only sources connected with the print media. More important, even when a privilege in this category appears to cover a particular reporter's situation, there is no certainty that the courts will uphold it when the reporter actually invokes it.

To summarize, the First Amendment provides increasingly greater protection against compelled disclosure of sources and unpublished information in the four situations below:

(1) Criminal case where a grand jury or prosecutor wants information (least protection);

(2) Criminal case where a defendant wants information (slightly more protection);

(3) Civil case where reporter is defendant (slightly more protection than in criminal cases);

(4) Civil case where reporter is not a party to suit (greatest protection).

b. Judicial Treatment

Despite acceptance of a qualified privilege by nine of the twelve U.S. Courts of Appeal and the existence of shield laws in 30 states, journalists have met with resistance regarding a reporter's privilege in lower state and federal courts.

Thus, journalists cannot rely with confidence even upon the plain language of their jurisdiction's shield law, but must also be aware of the case law construing such statutes. Even then, journalists should assume that in sensitive cases the courts will not uphold their claims to the statutory privilege and they should act as cautiously as possible consistent with "getting the story."

2. Administrative Protection for the Newsperson: Department of Justice Guidelines

Though no federal shield legislation has ever been enacted, the Department of Justice has adopted a set of guidelines that define when and how a U.S. attorney can obtain a subpoena against a working reporter. 28 C.F.R. § 50.10. In striking a balance between free dissemination of information and effective law enforcement, the following matters must be considered by Department of Justice personnel: (1) there should be reasonable belief based on nonmedia information that a crime has occurred: (2) there should be reasonable ground to believe that the information sought is essential to a successful investigation—particularly with reference to directly establishing guilt or innocence; (3) the government should have unsuccessfully attempted to obtain the information from alternative non-media sources; (4) except under exigent circumstances subpoenas should be limited to verification of published information; (5) even the appearance of harassment of media personnel should be avoided if at all possible; (6) subpoenas should, wherever possible, be directed at material information regarding a limited subject matter, should cover a reasonably limited period of time, and should avoid requiring production of a large volume of the newsperson's unpublished material. In 1980 the guidelines were extended to afford similar protection in civil actions and to telephone toll records of journalists.

While the guidelines reflect the Department's sensitivity to the problem of compelling testimony from newspersons, they provide only minimal and uncertain protection because they are limited in scope to federal criminal prosecutions and are construed by government officials whose main concern must, of necessity, be for effective law enforcement. Moreover, the protection afforded is by administrative grace and that protection can be modified or withdrawn by the Department of Justice almost at will.

C. LAWSUITS BY NEWS SOURCES

Journalists who promise confidentiality to a source will normally go to great lengths and even to jail to keep that promise. But in rare cases journalists or their editors may decide that a source's identity is so important to a story that they will name the source even when the source had been promised anonymity.

Such a situation led to the landmark Supreme Court decision of Cohen v. Cowles Media Co. (1991). By a 5–4 vote, the Court ruled that if a promise of confidentiality to a source is broken, the First Amendment does not protect the media from a common law contract action by that source, no matter how newsworthy or relevant the source's name may be to an important story.

The case began in 1982 when Dan Cohen, a public relations aide to Republican gubernatorial candidate Wheelock Whitney, gave several reporters documents revealing misdemeanors committed many years earlier (an arrest at a protest rally in the 1960s and a six dollar shoplifting conviction later set aside) by Marlene Johnson, the Democratic candidate for lieutenant governor. Without knowledge or approval from Whitney's campaign, Cohen leaked the information to the press just before the Minnesota gubernatorial election.

When Cohen's name was used, he was immediately fired from his advertising agency job. He sued for breach of contract, arguing that the promise of confidentiality was an enforceable contract under Minnesota law. A jury awarded him $700,000 in damages.

When the case reached the Supreme Court, it held that the First Amendment protects the media's right to publish truthful information, but only if it is lawfully obtained. Writing for the majority, Justice Byron White said Cohen's information was not lawfully obtained because of the broken promise of confidentiality: "[T]he First Amendment does not confer on the press a constitutional right to disregard promises that could otherwise be enforced under state law...." Cohen v. Cowles Media Co.

The Court observed that since journalists have insisted for over a century that they should have the same privilege not to reveal a source as that enjoyed by physicians and priests, the refusal of editors and reporters to keep promises of confidentiality damages the credibility of journalists' claim to a constitutional privilege. The Court thus remanded the case for further proceedings on the question of whether Cohen had a valid claim of promissory estoppel.

Four justices dissented, arguing that using Cohen's name was justified because voters had a right to know that the Republican gubernatorial candidate's public relations aide was leaking stories to the press about a Democratic candidate. In a dissenting opinion, Justice David Souter wrote: "There can be no doubt that the fact of Cohen's identity expanded the universe of information relevant to the choice faced by Minnesota voters ... [and] the publication ... was thus of the sort quintessentially subject to strict First Amendment protection."

See also Ruzicka v. Conde Nast Publication, Inc., (upholding judgment in promissory estoppel action against Glamour Magazine when reporter promised to mask source's identity but provided so many details that source was identifiable and suffered such severe emotional distress that she lost her job as a result of being identified).

Many journalists charged that Cohen left them between the Scylla of having to defend a lawsuit for revealing a source and the Charybdis of going to jail for not revealing a source when subpoenaed. Some media attorneys warned that Cohen could encourage news sources who are not pleased with how they appear in the news to sue the media, contending that they were promised confidentiality. But journalists must realize that if they abuse the privilege as in Cohen and Ruzicka, neither the courts nor the public will take them seriously.

D. CONTEMPT FOR UNPRIVILEGED REFUSAL TO TESTIFY

1. The Real Importance of the Privilege

The existence of a privilege in a particular case of a refusal to testify or produce material is important in shielding a newsperson from the sanctions associated with the contempt power of courts and legislatures. Without a privilege to refuse to comply with a judicial or legislative subpoena, the journalist will almost surely be held in contempt if the information sought is deemed relevant and material to the work of the government unit seeking the information. Depending on the type of contempt involved, the sanctions may include determinate and indeterminate jail sentences, criminal fines and civil payments to parties injured by the contemptuous conduct.

2. Types of Contempt

Traditionally, contemptuous conduct is categorized in two ways. First, there is the distinction between direct and indirect contempt. Direct contempt involves misconduct in or near the courtroom; for example, if a reporter without privilege refuses to testify at a trial or if someone violates the decorum of court or shows disrespect for the legal process, he or she may be cited for direct contempt.

If, on the other hand, the refusal to testify occurred in a grand jury proceeding, this would ordinarily be taken to be an indirect contempt outside the presence of the involved court. Before a sanction could be imposed by the court, the reporter would be entitled to some notice as to what was complained of together with a hearing on the matter before the appropriate judge.

The other major distinction is between civil and criminal contempt. This dichotomy is based on the purpose for which the sanction is imposed. If the sanction is designed, for example, to force the contemnor to testify, the sanction is viewed as coercive and nonpunitive and hence civil in nature. If the sanction is imposed to uphold the dignity and authority of the court and its orders without concern for coercion, it is deemed punitive in nature and thus the contempt is considered criminal.

3. The Impact of Contempt on Newspersons

The number of contempt citations issued against newspersons for refusal to testify before or otherwise cooperate with government units has increased dramatically in the last decade. But while the number of newspersons actually languishing in jails around the country is not yet great, the potential for such a situation is. The courts know that the imposition of fines or civil payments is not likely to intimidate or chasten the reporter who, on principle, refuses to cooperate in a grand jury or judicial proceeding.

Only imprisonment is at all likely to have the desired effect. Thus journalists who dig in their heels must be ready to accept incarceration of either determinate or indeterminate duration. About the only comforting note from the newsperson's perspective is that if the contempt is treated as criminal the likelihood of a sentence in excess of six months is remote because of the burden on the judicial system of granting the newsperson a jury trial.

4. Alternatives to Contempt Citations and Jailing of Newspersons

Courts are learning that even imprisonment for contempt is rarely effective in achieving the goal of disclosure by newspersons of confidential information. The courts are slowly changing tactics and choosing alternatives to contempt in an effort to enforce their disclosure orders.

In cases where reporters refuse to reveal the name of a source in libel proceedings, some courts have declared that such a refusal may allow an inference that no source exists. This is tantamount to saying the story was fabricated, making it much easier for the plaintiff to prove malice or reckless disregard for the truth. Courts have used this tactic in Caldero v. Tribune Publishing Co. (1977); Greenberg v. CBS Inc. (1979); Downing v. Monitor Publishing Co. (1980); and DeRoburt v. Gannett Co. (1981).

Another device to force compliance by reporters with judicial disclosure orders employed by at least one state trial court is to strike the newspaper defendant's pleadings and to enter a default judgment for plaintiffs in their libel actions. Because this device raises a serious question of deprivation of due process, courts must be very careful to employ it only when the information sought is absolutely essential to the plaintiff's case and cannot be obtained by less drastic means. For example, when the Twin Falls, Idaho Times–News refused to disclose confidential information, the trial judge ruled it in default and awarded $1.9 million to the plaintiff. The Idaho Supreme Court reversed this ruling, noting that the plaintiff's inability to discover the reporter's sources had not been shown to obstruct the plaintiff's ability to prove the story false. Sierra Life Insurance Co. v. Magic Valley Newspapers, Inc. (1980).

In another case, Jerry Plotkin, one of the Americans held hostage during 1980–81 in Iran, filed a $60 million lawsuit against the Los Angeles Daily News and two of its reporters, Adam Dawson and Arnie Friedman, when they published an article headlined: "Plotkin May Be Questioned in Drug

Probe." When the two reporters refused to disclose their sources, Judge Sara Radin entered a default judgment against the defendants. The Daily News then ordered Dawson and Friedman to disclose their sources (sparking a storm of criticism from other journalists). The reporters refused and hired separate attorneys to defend themselves. The default order was later vacated, but Judge Radin said that if no sources were named within 20 days, it would be "established as a matter of law" that no sources existed. One of the reporters finally identified two sources, both of whom were Drug Enforcement Administration agents. "News Notes," Med. L.Rptr. (Jan. 17, 1984).

The importance of source protection becomes apparent when one considers the fact that if Washington Post reporters Robert Woodward and Carl Bernstein could not have guaranteed confidentiality to their source "Deep Throat," the American public might never have learned the extent of the corruption involved in the Watergate scandal. In sum, it is important for courts to grant reporters the privilege not to reveal their sources because:

(1) The reporter's privilege encourages the free flow of information to the public; reporters' sources could dry up if they could not promise confidentiality;

(2) corruption in government might go unreported if whistle-blowers are afraid of being identified by reporters who are forced to reveal their identities;

(3) the physical safety or economic security of sources might be jeopardized by revelation of their identities, particularly if they are providing reporters with information about organized crime.

The strongest argument which judges can make against the reporter's privilege is that this privilege can conflict with the Sixth Amendment's guarantee of a fair trial in a case where the reporter has information crucial to the defense of an accused person, as in the life and death case of Kansas v. Sandstrom, discussed above. Except for this one particular situation, however, the arguments in favor of granting the reporter's privilege appear to outweigh any arguments against it.

E. THE EFFECT ON NEWSGATHERING OF SEARCHES AND SEIZURES IN THE NEWSROOM

1. Zurcher v. Stanford Daily

Searches and seizures in the newsrooms of the nation by law enforcement officers pursuant to properly issued search warrants have been rare in American history. Normally, prosecutors seeking evidence of crimes which they believe can be found in the desks or files of a newsroom have simply subpoenaed someone associated with the news operation to bring the evidence, if any, to court. This procedure avoids the disruption of a search of the newsroom, avoids the chilling effect on the gathering of sensitive news and information and gives the subpoenaed party an opportunity to move to quash the subpoena.

But in Zurcher v. Stanford Daily (1978), a local district attorney obtained a search warrant issued on a judge's finding of probable cause to believe that the Stanford Daily, a student newspaper, possessed photographs and negatives revealing the identity of demonstrators who assaulted and injured police officers who were attempting to quell a riot at the Stanford University Hospital. A search of the paper's newsroom was undertaken pursuant to the warrant but no incriminating evidence was found. Thereafter, the paper and certain staff members sought a judicial declaration that the search had deprived them of their constitutional rights and an injunction against further searches. The United States District Court denied the injunction but granted the declaratory relief sought. The United States Court of Appeals affirmed the judgment of the District Court.

In the Supreme Court, the Stanford Daily argued that such searches of newspaper offices for evidence of crimes committed by others seriously threatened the ability of the press to gather, analyze and disseminate news, thereby violating the First Amendment. More specifically the newspaper argued that (1) searches are physically disruptive to orderly publication; (2) confidential sources of information will dry up and access to various news events will be denied because of fear that press files will be readily available to law enforcement authorities; (3) reporters will be dissuaded from recording and preserving their recollections for verification and future use; (4) the processing of news and its dissemination will be chilled by the prospect that searches will disclose internal editorial deliberations; and (5) the press will resort to self-censorship to conceal its possession of information of potential interest to the police.

Although Justice Stewart in dissent generally agreed with the newspaper's contentions, a majority of the Court led by Justice White held that searches and seizures in newsrooms pursuant to warrant did not violate First Amendment guarantees because the drafters of the Constitution had not, under the Fourth Amendment, forbidden search warrants directed to the press, did not require special showings that subpoenas would be impractical before warrants could be issued to search the premises of the press, and did not insist that if a press organization was named in a search warrant, the police would first have to show the organization's complicity in the alleged offense being investigated.

Justice White argued in support of his conclusion that if law enforcement officers and the courts properly administer search warrants, the preconditions for their issuance—probable cause, specificity with respect to the place to be searched and the things to be seized, and overall reasonableness in searches and seizures—should afford sufficient protection against infringement of First Amendment interests. Further, Justice White doubted, in the face of numerous press organization affidavits to the contrary, that confidential sources would dry up or that the press would suppress news because of fears of warranted searches.

2. Federal Legislation in the Wake of Zurcher

Less than three years after the decision in Zurcher, a Congress less sanguine than Justice White about the dangers posed by searches and seizures in newsrooms enacted P.L. 96–449, the Privacy Protection Act of 1980, 42 U.S.C.A. § 2000aa–1 et seq. This act substantially restricts the situations in which a newsroom search and seizure may legally occur: generally law enforcement personnel must have a subpoena rather than merely a search warrant. In very limited circumstances the law allows searches and seizures of documentary materials such as photographs or videotapes with only a search warrant if 1) the person with the information is suspected of a crime, 2) law enforcement officers believe the materials must be seized immediately to prevent someone's death or injury, 3) there is reason to believe that giving notice with a subpoena would result in the materials being destroyed, changed or hidden, or 4) the materials were not produced pursuant to a court order that has been affirmed on appeal. A journalist's "work product" such as notes or rough drafts cannot be seized unless 1) the journalist is suspected of a crime, or 2) such seizure is necessary to prevent someone's death or bodily injury.

CHAPTER IX

REGULATION OF COMMERCIAL SPEECH

A. CONSTITUTIONAL HISTORY

First Amendment protection for commercial speech—particularly commercial advertising—has had a checkered history in the Supreme Court. First the Court refused to recognize any such protection. Then, after recognizing some protection utilizing the language of ad hoc balancing, the Court appeared to move toward absolutist protection of such speech qualified only by time, place and manner considerations. Now the Court, for the present at least, has settled upon a seemingly well-defined balancing approach that nevertheless leaves the Court great latitude in its specific application.

The chronology begins with Valentine v. Chrestensen (1942), in which the Court unanimously sustained an ordinance which banned the distribution of commercial handbill advertising. After being prohibited by local authorities from distributing a handbill announcing the exhibition of a submarine, the promoter had printed on the reverse side of the handbill a protest against an official refusal to allow him to use city wharfage facilities for such exhibition. The court found this supposed political protest to be a mere subterfuge to evade the ordinance and suggested that "purely commercial advertising" was not protected by the First Amendment. In short, the government could constitutionally regulate product or service advertising without abridging the First Amendment.

This distinction between types of expression has been a controversial one. In Cammarano v. United States (1959), Justice Douglas said that the Chrestensen opinion was "casual, almost offhand" and "has not survived reflection." But thereafter the Court reiterated the distinction between purely commercial advertising and all other expression in New York Times v. Sullivan (1964).

This was the state of commercial speech until Bigelow v. Virginia (1975). Jeffrey C. Bigelow was the managing editor of the Virginia Weekly, a newspaper published in Charlottesville, Virginia. The Weekly ran a referral service for an abortion clinic in New York City. Bigelow was convicted for violating a Virginia statute which made it a misdemeanor for any person by advertisement to encourage or promote the procuring of abortions. His conviction was reversed by the Supreme Court which held that merely because an advertisement is labeled commercial speech does not mean that it is stripped of all First Amendment safeguards, as had been implied in Valentine v. Chrestensen. Such speech retains some degree of constitutional protection which must be weighed against the state's interest in regulating the particular advertisement. Justice Blackmun, writing for the Court, then found some value in the abortion referral ad as a vehicle for conveying information of potential interest to Virginia Weekly readers. According to Justice Blackmun, the ad did more than fulfill Bigelow's profit motive. His interest coincided with the constitutional interests of certain of his audience who might need the service offered, or who were concerned about New York's laws or who were seeking abortion law reform in Virginia. Justice Blackmun noted that the availability of legal abortion in New York was information of value to the public and that, as previously decided, the right to early term abortion itself involved a woman's constitutional right to privacy. See Roe v. Wade (1973) and Doe v. Bolton (1973).

On the other side of the balance, Virginia contended that abortion referral agencies breed practices such as fee splitting that tend to decrease the quality of medical care and that advertising these agencies would encourage women to seek abortions from those interested only in financial gain and not in providing professional medical service. Virginia, however, made no claim that this advertisement would in any way affect the quality of medical care within its own boundaries, and the Court reasoned that the state was actually asserting an interest in regulating what Virginians hear or read about another state's services. This interest, in the Court's view, was entitled to little, if any, weight. Consequently, the state's interest was not sufficient to permit it to punish Bigelow for running the ad and his conviction was reversed.

Bigelow seemed to say that if First Amendment protection was to be accorded to commercial speech, it would be on an ad hoc balancing basis. But in Virginia State Board of Pharmacy v. Virginia Citizens Consumer Council, Inc. (1976), the Court appeared to adopt an absolutist approach to the protection of commercial speech in a case where the state statutorily prohibited pharmacists from advertising the prices of prescription drugs which they offered for sale—advertising which, unlike that in Bigelow, was *purely* commercial in nature.

In striking down the Virginia statute, Justice Blackmun, speaking for the Court, appeared to reject the balancing process when he said, "There is no claim ... that the prohibition on prescription drug price advertising is a mere time, place, and manner restriction. We have often approved restrictions of that kind provided that they are justified without reference to the content of the regulated speech, that they serve a significant governmental interest, and that in so doing they leave open ample alternative channels for communication of the information .... Whatever may be the proper bounds of time, place, and manner restrictions on commercial speech, they are plainly exceeded by this Virginia statute, which singles out speech of a particular content and seeks to prevent its dissemination completely." To similar effect are Linmark Associates, Inc. v. Township of Willingboro (1977) (local ordinance forbidding display of "for sale" signs in front of houses struck down); Carey v. Population Services International (1977) (statute prohibiting advertisement of contraceptives struck down).

B. THE FOUR–PART COMMERCIAL SPEECH ANALYSIS OF CENTRAL HUDSON

Following Bigelow, Virginia Pharmacy Board, Linmark and Carey, the issue was no longer whether purely commercial speech is protected expression but rather what First Amendment philosophy and analysis would govern the extension of such protection. That question appeared to be answered in Central Hudson Gas and Electric Corp. v. Public Service Commission (1980).

There, a regulation promulgated by the New York Public Service Commission banned electric utilities in the state from engaging in advertising which promoted the increased use of electricity. In striking down the regulation as violative of the First and Fourteenth Amendments, a bare majority of the Court enunciated a four-part test for determining the availability of constitutional protection for commercial speech. The test emphasizes the balancing of state interests in the regulation of commercial speech against individual free speech interests.

In short, the four-part test includes first a determination whether the expression is at all protected by the First Amendment. Commercial speech which involves or advertises unlawful activity or is false or misleading is *not* protected. For examples of this idea see Pittsburgh Press Co. v. Pittsburgh

Commission on Human Relations (1973) (ordinance prohibiting newspapers from carrying help wanted ads categorized by gender upheld); Princess Sea Industries, Inc. v. Nevada (1981) (statute prohibiting advertising of prostitution service in Nevada counties in which such service is illegal upheld); Friedman v. Rogers (1979) (statute prohibiting practice of optometry under a trade name upheld because ill-defined association of trade name with price and quality could be manipulated by user of trade name to mislead the public).

If the commercial speech does not involve illegality and is neither false or misleading, then the second part of the analysis comes into play. The test here is whether the asserted governmental interest in regulation or prohibition of certain commercial speech is substantial. If the state's interest is substantial, then regulation or complete prohibition of the particular commercial expression may be permitted, depending on the results of the third and fourth parts of the test.

The third part asks whether the state's regulation directly advances the asserted governmental interest. Such regulation will not be upheld unless it is actually effective in advancing the state's interest directly. Indirect or speculative advancement of the state's interest will not suffice.

The final part of the test and the one the New York Public Service Commission failed in the Central Hudson case is whether the state's regulation is only as broad as is necessary to serve the state's substantial governmental interest. In Central Hudson, the Court's five-member majority was not persuaded that the Commission's complete suppression of promotional advertising by New York electric utilities was necessary to further the State's interest in energy conservation. The majority pointed out that the Commission had made no showing that a more limited restriction on the content of promotional advertising would have been inadequate to serve the state's interests.

The second and third parts of the Court's four-part test clearly call into play the ad hoc balancing of First Amendment interests against conflicting legitimate state interests while the fourth part attempts to limit the degree of conflict and the extent of intrusion into the First Amendment area posed by the second and third parts.

In his concurring opinion Justice Blackmun pointed out the contradictions of the four-part balancing test with the more absolutist approach taken earlier in Virginia Pharmacy, Linmark and Carey. He noted that such test would permit a complete ban on utilities advertising, for instance, the advantages of air conditioning, assuming that a more limited restriction on such advertising would not effectively deter members of the public from cooling their homes.

Because the Central Hudson four-part test leaves each justice great latitude to insert personal views on the degree of protection to which specific commercial speech is entitled, subsequent decisions have not followed a clear direction or rationale. For example, in Metromedia, Inc. v. San Diego (1981), the Court struck down a city ordinance banning almost all off-site billboards. The decision featured five separate opinions, causing Justice Rehnquist to term it "a virtual Tower of Babel."

Three years later, in City Council v. Taxpayers for Vincent (1984), the Court was faced with another sign ordinance, this time a ban on posting signs on public property. By a 6–3 vote, the ordinance was found directly to advance the city's interest in limiting "visual clutter and blight." "By banning these signs, the City did no more than eliminate the exact source of evil it sought to remedy."

Although limiting visual clutter and blight is a sufficient government interest to justify restricting commercial speech, protecting people from offensive material is not. In Bolger v. Youngs Drug Products Corp. (1983), the Court unanimously struck down a postal regulation prohibiting the mailing of unsolicited advertisements for contraceptives. In addition to the offensiveness assertion, the government argued that the regulation was necessary to help parents control "the manner in which their children became informed about sensitive and important subjects such as birth control." The regulation there was deemed more extensive than necessary to accomplish the latter goal.

The seeming inconsistency of some of these cases illustrates the true ad hoc nature of the Central Hudson four-part test. The weight given the asserted state interest appears to depend more on the personal views of the justices and less on the degree of evidence offered by the government. A majority of the Court seems willing to defer to the legislative or administrative body's judgment, except where a justice personally disagrees with that judgment.

That view was again evident in Posadas de Puerto Rico Associates v. Tourism Company of Puerto Rico (1986). By a 5–4 vote the Court upheld a Puerto Rico statute prohibiting advertising of casino gambling directed at residents of Puerto Rico, while permitting similar advertising aimed at tourists.

Justice Rehnquist, writing for the majority, found that the speech in question met the first part of the four-part test because the advertising concerned a lawful activity and was not inherently false or misleading. He then accepted the government's contention that the substantial government interest served by the regulation was the reduction of casino gambling by the residents of Puerto Rico as well as the claim that casino gambling leads to increases in corruption, prostitution, local crime and organized crime. The application of the advertising ban solely to casino gambling was also seen as reasonable because other forms of gambling such as cockfighting, horse racing, and the lottery might be "traditionally part of the Puerto Rican's roots."

The government's assertion that the advertising ban directly advanced that interest was also accepted without much scrutiny. Justice Rehnquist observed that the Puerto Rico legislature believed that banning advertising would reduce demand and that in his opinion such a belief was reasonable.

Finally, the ban, in Justice Rehnquist's view, was no more extensive than necessary. He rejected an argument that counterspeech, speech aimed at reducing casino gambling, was a less First Amendment intrusive way to accomplish the same ends. Whether counterspeech would be effective in accomplishing the same end was a decision for the legislature, not the Court.

One of the more disturbing aspects of Justice Rehnquist's opinion was its extreme deference to the legislature. Essentially he seemed to be saying that as long as the government's assertions are plausible they will be accepted even though there is no direct evidence to support the assertions. Justice Brennan, in his dissent, argued that, at least where the government's asserted purpose is to influence citizen behavior, a stricter standard is needed. He would have required the government to show that casino gambling had serious harmful effects, that banning advertising would reduce the demand for casino gambling and that neither counterspeech nor strict regulation of casino gambling itself would accomplish the same end. He found no showing that the government had evidence for any of these assertions.

However, in Board of Trustees, S.U.N.Y. v. Fox (1989) the Court interpreted Posadas differently. In an opinion written by Justice Scalia, the Court held that the fourth part of the Central Hudson test merely requires a means narrowly tailored to achieve the desired objective, as opposed to the least restrictive means available. Thus, Justice Scalia viewed Posadas as holding that the legislature had only to show a reasonable fit between the means chosen by the legislature and the goal the legislature sought to achieve. He did emphasize, however, that the burden is on the government affirmatively to establish that reasonable fit.

The change from a least restrictive means test to a reasonable fit test did nothing to reduce the ad hoc nature of the Central Hudson test. Two 1993 cases illustrate the degree to which the Court is fragmented on this issue. In Cincinnati v. Discovery Network (1993), the Court struck down the city's prohibition against the use of newsracks to distribute "commercial handbills," while permitting the use of newsracks to distribute newspapers.

The majority, in an opinion written by Justice Stevens, held that the ban failed the reasonable fit test. The city argued that the ban served its interests in safety and esthetics. First, the ban affected 62 newsracks, while allowing between 1,500 and 2,000 newspaper newsracks. Thus, the ban only minimally advanced the city's asserted interests. Second, the distinction between those newsracks banned and those permitted was totally unrelated to the city's asserted interests. In Justice Stevens' view one requirement for a "reasonable fit" is that the distinction between regulated and unregulated speech must be related to the interests the regulation is designed to advance. Unless the commercial speech is being regulated because of its content or adverse effects stemming from its content, it cannot be singled out for restrictions that are not placed on other speech.

In his dissent Chief Justice Rehnquist flatly rejected this interpretation of reasonable fit. According to Rehnquist the city, in its quest to improve safety and esthetics had decided to burden low value speech without imposing a similar burden on high value speech. By restricting the ban to commercial handbill newsracks, Rehnquist argued that city was advancing First Amendment interests.

United States v. Edge Broadcasting Co. (1993) involved a North Carolina station that wished to carry advertisements for the Virginia state lottery. 18 U.S.C.A. § 1304 prohibits the broadcast of lottery information. Although there are exceptions for advertising state-run lotteries, discussed in Chapter 11, the ban does apply to broadcasters located in states such as North Carolina that do not themselves have a state lottery.

Both the district and appellate courts found the statute unconstitutional as applied. The Supreme Court reversed. Applying the Central Hudson test, the Court rejected the lower courts' finding that the regulation did not advance the government's interest in supporting each state's right to implement its own policy with regard to lotteries. The Court's analysis focused on whether the statute in general advanced the government's interest, whereas the lower courts had focused on the statute as applied to Edge. The Court argued that the question of the statute's application to Edge was more properly addressed in assessing whether or not there was a reasonable fit between the regulation and the governmental interest.

Here the Court held that despite the fact that the vast majority of Edge's listeners were in Virginia and that its North Carolina listeners had access to all kinds of Virginia media carrying advertisements for the Virginia lottery, there was a reasonable fit. The ban still reduced the amount of lottery advertising to which the station's North Carolina listeners were exposed.

In dissent, Justice Stevens argued that the lottery advertising restriction was "a ban on speech imposed for the purpose of manipulating public behavior." As such its effect on Edge's First Amendment rights was disproportionate to the federal government's "asserted interest in protecting the antilottery policies of nonlottery States."

C. ATTEMPTS TO BAN ADVERTISING OF LEGAL PRODUCTS

In Posadas the Court finally addressed another important commercial speech question. Can the government consistent with the First Amendment ever ban advertising for a legal product? The question has received increased attention in the past few years with the proposals by SMART (Stop Marketing Alcohol on Radio and Television) to ban broadcast advertising for beer and wine and the American Medical Association to ban all advertising for tobacco products. The latter proposal has been incorporated in proposed federal legislation.

In response to arguments that it was unconstitutional to ban advertising of a legal product, Justice Rehnquist stated that whenever the state has the authority to ban an activity it has the right to take the less intrusive step of banning advertising for that activity. He thought it would be "strange" to hold the state can ban an activity outright, but not reduce demand for that activity by banning advertising. He also cited with approval several lower court cases upholding advertising bans on legal activities or products. See Dunagin v. Oxford, Mississippi (1983) (Mississippi ban on alcoholic beverage advertising held constitutional under the Central Hudson test.); Capital Broadcasting Co. v. Mitchell (1971) (Federal ban on cigarette advertising on electronic media found constitutional).

Justice Brennan strongly disagreed. He argued that the advertising ban was not less intrusive than a prohibition of the actual activity. "The 'constitutional doctrine' which bans Puerto Rico from banning advertisements concerning lawful casino gambling is not so strange a restraint—it is called the First Amendment."

Opponents of advertising bans have argued that because Posadas involved a Puerto Rico statute, the unique history and status of Puerto Rico provides a basis for limiting Posadas to the facts of that case.

Nevertheless, Posadas clearly was a blow to industries such as liquor and tobacco that are currently threatened with advertising bans. The Court's approving references to Capitol Broadcasting and Dunagin are especially disturbing for those industries.

D. THE SPECIAL PROBLEM OF PROFESSIONAL ADVERTISING

Advertising by professionals had been generally frowned upon in the twentieth century and individual members of a number of the learned professions such as law and medicine were prohibited by the states at the behest of professional organizations such as the ABA and the AMA from advertising their services, ostensibly because such advertising was unseemly and unprofessional but more realistically because such bans reduced economic competition within the professions.

1. Advertising by Lawyers: A Case Study

After the Supreme Court's decisions in Bigelow and Virginia Pharmacy Board according First Amendment protection to commercial speech, it was inevitable that bans on professional advertising would come under attack. As might be expected the first legal challenges came from members of the legal profession.

As the legal profession began to change and develop new forms of delivery systems for legal services such as legal clinics for the less affluent in society, advertising became an important tool in achieving volume business to sustain lower fee schedules. But the use of such a tool was in direct conflict with established law.

In Bates v. State Bar of Arizona (1977), two Phoenix legal clinic attorneys, in seeking business from persons of modest income in need of legal services, placed an ad in the Arizona Republic, a daily general circulation newspaper saying "Do You Need a Lawyer? Legal Services at Very Reasonable Fees" and listing the services available, the charges for such services and the name of the clinic, the address and the telephone number. The ad clearly violated the American Bar Association Disciplinary Rule 2–101(B), embodied in Rule 29(a) of the rules of Arizona Supreme Court. The president of the state bar immediately filed a complaint with the Arizona Supreme Court and ultimately that court censured the two attorneys.

By a 5–4 vote, the United States Supreme Court reversed that portion of the state court order which had upheld the total ban on advertising. In so ruling the majority emphasized the consuming public's First Amendment interest in receiving truthful information about available services and products. Justice Blackmun, writing for the majority, noted that the ABA itself had reported that the middle 70 percent of the population on the economic scale was not being reached or adequately served by the legal profession. According to Justice Blackmun, advertising could help solve that problem.

But in holding that lawyer advertising could not under the First Amendment be subjected to blanket suppression, Justice Blackmun made clear that such advertising was too risk-filled not to be regulated. Regulation would be permitted to insure truthful advertising by lawyers for the protection of the public. Reasonable restrictions on the time, place and manner of advertising would be permitted, as would the suppression of false and misleading information and even accurate advertising concerning illegal transactions. In addition, advertising via electronic broadcast media might warrant special consideration and control. Justice Blackmun expected that the organized bar would have "a special role to play in assuring that advertising by attorneys flows both freely and cleanly."

Emphasizing cleanliness over freedom, the American Bar Association responded to the Bates decision by promulgating two alternative substitutes for the now dead letter DR 2–101(B). "Plan A"—the preferred alternative—listed 25 categories of information that a lawyer could include in his or her advertising. Nothing more could be included. The less restrictive "Plan B" simply permitted advertising that did not run afoul of a small number of general guidelines designed to prevent fraud, deception or the misleading of the public.

Despite warnings from legal scholars that "Plan A" was too restrictive to pass constitutional muster, a majority of the states that considered the ABA's alternative proposals adopted "Plan A" or some variation of it.

Missouri was one of them. The Missouri Supreme Court's Rule 4 listed only ten categories of information that could be included in newspaper, periodical and telephone directory ads. When attorney R_____ M. J_____ placed ads in local newspapers and the St. Louis telephone directory containing material not included in Rule 4 such as the fact that he was licensed in Illinois and had been admitted to practice before the United States Supreme Court, the Advisory Committee of the Missouri Bar filed a complaint in the Missouri Supreme Court seeking the imposition of sanctions. Following a hearing the attorney was officially reprimanded by the Missouri Supreme Court and required to pay the costs of the action despite his contention that his advertising was protected speech.

On appeal the United States Supreme Court, reflecting the principles laid down in Central Hudson and Bates, voted unanimously to reverse the judgment of the Missouri court. First Amendment protection was accorded the lawyer's advertising because none of the information contained therein was shown to be misleading nor did the Missouri Supreme Court identify any substantial state interest in so sharply limiting lawyer advertising that would outweigh the lawyer's or the public's interest in such advertising. In the Matter of R.M.J. (1982). As a result of this decision the constitutionality of state bar advertising rules based upon restrictive "Proposal A" of the American Bar Association is now in doubt.

A slightly different question was presented in Peel v. Attorney Registration and Disciplinary Counsel (1990). Attorney Peel had placed on his letterhead a notation that he was a "Certified Civil Trial Specialist By the National Board of Trial Advocacy," as well as one that he was licensed in Illinois, Missouri and Arizona. The Illinois' Attorney Registration and Disciplinary Commission held that this violated an Illinois prohibition on attorney's holding themselves out as "certified" or "specialists." On appeal the Illinois Supreme Court found that the letterhead was inherently misleading, that it implied that the state had authorized this certification, and that there was an implied claim of superiority of the quality of the lawyer's services.

The United States Supreme Court reversed. Justice Stevens, joined by three other Justices found that the letterhead was not actually or inherently misleading. Even if there was a danger of confusion, less restrictive means such as screening certifying organizations or requiring disclaimers regarding the certification would be sufficient to prevent such confusion. Justice Marshall concurred in the judgment finding the state rule unconstitutional as applied to attorney Peel, but expressed concern that placing certifications on letterhead could be potentially misleading.

One of the special problems of professional advertising is that at some point it shades off into personal solicitation of business. The prohibition of these personal attempts by professionals to generate business has been upheld by the Supreme Court in the face of First Amendment claims because of the inherent dangers of fraud, undue influence, intimidation, overreaching and vexacious conduct. See Ohralik v. Ohio State Bar Association (1978).

In Zauderer v. Office of Disciplinary Counsel (1985), an attorney had been disciplined for running a newspaper advertisement stating that he was available to represent on a contingent fee basis women injured through use of the Dalkon Shield, an intra-uterine contraceptive device. The advertisement stated that there would be no legal fees unless there was some recovery. The advertisement was accompanied by a drawing of the Dalkon Shield. The Ohio Supreme Court held that the advertisement violated Ohio Disciplinary Rules prohibiting self-recommendation and banning the use of illustrations in lawyer advertising.

By a 5–3 vote the United States Supreme Court struck down the self-recommendation prohibition as overbroad because it applied even to nondeceptive advertising. The Court distinguished Ohralik as applying to face-to-face solicitation, which in its view posed a much greater threat of undue influence and intimidation. Using the same reasoning the Court also struck down the ban on all illustrations. The Court did, however, find one aspect of the lawyer's ad misleading in that he stated no legal fees would be charged without some recovery, but failed to mention that court costs could be charged. The Ohio court's finding that this violated a full disclosure requirement for contingency fee rates was therefore upheld.

Similarly, in Shapero v. Kentucky Bar Association (1988), the Court struck down a total ban on targeted direct mail solicitation. The Court distinguished targeted direct mail from in-person solicitation in two ways. First, direct mail did not present the same potential for "overreaching, invasion of privacy, the exercise of undue influence, and outright fraud." Second, there are means of ensuring public scrutiny of direct mail that are not applicable to in-house solicitation. For example, submission of a sample letter for screening could be required.

The separation between protected commercial speech and prohibited solicitation appears to be at the point where the expression is so immediate and personal that danger exists that the potential client's privacy may be invaded or the potential client may not be able to exercise his or her free will in deciding whether to accept a particular professional's services.

2. The Effect of the Lawyer Advertising Cases on the Other Professions

The principles espoused in the lawyer advertising cases seem generally applicable to restraints on advertising imposed on the other professions. Responding to these cases, the American Dental Association, for instance, has entered into a consent decree with the Federal Trade Commission agreeing not to engage in unfair competition by unduly restricting the advertising of its members. This

agreement was contingent upon the success of the
FTC's litigation with the American Medical Association to eliminate the AMA's restrictions on price
advertising and advertising of the availability of
individual and alternative medical services. The
FTC prevailed in American Medical Association v.
FTC (1982).

Not all the restrictions on lawyer advertising
have been upheld when applied to other professions.
For example, in Edenfield v. Fane (1993), the Supreme Court struck down a Florida statute prohibiting personal and telephone solicitation by CPAs.
The Court distinguished Ohralik on the basis both
of the difference in training for the two professions
and the type of clients each has. First, lawyers
serve as advocates and are trained in the art of
persuasion. CPAs' training emphasizes independence and objectivity. Also, lawyers' potential
clients are often injured, distressed or unsophisticated. A CPA's potential clients are most often
sophisticated and experienced business executives.
Thus, the potential for harm to the people solicited
by CPAs is much less than in the case of lawyers.

Overall, there has been a decided loosening of
strictures on professionals advertising their services. This trend was given fresh impetus by the
Supreme Court's affirmance of the FTC's victory
over the AMA in the Second Circuit and the Court's
decision in Edenfield v. Fane.

E. ACCESS OF THE PUBLIC TO THE PRIVATE ADVERTISING MEDIA

Thus far in this chapter the thrust of discussion has been the constitutional protection afforded to individual and corporate commercial speech. But it is important to remember that the First and Fourteenth Amendments are directed only to governmental action and do not compel private media interests to communicate commercial expression. Indeed, the Supreme Court has held that those Amendments do not require newspapers and broadcasters to accept paid editorial messages let alone purely commercial advertising. See CBS, Inc. v. Democratic National Committee (1973); Miami Herald Publishing Co. v. Tornillo (1974).

Thus, while the Constitution limits governmental regulation of commercial speech, there is no guarantee that it will be heard if the speaker is dependent on private means of communications controlled by others. The exception occurs where the media outlet in question has monopoly power and refuses advertising for the purpose of furthering that monopoly. For example, in Home Placement Service, Inc. v. Providence Journal Co. (1982), the Providence Journal refused to accept advertising for a rental referral service. Because the newspaper was the only daily newspaper in the city and Home Placement was a direct competitor for real estate advertising, the court held that the refusal to accept

Home Placement's advertising violated § 1 and § 2 of the Sherman Act.

————————

The fact that until recently commercial speech generally was not accorded First Amendment protection, and false and misleading speech specifically has never been constitutionally protected accounts, at least in part, for the rise of statutory and administrative controls on advertising at both the state and federal levels designed to protect the public from commercial loss. In the remaining sections of this chapter we consider the agencies that exercise these controls, the nature of the controls, available sanctions against commercial wrongdoers and limitations on the imposition of these sanctions.

F.   STATE STATUTORY REGULATION

As manufacturing began to dominate the early American agrarian economy and the frontier pushed westward, the distances between the manufacturers and their markets constantly expanded, making regional and national advertising increasingly necessary. Gradually the use of brand names, trademarks, magazine advertising and even advertising agencies grew to fulfill this need. Along with this dramatic growth of advertising use came flagrant advertising abuses. The patent medicines were the epitome of this advertising era, with elixirs such as Dr. J. W. Poland's White Pine Compound, claiming to cure "sore throat, colds, coughs, diphtheria, bronchitis, spitting of blood, and pulmonary afflictions generally." Flamboyant misleading copy writing, false testimonials, slogans, jingles and trade characters quickly became the rule in local and national advertising. Advertisers could, and did, promise anything and everything.

Common law and early state statutory remedies proved inadequate to curb advertising abuses. See E. Kintner, A Primer on the Law of Deceptive Practices: A Guide for the Businessman 7–8, 405–407. Today a majority of the states have added legislation similar to the Federal Trade Commission Act, discussed below, to encourage criminal prosecutions and to provide civil remedies for aggrieved consumers.

G. FEDERAL STATUTORY AND ADMINISTRATIVE REGULATION

1. The Federal Trade Commission

a. *Nature and Jurisdiction*

The original Federal Trade Commission Act was not directed toward false advertising but rather toward the prevention of monopolistic and unfair methods of competition in interstate commerce. Despite the absence of a clear congressional mandate in the advertising area, the early commissioners regulated deceptive ads by labeling them "unfair methods of competition." They took the position that exaggerated or misleading claims for an advertiser's product gave him or her an inequitable competitive advantage over those sellers who told the truth. This position was affirmed by the Supreme Court in Federal Trade Commission v. Winsted Hosiery Co. (1922). Justice Brandeis, speaking for the Supreme Court, upheld an FTC determination that when a manufacturer labels its underwear "Natural Wool" and "Natural Worsted" the product must be all wool, not merely 10 percent wool. The Court agreed that when misleading ads are marketed in competition with truthful ads, potential customers are unfairly diverted from the honest advertiser's products. By 1925 three quarters of the Federal Trade Commission's orders concerned false and misleading advertising.

All of the Federal Trade Commission's orders of this period were tied to the concept of unfair competition. The question remained whether the Commission could protect the public from false advertising directly, without having to demonstrate economic injury to a business competitor. Finally, in Federal Trade Commission v. Raladam Co. (1931), the Supreme Court answered that question in the negative. In a unanimous decision the Court held that the Commission had no authority to ban purely false advertising unless it could be shown to be an unfair method of competition. The Raladam decision prompted Congress in 1938 by the Wheeler–Lea Act to amend the Commission's enabling act to permit regulation of "unfair or deceptive acts or practices in commerce" that injure the consumer.

Congress also provided for substantial civil fines for violations of Commission orders to "cease and desist" from proscribed advertising practices and for criminal penalties for and injunctions against the dissemination of false advertising pertaining to cosmetics, therapeutic devices and drugs.

b. Organization and Enforcement

The Federal Trade Commission is an independent regulatory agency with five commissioners appointed by the President for renewable seven-year terms. No more than three members can belong to the same political party. It has more than 1200 employees divided primarily among four bureaus. The one most concerned with advertising is the Bureau of Consumer Protection. Through this bureau the Commission may institute an investigation upon the receipt of even a single letter of complaint from a member of the public. Unfortunately, because of its large work-load and reduced budget, investigations often take a considerable length of time to start and complete, if begun at all.

If, as a result of the investigation, the Commission feels a formal hearing is necessary to determine the issues, it will draft a detailed complaint specifying the alleged false or deceptive practices and will hold a hearing. At the hearing an administrative law judge will make an initial decision after both sides present their respective positions. The judge's decision is final unless it is reviewed by the Commissioners. If the decision is unfavorable to the advertiser the Commission may issue a cease and desist order which, if violated, will subject the advertiser to an action in a federal district court for civil fine. The advertiser may seek review of the cease and desist order in the United States Court of Appeals.

Because of the delays inherent in such formal proceedings, the Commission has developed faster, less expensive methods of halting or preventing deceptive advertising. Indeed, the general policy has been to avoid litigation if possible by offering some form of settlement to offenders. This settlement can be effected through an "assurance of voluntary compliance" wherein the advertiser merely signs an affidavit that it will discontinue the practices involved. A second and more common approach is the use of the consent decree. Under this procedure the Commission drafts a proposed complaint together with a cease and desist order and attaches them to a notice of intent to commence formal proceedings. This package is sent to the alleged offender who must advise the Commission within 10 days if it is willing to forego a formal hearing and have the issues resolved by consent decree. Once a settlement is negotiated and accepted by the parties, it has the same effect as an order issued after a formal proceeding.

These settlement methods are made palatable to the businesses involved because they do not have to admit any violations of law. Another individualized approach, involving anticipatory regulation, is the advisory opinion. This is simply an informal non-binding statement of advice from a responsible member of the Commission staff to assist the businessperson in determining in advance the legality of proposed conduct such as a future advertising campaign. The request must anticipate the act; the Commission will not give advice concerning current business practices.

The Commission also employs certain industry-wide approaches to illegal advertising and other business practices. One generalized method the Commission utilizes to promulgate its views on advertising is the publication of practical manuals or "Guides." The Guides, in pamphlet form, are disseminated to both industry and public to inform them of the Commission's position on certain business practices such as bait and switch advertising, testimonial advertising and deceptive pricing. These Guides reflect the view of the Commission as to what might be considered illegal practices. Violation of a guideline is not itself a violation of law. Rather, where a guideline has not been followed, the Commission must plead and prove that the accused business violated a provision of the Federal Trade Commission Act itself. For litigation purposes, it is as if the Guide did not exist.

This is in marked contrast to cases involving violations of Commission Trade Regulation Rules which state the types of conduct that will be deemed unfair or deceptive by the Commission under the Federal Trade Commission Act. In these cases the Commission need only show that its Trade Regulation Rules have been violated. Thus, these Rules are treated as having the force of law and their violation may result in civil penalties of up to $10,000 for each offense.

c. The Federal Trade Commission Improvement Act of 1974

Another major grant of power to the Commission was effected by the Magnuson–Moss Act, 15 U.S.C.A. § 2301 (1975). The 1938 amendments to the Federal Trade Commission Act had placed deceptive advertising squarely within the Commission's jurisdiction, but the advertising was required to be "in commerce." In most other areas of federal regulation the quoted phrase, drawn from the Constitution, has been expanded by court decision to allow federal regulation of matters which merely "affected" interstate commerce. This liberal interpretation was denied to the Commission in Federal Trade Commission v. Bunte Brothers (1941). The Bunte Brothers decision declared that only a congressional amendment could expand the scope of the Commission's powers to permit regulation of local business activity "affecting" interstate commerce. Thirty-three years later that amendment was made in the Magnuson–Moss Act. Accordingly, the Commission now has clear regulatory power over advertising reaching down to the local level and may, of course, control local advertising by Trade Regulation Rule, if necessary. In addition, as a result of a "rider" attached to the Trans–Alaskan Pipeline Act of 1973, violations of Commission rules outlawing certain trade practices can now be enjoined. See 15 U.S.C.A. § 53 (Cum.Supp.1976).

Industry claims that the FTC was abusing its powers by using the unfairness standard to regulate truthful, nondeceptive advertising led Congress in its 1980 FTC reauthorization bill to remove the FTC's authority to use that standard to initiate any new rulemakings. In subsequent years the House and Senate have been unable to agree on an FTC authorization bill, but each year have included the unfairness prohibition in the Continuing Resolutions providing operating funds for the FTC.

d. *Constitutional Limitations on the Federal Trade Commission's Power to Impose Sanctions*

Even before the Central Hudson case, supra, it was accepted constitutional doctrine that no protection was afforded false or deceptive advertising. Nevertheless, several United States Courts of Appeal have held that the First Amendment limits the *remedies* the Federal Trade Commission can fashion to protect the public against the risks created by such advertising. And thus it is not correct to assume that the FTC (and state agencies as well) are free to wield unlimited power against fraudulent or misleading advertising. These courts, while mindful that the First Amendment does not shield false or deceptive commercial speech from governmental control, insist that the Commission's exercise of that control be no greater than necessary to protect the public.

For example, in Beneficial Corp. v. FTC (1976), the Commission ordered a combined loan and income tax preparation company to stop using the words "Instant Tax Refund Plan" or "Instant Tax Refund Loan" in its advertising because such terms mislead the public as to the nature of the transaction by which consumers received amounts of money from the company equivalent to their prospective tax refunds (actually loan transactions with a substantial interest charge). While not questioning the correctness of the Commission's findings that Beneficial's ads were misleading, the Court refused to approve the Commission's complete ban on the use of the delineated phrases. Rather, the court permitted advertising with the inclusion of those phrases provided they were sufficiently qualified so as not to mislead the audience. The Court said, "The Commission, like any governmental agency, must start from the premise that any prior restraint is suspect, and that a remedy, even for deceptive advertising, can go no further than is necessary for the elimination of the deception."

Similar rulings modifying FTC remedial orders were made in National Commission on Egg Nutrition v. FTC (1977) (FTC order requiring a trade association whose advertising on the risks of egg consumption was misleading to present arguments in its future advertising in opposition to its own position disapproved); Warner–Lambert Co. v. FTC (1977) (FTC order requiring corrective advertising to counteract previous false claims that a mouthwash prevented or moderated the common cold modified so as to delete the prefatory phrase "Contrary to prior advertising").

2. The Federal Communications Commission

The Federal Communications Commission licenses radio and television broadcasters to operate in the "public interest, convenience and necessity." This includes broadcast advertising, but historically the FCC has relied on self-regulation by the broadcasters to avoid the specter of government censorship forbidden by Section 326 of the Federal Communications Act of 1934. For a long time there was an absence of any clear boundary between the FCC's authority over advertising through commercial broadcasting facilities and the FTC's general authority over advertising. This issue was finally resolved by agreement between the two agencies. The FCC has responsibility for assuring that commercials are neither objectionably loud nor excessive in number and that a separation is maintained between advertising and programming, especially during children's programs. Misleading or deceptive advertising on radio or television is to be controlled by the FTC.

PART TWO

REGULATION OF THE ELECTRONIC MASS MEDIA

CHAPTER X

THE FEDERAL COMMUNICA-TIONS COMMISSION—WHAT IT DOES AND DOES NOT DO

One of the most important government agencies which affects the communication of information, and which has played an increasingly important role in shaping what we see and hear is the Federal Communications Commission. However, because its activities are often so technical, and because much of its work is phrased in language not susceptible to easy comprehension, there is much confusion in the public mind as to the precise role which the Commission plays in communications regulation.

A.   HISTORY OF THE FEDERAL COMMUNICATIONS COMMISSION

The existence of the Commission is, in effect, a typical American reaction to a practical and scientific problem. Government regulation of radio began in 1910 at a time when radio was perceived primarily as a safety device in maritime operations and as a potential advance in military technology. The government's primary concern was to assure itself of efficient use of this safety and defense technology, and its role was roughly analogous to that played by the police in registering automobiles. Persons desiring to use radio frequencies would register with the Department of Commerce and frequencies would be assigned to them. Pervasive regulation of the type we have come to accept as routine did not exist because there was no need.

Radio technology made quantum leaps during World War I and the commercial possibilities of radio began to be recognized by entrepreneurs. By the mid–1920's there were hundreds of radio stations operating for commercial use, and frequencies were set aside by the Secretary of Commerce for commercial application. However, the powers of the Secretary to regulate such broadcasting were questionable, particularly the Secretary's power to require a radio applicant to broadcast on a particular frequency at a particular power. Two opinions, one by the courts (United States v. Zenith Radio Corp. (1926)) and one by the Attorney General, (35 Ops.Atty.Gen. 126 (1926)), concluded that the legislation then in force did not permit the Secretary to limit applicants in the use of power and frequencies. The Secretary could only record the applications and grant frequencies, but he did not possess the expansive powers required to regularize radio operations.

These decisions threatened to throw the emerging radio industry into chaos and led to repeated requests by the industry itself for a government agency with greater power than had been possessed by the Secretary of Commerce—an agency which could assign applicants to specific frequencies, under specific engineering rules and with the power to enforce these rules through its licensing function. These efforts culminated in the Radio Act of 1927, which established the Federal Radio Commission and which transformed licensing from a ministerial act to a judgmental one, empowering the Commission to create and enforce standards for the broadcasters' privilege of using the public's airwaves.

The Federal Radio Commission created by the Radio Act of 1927 to supervise broadcasting was, pursuant to the Communications Act of 1934, merged into what is today the Federal Communications Commission. The 1934 Act, modeled largely after the Interstate Commerce Commission Act, and embodying much of the law that had already been made by the 1927 Radio Act, remains the organic legislation which controls American commercial and non-commercial ("Public") broadcasting. The Communications Act prescribes the basic task of the Federal Communications Commission to be that of "regulating interstate and foreign commerce in communication by wire and radio so as to make available, so far as possible, to all the people of the United States a rapid, efficient, nationwide and world-wide wire and radio communication service with adequate facilities at reasonable charges for the purpose of the national defense, for the purpose of promoting safety of life and property through the use of wire and radio communication . . ." 47 U.S.C.A. § 151. The standard to which the Commission must conform in carrying out this responsibility is that of action "consistent with the public interest, convenience [and] necessity." 47 U.S.C.A. § 307. The courts have repeatedly emphasized that the standard is sufficiently broad to allow the Commission to act dynamically in areas of changing or emerging technology while, at the same time, sufficiently precise to prevent the Commission from acting in a wholly arbitrary, unreasonable or capricious manner.

B. SCOPE OF THE COMMISSION'S POWER

It is important at the outset to recognize that the Commission's jurisdiction and power are strictly limited in scope to that which is granted by its enabling legislation, the Communications Act of 1934. It can only act in those areas in which it is specifically empowered to act.

This limitation is important. There are many areas which might be considered part of the "communications realm," but over which the Commission has no jurisdiction. Perhaps most important, and least known, is that the Commission does *not* have jurisdiction and power over the entire radio spectrum space available to the United States under international treaty. In fact, the Commission has jurisdiction of only approximately one-half of this available radio space. Section 305 of the Communications Act exempts from the Commission's power or jurisdiction all "radio stations belonging to and operated by the United States." The United States government, through its various agencies, offices and departments (military and civilian), operates a host of radio services occupying approximately one-half of the total available frequency space. Allocation of spectrum space among the various governmental branches is made through a governmental coordinating group which is now housed in the National Telecommunications and Information Administration (NTIA), a division of the Department of Commerce. The FCC coordinates with this group but exercises no jurisdiction over the government's stations. It is only that part of the spectrum allocated to non-federal government use over which the FCC exercises jurisdiction. It is instructive to recall this fact when the concept of a "scarcity" of frequency space is discussed. At least in part, the scarcity of frequency space for commercial broadcasting is man-made and its dimensions are initially defined by the Executive Office of the White House. For a fuller discussion of the problem of radio frequency allocation between governmental and non-governmental uses, see Metzger and Burrus, "Radio Frequency Allocation in the Public Interest: Federal Government and Civilian Use," 4 Duquesne L.Rev. 1 (1966).

But even with those frequencies over which the FCC clearly possesses jurisdiction, there are large areas in which the FCC is forbidden to or has chosen, as a matter of policy, not to exercise power. Thus, for example, the Commission is not empowered by the Act to enforce or decide antitrust issues as embodied in the Clayton and Sherman Antitrust Acts; it has been explicitly forbidden to do so by the courts. United States v. Radio Corp. of America (1959). Although the Commission may, and sometimes must take into consideration, as part of its public interest standard, economic considerations involving such matters as competition, merger, market share, and the like, it is nevertheless free to ignore the policies favoring competition underlying the Sherman and Clayton Acts if to do so would be in the public interest, convenience and necessity. Federal Communications Commission v. RCA Communications, Inc. (1953).

Similarly, the Commission does not determine whether a particular advertising message is "false and misleading." That question has been delegated by law to the Federal Trade Commission. Of course, the FCC would act where a licensee continues to broadcast an advertisement which has been finally adjudicated by the FTC to be false and misleading. But the Commission regularly refuses to make the initial determination as to the nature of the advertising. See FTC–FCC Liaison Agreement, Current Service, Pike and Fischer Radio Reg., p. 11:212 (hereafter cited as R.R.).

The FCC does not ordinarily become involved in civil or contractual litigation between broadcasters. It does not set advertising rates or oversee ordinary and usual business practices such as production charges, commission arrangements, and salaries of artists. It does not regulate rates which may be charged the public by pay television. It does not regulate closed circuit television or radio. It does not license radio or television networks. It does not license cable system franchises. There are many other areas which might appear to fall within its power but which do not.

The reason is at once simple and complex. The American system of broadcasting is an attempt to introduce state regulation of the radio spectrum while, at the same time, allowing as much free market play as possible. The Commission sets the ground rules by which stations can be licensed. It will choose between applicants for conflicting licenses, set up a framework which attempts to insure some competition, and then allow the free market to determine, as well as possible, such matters as advertising costs, expenses, cost of equipment and, perhaps most important, choice of programming by broadcasters. The simplicity of the system breaks down at those points where free market considerations may not work well. A free marketplace may not automatically serve up programming for minority, ethnic or cultural groups. At a number of points (many of which are discussed later), the government has chosen to intervene; more recently (as the number of media types and outlets have grown) the government has "deregulated" many areas and given market forces more scope. Much of communications law cannot be understood unless it is recognized that the basic bias of our communications system is toward allowing, where possible, the free market to determine matters. See Report and Order, Deregulation of Radio, 46 Fed.Reg. 13888 (1981). Government regulation is, in essence, a last resort, to be used when the free market cannot deliver.

C. STRUCTURAL ORGANIZATION OF THE COMMISSION

Having been delegated broad powers to make rules and regulations necessary to carry out the mandate of its enabling legislation, the Commission faces the task, first, of attempting to satisfy the differing demands for communications frequency space in a modern industrial (indeed, post-industrial) economy. Although most familiar to the public in the role of a regulator of commercial and "public" broadcasting, the Commission has the equally demanding responsibility of regulating non-broadcast use of communications facilities such as interstate common carrier systems, radio systems for industrial use such as truck-to-truck communications, taxi cab networks, communications between central plant and repairmen or servicemen, communications between hospital and doctor, marine and ship radio, aviation frequencies, citizen band radio, international "ham" communications, police and fire communications networks, computer to computer communications, and emerging technologies such as cable, pay television, satellite communications, computer networks, cellular telephones, personal communications networks, etc. In the case of common carriers, the FCC acts as a rate-making agency for interstate common carriage in a manner similar to state public utilities commissions. The reach of its jurisdiction is quite remarkable.

The Commission itself is composed of five commissioners, appointed by the President with the advice and consent of the Senate. The President designates the chairman. Not more than three members of the Commission can be members of the same political party. Commissioners are appointed for a term of five years on a staggered basis. See 47 U.S.C.A. § 154(a).

To meet its responsibilities, the Commission has established a number of bureaus. The most important of these bureaus and a description of the matters with which they deal are:

   1. *Mass Media.* This bureau handles all matters which we normally associate with commercial and "public" (non-commercial) broadcasting, i.e., the initial licensing of applicants, the processing of applications for periodic renewal of licenses, inspection and supervision of stations to determine compliance with technical and operational

rules and regulations, and development of rules covering broadcasting. We will emphasize the work of this bureau and its review by the courts in the pages that follow.

2. *Cable Services Bureau.* This bureau regulates cable television related matters, particularly the rate regulatory and pro-competitive provisions of the 1992 Cable Television Consumer Protection and Competition Act. The bureau has three divisions: the Consumer Protection Division, the Competition Division and the Policy and Rules Division.

3. *Common Carrier Bureau.* This bureau regulates the interstate and foreign common carrier wire and radio system (telephone, telegraph, facsimile, telephoto and satellites), and acts not only as a licensing and regulatory agency, but also as a rate-making agency for interstate and foreign services. It also acts, in some respects, as a coordinating body for the various state public utilities commissions which regulate intrastate common carrier services.

4. *Private Radio Bureau.* This is the bureau which handles other types of radio uses not regulated by the other three. This bureau regulates such matters as industrial use, police and fire use, aviation and marine use, and citizens band radio.

D. ALLOCATION OF FREQUENCIES

The Commission handles the problem of allocation of frequencies between uses in a rather straightforward manner. Certain frequencies are specifically allocated to commercial "broadcasting uses"; other frequencies are specifically allocated to common carrier uses (i.e., telephone, telegraph and other communications services for hire); other frequencies are dedicated to uses such as industrial communication, marine and ship radio, aviation and medical services. These initial allocations are quite important for a number of reasons: (1) they help establish the relative "scarcity" of frequencies which, as we will see, is the basic justification for governmental action in the broadcasting realm, and (2) they are the warp and woof of the nation's communication's system. As much as any single factor, the FCC's allocations policy determines the shape and content of our communications capabilities.

E. JURIDICAL BASIS FOR COMMISSION REGULATION OF BROADCASTING

Government regulation of broadcasting is anomalous. We accept a depth and type of regulation over broadcast facilities which we do not, as a Constitutional matter, tolerate with respect to print media. The most obvious example is governmental licensing of broadcast stations. The First Amendment flatly forbids any such licensing requirement for newspapers, books or magazines. See Near v. Minnesota (1931); New York Times Co. v. United States (1971). Yet the licensing of radio stations has long been upheld. Federal Radio Commission

v. Nelson Brothers Bond and Mortgage Co. (1933). Broadcasters at one time operated under the constraints of the Fairness Doctrine (and may yet again), requiring them to air controversial issues of public importance, and to do so in a manner allowing presentation of contrasting views. See Red Lion Broadcasting Co. v. Federal Communications Commission (1969). No such requirement could constitutionally be enforced against the print media. Moreover, "indecent" (though not obscene) material, which would be protected under the First Amendment if seen in a movie or magazine, may nevertheless be channelled into certain hours for broadcast over the air. The Supreme Court has noted that " . . . of all forms of communication, it is broadcasting that has received the most limited First Amendment protection." Federal Communications Commission v. Pacifica Foundation (1978).

Although the courts have justified these apparent contradictions on the ground that different media present different First Amendment considerations, they do not often explain in any rigorous analytical detail how the differences in media result in constitutional distinctions. It is even rarer for a court to test the breadth or scope of its holding against the constitutional justification for differences in regulation. For example, the United States Supreme Court in Miami Herald Publishing Co. v. Tornillo (1974) struck down a type of political "equal time" legislation imposed by the Florida legislature on Florida newspapers, without ever mentioning or attempting to distinguish the cases that allow precisely such regulation in the broadcast area.

The justification for broadcast regulation has been stated in terms of the "scarcity" of broadcast frequencies. The leading case discussing this point (National Broadcasting Co. v. United States (1943)) set the formulation:

> The plight into which radio fell prior to 1927 was attributable to certain basic facts about radio as a means of communication—its facilities are limited; they are not available to all who may wish to use them; the radio spectrum simply is not large enough to accommodate everybody. There is a fixed natural limitation upon the number of stations that can operate without interfering with one another. Regulation of radio was therefore as vital to its development as traffic control was to the development of the automobile.

Use of the term "scarcity," however, to describe the legal rationale for broadcast regulation has caused much unnecessary confusion. The confusion derives from the fact that the term can be used in two quite different senses: "numerical scarcity," on the one hand, and "allocational scarcity," on the other. "Numerical scarcity" simply means measuring the government's power to regulate the broadcast media by gauging the number of broadcast and other competing media facilities which exist at any one time. The smaller the number of media facilities, the greater the government's power to regulate and, conversely, the government's regulatory power shrinks as the number of media outlets increases. Advocates of this viewpoint have interpreted the *National Broadcasting Co.* case to rest simply on numerical scarcity. As the number of broadcasting stations and other media outlets have increased, they have used the increase as justification for decreasing (indeed, abandoning) government regulation.

We believe that the "numerical scarcity" rationale is a misreading of the Supreme Court's *NBC* decision. The Court in *NBC* did not rely upon "scarcity" in any numerical sense as the foundation on which Commission jurisdiction is based. This is plain enough simply by considering "numerical scarcity" as applied to daily newspapers. There are far more broadcasting stations than daily newspapers in the United States and it is more difficult (from an economic point of view) to start a newspaper than a radio station. By numerical standards, newspapers are "scarcer." The FCC itself has noted that cable broadcasting, multipoint distribution services using microwave frequencies, satellite transmission direct to privately owned satellite reception dishes and a host of other new technological innovations all demonstrate that broadcasting is, indeed, no longer a numerically "scarce" resource. See FCC Report: General Fairness Doctrine Obligations of Broadcast Licensees, 50 Fed.Reg. 35418 at 35421 (Aug. 30, 1985); 58 R.R.2d 1137. Yet the Commission has never suggested that this lack of scarcity has deprived it of regulatory jurisdiction, nor can anyone seriously argue that the relative scarcity of newspapers vis-a-vis broadcast media would allow the government to regulate the press. The difference between broadcasting and print media lies not in numerical scarcity, but rather in the other use of the term, i.e., "allocational" scarcity.

Justice Frankfurter in *NBC* grounded the regulatory distinction between broadcasting and other media not upon numerical scarcity, but rather, upon the fact that broadcasting imposes a duty upon the government which it does not face in the print media—the duty of making choices between two or more potential broadcasters wishing to utilize the same broadcast space. Two newspapers can, without governmental intervention, physically operate in the same community at the same time; their survival would depend on competitive market forces. In broadcasting, however, if there is but one frequency available for use in a particular community, then, by the laws of physics, two stations cannot physically operate on it, for to do so would result in neither being heard. And since it has been determined to be important to the society at large that *someone* be heard, at base it is "allocational scarcity" which imposes the necessity for governmental choice and this, in turn, distinguishes broadcasting from other types of media. Stated another way, broadcasting is unique because it is the only communications medium which requires some type of governmental intervention as a practical *sine qua non* of its existence. So long as there are more persons desiring to broadcast than there are frequencies available to accommodate them, a broadcast frequency is a "scarce" resource.

Despite sharp criticism of the scarcity rationale from some quarters, the Supreme Court has refused to reconsider it without some signal from Congress or the Commission that revision of the long-standing regulatory system is required. See League of Women Voters, supra.

This, then, is the rationale for government regulation: There is a clear public need that some form of broadcasting exist. Broadcasting must be recognized as a public resource, analogous to an interstate traffic system, or a national park system, or a national environmental policy. Technical considerations make broadcast frequencies allocationally "scarce" and impose an obligation on the government to (a) make choices and (b) set standards to make certain that the "resource" is not wasted or misused. Because the government grants broadcasters a limited monopoly in the sense that it will protect a broadcaster's right exclusively to use a frequency, it is not inappropriate to extract a quid pro quo in the form of requiring that broadcasters operate in the "public interest." The government's traditional "police power" further allows it to impose certain limitations (as, for example, to protect children from "obscene or indecent" material). All governmental regulation of broadcasting can be traced to at least one of these considerations and, although they are not present at all times, together they represent the foundation of broadcast regulation.

To assert, however, that the uniqueness of broadcasting allows some form of government regulation is merely to begin the inquiry. For it is quite clear that the NBC rationale will not support any and every form of governmental action. The First Amendment places limits even upon government regulation of allocationally "scarce" resources. See Columbia Broadcasting System, Inc. v. Democratic National Committee (1973). Congress, for example, cannot forbid a station from editorializing in favor of a particular candidate or issue. Nor (except, perhaps, in the very limited circumstances of appearances by political candidates or the rather unique worlds of "indecency" or pornography) can the Commission regulate the content of broadcasting material. Restrictions on broadcasting can be upheld only when the courts are satisfied that the restriction "is narrowly tailored to further a substantial governmental interest, ..." Federal Communications Commission v. League of Women Voters of California (1984). And although numerical scarcity is not the foundation for the government's control over broadcasting, nevertheless, numerical scarcity can, and does, affect the type of regulation which the Commission has imposed. For example, in the 1950's the Commission created the so-called "Fairness Doctrine," which imposed certain obligations upon licensees to cover controversial issues of public importance and to do so in a fair and "balanced" fashion. Such regulation was justified (and approved by the Supreme Court as constitutional) as necessary to insure that the public have before it a broad diversity of viewpoints. But as the number of broadcast outlets dramatically increased in the past decade through such technological advances as cablevision and direct satellite cable distribution, the need for such governmentally imposed requirements appeared to the Commission to decrease (the marketplace being viewed as diverse enough to insure broad issue coverage) and the Commission repealed the Doctrine as (a) no longer necessary and (b) constitutionally suspect. See Syracuse Peace Council v. FCC (1989). This is but one example of the fact that the tension between the necessity for governmental regulation and the common recognition of the dangers posed by such regulation forms the matrix in which broadcast law has developed.

F.   NATURE OF THE BROADCAST RIGHT

Although there may have been other methods of insuring the existence of a nationwide communications system, as, for example, by lottery or by auctioning off frequencies to the highest bidder and granting the winner a broadcast right in perpetuity subject to defeasance for misconduct, Congress nevertheless chose to institute a licensing procedure by which broadcasters are granted a limited privilege to broadcast over a particular frequency at a particular power for a fixed term. The grant of the privilege gives the licensee no vested property interest in the frequency. 47 U.S.C.A. § 309(h). Section 307(d) of the Communications Act limits the license of a radio broadcasting station to a maximum of seven years, with a requirement that the broadcaster file for renewal of that license every seven years if it wishes to continue broadcasting. Television station licenses are granted for a period of five years, with provisions for renewal every five years (see Omnibus Budget Reconciliation Act of 1981, 95 Stat. 736–37). Licenses will be granted only if the "public convenience, interest, or necessity will be served thereby." Section 310(b) of the Act provides that no license may be transferred to any person or entity, directly or indirectly, without the prior approval of the Commission, and Section 310(a) of the Act mandates that station licenses shall be granted only to U.S. citizens and cannot be held by aliens, foreign governments, or corporations of which any officer or director is an alien or of which more than a minority of the stock is voted by aliens or representatives of foreign governments. Interestingly, there is no restriction on foreign individuals or corporations holding ownership interests in cable systems.

Although a licensee who has given "meritorious service" has a "legitimate renewal expectancy," nevertheless, there is no guarantee that a license will be renewed or, indeed, that there will even be an available frequency over which to operate at the expiration of the license term. Transcontinent Television Corp. v. Federal Communications Commission (1962). Nor is the Commission required to grant a license for the full five- or seven-year term. It may, and occasionally does, grant a license for a shorter term if it believes that action would be more appropriate or if it has doubts about the qualifications of the licensee sufficient to desire an opportunity to review its operation for an interval shorter than five or seven years. Moreover, the license carries obligations which have been held to be constitutional even though "content based." Thus, for example, a licensee must make equal time available for political candidates; it cannot broadcast material which is "obscene" or indecent; it cannot broadcast lottery information (except for state-run or charity lotteries under certain conditions); it must meet certain equal employment opportunity guidelines and, in general, it must "operate in the public interest."

Licensees do possess certain constitutional and statutory protections which derive not from any "right" in the license itself, but rather from general constitutional and statutory protections against arbitrary action of government. Although a license can be revoked during its term, the Commission can only do so after giving notice to the licensee and a full opportunity to be heard. 47 U.S.C.A. § 312(c). The Commission carries the burden of proof in such a revocation proceeding whereas in the initial licensing phase and in the renewal phase it is the applicant who must carry the burden of persuading the Commission that it is qualified. The Commission cannot act arbitrarily or capriciously and must explain its decisions through written findings (Saginaw Broadcasting Co. v. Federal Communications Commission (1938)) on a public record containing full explanation of its rationale and actions. Greater Boston Television Corp. v. Federal Communications Commission (1970). Its actions are subject to the requirements of the Federal Administrative Procedure Act, 5 U.S.C.A. §§ 500–576. The Commission's decisions are appealable to the United States Court of Appeals and the court must be satisfied that the Commission has exercised its decision-making powers in accordance with constitution and statute.

G. COMMISSION FUNCTIONS IN BROADCASTING REGULATION

Analytically, the Commission exercises three different types of functions in the regulation of broadcasting: (1) licensing, which involves the choice of licensee either initially or at renewal time; (2) operational supervision, which involves oversight as to whether a licensee is meeting the conditions of its license; and (3) planning, by which the Commission attempts to integrate new and emerging technology into the broadcast regulatory scheme. These functions will be discussed in this and the following chapters.

H. LICENSING POLICIES OF THE COMMISSION

The Commission's primary statutory function is licensing; indeed, licensing is the linchpin on which all Commission broadcasting functions depend. Section 301 of the Communications Act mandates that no person shall use or operate any apparatus for radio transmission except by virtue of a license to operate granted by the Commission. Section 307(a) requires that licenses be granted to applicants only "if public convenience, interest, or necessity will be served thereby." Section 303 gives the Commission the power to classify different types of stations, to prescribe the nature of the service to be rendered by different types of stations, and to assign the bands of frequencies for each individual station. A license from the Commission is, in essence, an exclusive right to operate a station on a particular frequency at a prescribed power.

Before turning to the intricacies of the licensing process, it is instructive to consider the Commission's frequency allocations policy. The nature of that policy has a profound impact upon licensing and upon the type of communication's system that the public enjoys. The power to determine which type of broadcaster will be allowed on which frequency is, perhaps, the most potent power the Commission possesses. It affects not only the content of the material (for example, a policy prohibiting commercial advertising on frequencies allocated for non-commercial use obviously is content based) but it also sets the ground rules for the competition between prospective users. Often overlooked is the very simple fact that the present regulatory structure arose in a context where frequency space was a terribly precious commodity while demands for communications capability increased dramatically. The Commission must mediate between competing potential users. The choice of whether particular frequencies would be used for broadcasting, common carriage, industrial uses, airlines, maritime use, etc., is perhaps the most significant determinant of what and how the public will receive as broadcast service.

1. Frequency Allocation

The Commission has designated a portion of the spectrum for "broadcast" use, and has further subdivided the broadcast "band" into distinct portions. One set of frequencies is set aside for standard (or AM) broadcast stations, another group for frequency modulation (FM) stations, and a third for use by television stations. But the manner in which it chooses to assign specific frequencies within these groupings is not the same.

a. AM Allocation

The Commission immediately confronts a fact of physics: because of electrical interference considerations, the number of individual broadcast stations which can operate in a particular bandwidth varies inversely with their power. The higher the power, the smaller the number of stations which can be accommodated and vice-versa. The Commission could have chosen an allocations policy which would have led to a small number of very powerful stations, each being given the task of covering very large distances. This system was rejected on policy grounds, i.e., that the nation should have a large rather than a small number of individual voices.

Conversely, the Commission could have allowed a very large number of stations, giving each low power. The difficulty here was that the coverage area of such stations might be so small as to preclude financial viability. Instead, the Commission opted for a compromise. The present AM allocation policy allows three classes of stations;

(1) The so-called "clear channel" stations, approximately 25 in number, which operate at 50 kilowatts (the highest permissible power for any commercial AM station), cover a radius of approximately 80 to 90 miles during daytime hours and (because of a scientific phenomenon) can be heard during the night at distances which sometimes reach 500 or 600 miles. These few "clear channel" stations are heavily protected from interference by other stations;

(2) Lower power, so-called "regional" stations which operate at a power usually of 5 or 10 kw and which cover a radius of approximately 25 or 30 miles (depending on the terrain); and

(3) So-called "local" stations which operate at a power no greater than 1 kw, cover an area of approximately 8 to 10 miles in radius, and many of which (because of interference considerations) are allowed to operate only during daytime hours. By far the majority of standard broadcast stations in the United States are local stations which operate on a "local" frequency.

See 47 C.F.R. §§ 73.21–73.29 and Regulations of the Commission for a full exposition of the AM broadcast allocations rules.

The second characteristic of the AM allocation system is that, unlike FM or TV, it operates on a "demand" basis. To illustrate, the Commission could have taken all of the available frequencies in the AM band and allocated specific frequencies to specific communities. New York City could have been allocated 5 clear channel stations, 6 regional stations and 13 local stations. Chicago could have been allocated a different number of specific classes of stations, Des Moines, Iowa yet a third, and so on throughout all communities in the United States. This type of specific allocation by city has the advantage of ensuring that significant cities have a certain number of broadcast stations, and it also has the virtue of reserving frequencies for future use in areas which are now relatively sparse in population, but which later might become more heavily populated.

Instead, in AM the Commission opted for an allocation policy which allowed maximum scope for a "market type" of demand. The Commission first established engineering ground rules stipulating certain power requirements, and also stipulating the amount of allowable interference which a proposed station could cause or accept. Within these ground rules, applicants were entitled to apply for any of the various classes of stations in any community. It was believed (and proved to be the case) that the larger population centers, being able to support the larger number of stations, would attract the largest number of applicants. The Commission put as few restrictions as possible on the number of applicants so that the benefit of radio communication could be realized throughout the country as quickly as applicants could design proposed facilities which would fit within the Commission's overall engineering guidelines.

The "demand" system still governs the allocation of AM stations, although the engineering ground rules are now such that (in light of the number of existing AM stations) it is virtually impossible to design a new AM station which will fit within them. Moreover, as FM stations continue to multiply, their superior technical performance has made them the dominant radio medium, to the economic detriment of AM broadcasting. The number of AM stations has not significantly increased in the past decade, and (absent a radical policy change) is not likely to do so in the future. Indeed, the Commission has suggested (in a rather radical policy change) that there now may be too many operating AM stations, creating technical degradation to their economic detriment. In 1991 the Commission allocated an additional 1000 KHz to the AM band so as to allow some existing stations to migrate to the new band to relieve congestion in the AM service. See, e.g., Report and Order, MM Docket No. 87–267, released October 25, 1991.

b. *Television Allocation*

Although television technology was virtually fully developed by 1934, a number of factors (including WW II) delayed its entry into the marketplace until the late 1940's. By that time the Commission had considerable experience with the "demand" allocation system and had identified shortcomings in it, particularly that it engendered a great deal of complicated, lengthy and difficult engineering litigation. It tended to favor the more populated areas over the less populated, since a station granted to a larger community, by necessity precluded use of that frequency in smaller communities which had not as yet stimulated entrepreneurs to view them as places for radio stations. The demand system was essentially an "unplanned" one in which future growth might not adequately be accommodated.

The Commission therefore discarded the demand system in television and turned towards a simplified, more specific allocation policy which assigned specific frequencies to specific communities. Certain frequencies were reserved for non-commercial, educational (now termed "public") stations. There are no different *classes* of television stations. All television stations are either on VHF or UHF frequencies. They can all operate day and night, and all have the same maximum power limitations (though, for technical reasons, VHF stations can cover a larger area than UHF stations).

Each city only has available to it those specific frequencies which the Commission has chosen to assign. These allocations are part of the Commission's rules, and any change in them requires a formal request for the Commission to institute a rule-making proceeding in accordance with the Administrative Procedure Act. Certain frequencies are reserved for use only by non-commercial stations, and some of these frequencies, even now, lie fallow, an example of the Commission allowing for future growth. Because there are no interference "ground rules" for television, there is much less engineering litigation in television cases, and there is no need for the Commission to compare in the hearing process (as it does in AM) the relative needs of different communities for a particular frequency. The needs of the various communities have already been evaluated in the rule-making process by which the frequencies were assigned.

The exception to the above TV allocation scheme is the low power television service (LPTV) inaugurated in 1982. The LPTV service allows low power stations (maximum power of 100 watts VHF and 1000 watts UHF, encompassing a coverage area of approximately 10–15 miles) to operate on any available channel, on a secondary (i.e., non-interference) basis to regular full service stations. "Secondary basis" means that any low power station creating interference to a full service station must either eliminate the interference or cease operations. See Final Rule, LPTV General Docket No. 82–107, 47 Fed.Reg. 21468, May 18, 1982.

c. *FM Allocation*

FM allocation, though originally on a "demand" basis, is now handled in the same manner as television allocation. Specific frequencies are assigned to specific cities according to a table of allocations, which can be changed only through the institution of a formal rule-making proceeding. The only essential difference is that in FM there are essentially four classes of stations, higher powered ones (which can operate up to 100 kw) and lower powered ones (which are limited to 50 kw, 25 kw or 3 kw). There are also channels reserved strictly for educational ("public") use. The number of FM stations has been increasing at a rapid rate and the Commission in 1985 allocated hundreds more.

2. The Showing an Applicant Must Make— Basic Qualifications

Having found a frequency which can be used in accordance with the Commission's rules, what type of showing must be made by an applicant in order to convince the Commission that the public interest requires a grant of the license?

The Commission is not always faced with the necessity of choosing between particular applicants; there may be only one applicant. But whether or not a choice is required, there are certain basic qualifications which *all* applicants must meet, some specifically required by the Communications Act and others by the Commission under its policy making authority.

a. *Citizenship*

Section 310 of the Act mandates that a broadcast license may not be held by a non-citizen, a foreign government, a foreign corporation, or any corporation of which any officer or director is an alien or of which more than one fifth of the capital stock is owned by non-citizens. The above restrictions are mandatory. They cannot be waived by the Commission and can be changed only by Congress. If the corporation is a holding company, no more than one-fourth of the capital stock can be owned by non-citizens, unless the Commission finds that the public interest will be served by allowing the increased foreign ownership. Other provisions of Section 310 specifically allow licenses to be held by foreign pilots, ships and radio ham operators under certain circumstances. There are no similar restrictions on foreign ownership of cable systems.

b. *Character*

By statute (Section 308(b) of the Act), the Commission must determine whether an applicant possesses the requisite "character" qualifications. But neither the Act nor the Commission's rules spell out the requirements that constitute "good character" or those that will be deemed "bad." The matter is left to the Commission's discretion. Because "bad character" could be as extensive as human experience and considerations of "character" per se could involve the Commission in abstract value judgments which it would rather avoid, the Commission's policy is to concern itself only with the type of bad character traits that would raise questions as to the honesty of the applicant, its potential performance as a broadcaster, or its proclivity towards obeying or violating Commission regulations. See Matter of Policy Regarding Character Qualifications in Broadcast Licensing (1986).

Honesty and candor are essential. The Commission could not function effectively if its licensees were dishonest. It has neither the staff nor the budget to check independently every licensee representation. The information with which it deals is almost always information given to it by its licensees; it relies upon their veracity to do its work. Therefore, a licensee or an applicant who has been found to have knowingly misrepresented a fact to the Commission is in serious danger of having its license application denied, even if the misrepresentation is in an area of little significance. The significance of the misrepresentation is far less important than the fact that the misrepresentation occurred. Federal Communications Commission v. WOKO, Inc. (1946). A review of the cases where the Commission either denied or revoked an application or license shows that by far the greatest percentage of denials occurred where the Commission found knowing misrepresentation to have occurred.

Violations of criminal law also raise character issues, although here the Commission has adopted a more flexible attitude. Felonious violation of criminal law involving moral turpitude (such as murder, robbery, rape, etc.) almost certainly would result in denial. But disqualification is not automatic. There have been instances of felony violations that have not resulted in outright denial. See Las Vegas Television, Inc. (1957). The Commission is likely to be forgiving if the crime occurred years ago and involved a law that had been routinely disregarded, for example, operating a speakeasy during Prohibition at a time and place where such operation was not uncommon. See WGCM Broadcasting Co. (1947). In general, the Commission's policy is that criminal convictions not involving fraudulent conduct are not relevant unless it can be demonstrated that there is a substantial relationship between the criminal conviction and the applicant's proclivity to be truthful or comply with the Commission's rules and policies.

Somewhat related are violations of regulatory statutes of other government agencies. An applicant convicted of having repeatedly violated federal regulatory laws in his non-communications related business has had his application denied on basic character grounds (Bulova and Henshel (1946), affirmed sub nom. Mester v. United States (1947), because the nature of the violation showed a knowing disdain for governmental regulations. But an unintentional violation of the Food, Drug, and Cosmetic Act did not result in denial in another case. Brown Radio & Television Co. (1965). As a general rule, the FCC believes that non-FCC regulatory violations do not have sufficient relationship to the Commission's concerns to be relevant unless they involve a specific adjudication of misrepresentation to another government unit.

Nor are criminal violations of the Federal antitrust laws necessarily grounds for disqualification. A number of nationwide companies (among them General Electric and Westinghouse) were found to have violated the Sherman Act through price fixing in their non-communications-related businesses. In considering whether to take away their broadcast licenses, the Commission found that the communications sections of these companies were separate from the other areas, were not handled by any of the persons involved in the price fixing, and were characterized by a history of meritorious programming and pioneering broadcast efforts. Weighing these factors led the Commission to renew the licenses. Westinghouse Broadcasting Co., Inc. (1962); General Electric Co. (1964).

But violations of the Sherman Act by a newspaper which engaged in predatory competitive tactics against a radio station, and with no past broadcasting history against which to weigh them, could be grounds for refusal to grant a license to the offender (see, e.g., Mansfield Journal Co. v. Federal Communication Commission (1950)). Obviously, the outcome of these cases depends upon their individual facts. The Commission will not adjudicate controversies that are the subject of other court proceedings. In such cases the Commission will condition its actions upon the outcome of the adjudication in the courts. See, e.g., RKO General, Inc. (1969). The general rule is that where non-broadcast related antitrust or anticompetitive activity is involved, even adverse adjudications will not be considered relevant unless they suggest a proclivity toward fraud or unreliability. The factors which weigh most heavily in the analysis are the willfulness of the misconduct, the frequency of such behavior and its currency.

At one time, the Commission considered character not only as a *basic* qualifying condition but also as a factor to be weighed on a *comparative* basis. If the alleged misconduct was not sufficient to totally disqualify an applicant, nevertheless, it could be used as a standard to choose one competitor over another. This is no longer the case. The Commission's present policy is that a character defect either disqualifies the applicant or is irrelevant. See Matter of Policy Regarding Character Qualifications in Broadcast Licensing (1986).

c. *Financial Qualifications*

An applicant must demonstrate its financial capability to construct and operate its proposed facility. The theory is that a "scarce" public resource should not be wasted in the hands of an operator that does not have the financial capability to run it. The Commission has established a minimum standard which applicants must meet. Applicants for new stations (AM, FM or television) must demonstrate financial capability to construct and operate the station for 90 days, even assuming that the station earns no revenue. Financial Qualifications (1978); (1979). Similarly, purchasers of a broadcast station must have sufficient capital to consummate the transaction and to meet expenses for a three-month period. See Financial Qualifications (1981).

Although applicants are not required to demonstrate their financial capabilities through the filing of balance sheets or other documents, nevertheless, they are required (a) not only to certify that they have sufficient assets on hand and/or available to meet their financial obligations, but (b) they must also specifically identify the sources from which the applicant expects these funds to be available. An erroneous certification as to sufficiency of assets or the source of funds could lead to a misrepresentation issue being added to any hearing held on the application.

Financial qualifications are *not* considered on a comparative basis. The fact that one applicant may have more finances available than a competing applicant will not result in a preference for the former, because to do so would reward wealth alone, a result which the Commission does not desire. Scripps–Howard Radio v. Federal Communications Commission (1951). Every applicant need meet only the minimum qualifications. Once it has done so, additional financial capability per se is ignored as irrelevant.

d. Technical Showing

All applicants must demonstrate that they will meet the applicable technical requirements such as, for example, using equipment that has been appropriately "type approved" by the Commission, proposing to operate within the height and power limitations for the station sought, operating during the hours appropriate for the frequency sought and causing or receiving no more than the allowed amount of interference. This showing of technical qualifications has extremely important procedural ramifications. Although the Commission cannot normally deny a broadcast application without giving the applicant a hearing, the Commission may properly refuse even to consider an application if it fails to meet technical requirements. As a matter of practice, an application is not "filed" with the Commission; it is only "tendered" for filing and must first be "accepted" for filing even before the processing stage is reached. If an application, on its face, patently fails to meet certain technical minimum requirements, it will not even be "accepted" for filing, much less processed. For example, in AM radio the Commission has established a set of engineering "ground rules" which every applicant must meet. In FM and television allocations, the Commission has allocated specific frequencies to specific cities. If an AM application fails to meet the ground rules, or if an FM or TV applicant specifies a frequency other than one already assigned to the particular community involved, the Commission need not (and will not) accept these applications for filing. United States v. Storer Broadcasting Co. (1956); Ranger v. Federal Communications Commission (1961). And the Commission is becoming increasingly insistent upon applications being filed in a letter-perfect manner. In the past, the Commission was lenient in allowing perfecting amendments to cure facial defects. The Commission will no longer permit this. It has, at least with respect to applications for newly designated FM frequencies and for low-power television stations, adopted a so-called "hard look" policy under which an application will not be accepted for filing unless it includes *all* required information in the required form and format. See Salzer v. FCC (1985). Although the Commission has somewhat relaxed its "letter-perfect" rules, nevertheless, it still gives each application a very careful acceptability review. Because many applications must be filed by a specific date or be forever barred, failure to file an almost letter-perfect application can be, and in many cases has been, fatal.

There is one caveat to this general rule. The Commission cannot refuse to accept an application failing to meet minimum technical requirements where the applicant makes a strong prima facie showing that because of its particular situation, the requirements should be waived. See Storer Broadcasting Co., supra. Thus, for example, where the Commission's rules did not permit AM applications for nighttime operation of local stations on "clear channels," an applicant which sought such operation argued that its application should be considered because it was a unique "good music" station which would directionalize its antenna to protect the clear channel station. The Commission's refusal even to accept the application for filing was reversed by the court of appeals on the grounds that the applicant had at least made a prima facie showing that the rule should be waived in its case, and the Commission was required to give the application "reflective consideration." WAIT Radio v. Federal Communications Commission (1969). But such a holding is quite unusual. Absent special circumstances, an application which does not meet fundamental technical standards will not be processed.

e. Diversity of Media Ownership

Perhaps the major premise upon which the First Amendment is based is the societal necessity of a flourishing marketplace of ideas, with truth emerging not by governmental fiat but, rather, from the clash of many voices. Associated Press v. United States (1945). Where no government regulation is constitutionally permitted, the economic marketplace determines the number of voices to be heard. The government's role is limited to ensuring (through appropriate antitrust involvement and legislation) that the economic model succeeds. Where, as in broadcasting, government regulation is allowed, and where inherently it creates market monopolies, the question arises as to how the Commission should act to ensure hoped-for multiplicity, competition and diversity.

The Commission has historically responded to the problem by enacting "multiple ownership rules" which restrict persons or entities from acquiring excessive power through ownership of too many radio or television facilities. Congress (or the Commission) might, of course, have limited applicants to only one radio facility, either AM, FM or television, so that no one could own more than one station anywhere in the United States; neither has done so. Yet, the absence of any limitation posed the threat that broadcast economics might well follow the path of newspaper economics where a relatively small number of entities control a large number of daily newspapers throughout the country, and sometimes control all of the daily newspapers in a particular community. The Commission's multiple ownership rules attempt to strike a balance between these extremes, allowing multiple ownership of commercial media by a single entity in certain instances, and forbidding it in others. Non-commercial stations are exempt from the operation of these rules. The multiple ownership rules operate in much the same way as the engineering rules. If an applicant attempts to apply for more radio or television facilities than the rules allow, its application will not be accepted for filing, excepting special circumstances requiring waiver.

There are basically three types of multiple ownership rules: (a) those forbidding multiple ownership of facilities in the same community or area; (b) those limiting ownership of broadcast facilities by single entities no matter where the facilities are located; and (c) those forbidding newspapers from owning television stations in the same community in which they publish. There are also rules prohibiting telephone companies from owning cable systems in the areas where they provide telephone service, although at least one federal district court has held such rules unconstitutional as violating the First Amendment. The multiple ownership rules generally operate as follows:

(1) Ownership in a single community. The Commission's multiple ownership rules (47 C.F.R. § 73.3555) place limits upon the number of radio

or television stations that can be awarded in the same market, depending upon the number of stations in the market, the combined audience share of the commonly-owned station and whether the stations are radio or television facilities. 47 C.F.R. § 73.3555. A "market" is defined by the degree of overlap of the station's operating contours. In markets with 14 or fewer commercial radio stations, a single licensee can now own up to three radio facilities, no more than two of which can be in the same (i.e., AM or FM) service, so long as the combination represents less than 50% of the total number of stations in the market. In markets with 15 or more commercial radio stations, combined ownership can increase to two AM and two FM stations, with a 25% combined market audience level cap. The cap can be increased if the owner makes a special showing overcoming a presumption of lack of diversity at that audience level. See Revision of Radio Rules and Policies, 7 FCC Rcd. 2755 (1992).

The allowable common ownership in television is more restricted, reflecting the fact that there are fewer TV than FM or AM stations. The Commission's rules still prohibit combined ownership of two television stations in the same community or area (measured by contour overlap) or combined ownership of a VHF–TV/AM combination or a VHF–TV/FM combination (UHF–AM and UHF–FM combinations are allowed in certain cases depending upon particular market circumstances; UHF–AM–FM overlap is handled on a

case-by-case basis and is not subject to the same
blanket prohibitions as VHF/AM–FM combinations).   The Act and the Rules also prohibit common ownership of a television broadcast station
and a cable system that lies within that station's
local service area (see 47 C.F.R. § 76.501 (1986)),
although the Commission has recommended that
this rule be relaxed.   See Review of Regulations
Governing Television Broadcasting, MM Docket
No. 91–221, FCC 92–209 (June, 1992).

(2) The second aspect of the multiple ownership rules is an absolute limit on the number of
commercial AM, FM or television stations which a
single entity can own, no matter where located.
A single entity can own no more than 20 AM, 20
FM and 12 television stations anywhere in the
United States—a total of 52 stations.   These
numbers can be increased (for television stations)
from 12 to 14 and for AM and FM stations from a
total of 40 to 46 if two of the television stations or
three of the AM or FM stations are controlled by
minority groups or small business entities, a relaxation of the rules mainly aimed at increasing
ownership of broadcast stations by members of
recognized minorities.   There is one further limitation.   No single group or entity can directly or
indirectly have an interest in television stations
which have an aggregate national audience ex-
ceeding 25% (or 30% if the stations are minority
controlled).   See 47 C.F.R. § 73.3555(d).   In
counting the number of permissible stations, the
Commission will include in the total any station

in which the same person is an officer, director or voting shareholder owning 5% or more of the station's outstanding shares. If the corporation, however, has one stockholder holding more than 50% of the voting stock of the company, then the Commission will not consider any other stockholders as "owners" for purposes of the rule. If the stockholder is a mutual fund or other type of purely investment vehicle, then it is considered only if it holds more than ten percent of the voting stock of the company or if its representatives are officers or directors of the company.

Determining whether or not a party holds a "cognizable interest" for purposes of the various multiple ownership rules, and the impact of such a "cognizable interest" upon whether or not a combination falls within or without the multiple ownership rule caps, can cause quite complex problems which cannot be adequately covered in this work. The reader is referred to 47 C.F.R. § 73.3555 for a more detailed exposition. The key point to remember, however, is that there is an absolute limit to the number of commercial broadcast facilities that can be held under common ownership.

(3) Broadcasting/Newspaper Combinations. Until 1975, there was no prohibition against ownership of a broadcast station by a newspaper in the same community. Although the Commission acknowledged as early as 1944 that such ownership might lead, at least in certain circumstances, to a monopoly both in the economic and the

informational senses, nevertheless, it was not persuaded that the feared results were inevitable nor
that the problem could not be handled in ways
other than outright prohibition. In 1975, though
still finding no specific evidence of monopoly
abuse, the Commission nevertheless concluded on
policy grounds that the public interest would be
best served, and the twin goals of economic competition and competition in the marketplace of
ideas furthered, if future newspaper-broadcasting
combinations were prohibited by rule. Therefore,
it prohibited the ownership of either AM, FM, or
TV stations by daily newspapers in communities
over which the AM, FM or TV stations place a
signal of a particular strength. See Second Report and Order, Docket No. 18110, 50 FCC 2d
1046 (1975). Existing combinations were almost
all grandfathered with the proviso that they could
not be sold as a unit to a third party. In 16
instances, the Commission actually ordered dives-
titure by newspaper-broadcaster owners. See
FCC v. National Citizens Committee for Broadcasting, et al. (1978).

It should be recognized, of course, that joint or
common ownership is only one method by which the
number of potential broadcast voices can be limited.
Diversity can be affected by other types of joint
ventures between independently owned stations in
the same community such as, for example, cooperation between separately owned stations in terms of
advertising sales, joint use of technical facilities,
joint program formats and joint sales of commercial

time. The Commission has considered whether these types of joint arrangements should be brought under (or made subject to) the multiple ownership rule caps but in 1992 rejected this approach. See Revision of Radio Rules and Policies (1992). The Commission now generally allows such activities, so long as each licensee retains ultimate control of its station. The Commission is content, in these circumstances, to allow the question of competition (and, thus, program diversity) to be left to the federal antitrust laws enforced by the Department of Justice. The Commission did, however, place restrictions on one type of joint venture, local "time brokerage" arrangements. Time brokerage involves the sale by a licensee of discreet units of time to a "broker," who then supplies the programming to fill that time and sells commercial spot announcements to run within that time unit. The profits from the sale of these spot announcements go to the broker so that, in a sense, he becomes a "mini-licensee" for the time involved. The Commission recognized that widespread and substantial time brokerage agreements could adversely affect its multiple ownership restrictions. Therefore, in order to prevent the use of such agreements to circumvent its ownership limits, the rules provide that where an individual owns (or has a cognizable interest) in one or more stations in a market, time brokerage of more than 15% of the programming of any other station in that market will result in counting the brokered station toward the broker's permissible ownership limits, either with respect to

local market totals or to national multiple ownership limits.

The Commission's trend during the past fifteen
years has been to relax the stringency of the multiple ownership rules so as to allow common control
of a larger number of stations than previously was
the case. During the past decade, the number of
stations allowed under common control has increased dramatically (in the case of radio stations
from a total national limit of 12 AM and 12 FM to
the point now where a common owner can own a
total of 20 AM and 20 FM stations). The Commission is now considering rulemaking which would
significantly increase the national limit for television stations far beyond the 12 (14 if owned by
minorities) station market limit now in place. The
clear reason for the relaxation is the increase in
competing media (primarily cable) which has (a)
siphoned audiences away from over-the-air traditional broadcasting and has put AM, FM and TV
stations under increasing economic pressure, and
(b) increased the total available pool of media
voices. The Commission's stated purpose in deregulation is to allow the economic marketplace greater sway in ownership decisions and to improve
competition by allowing broadcast combinations to
become economically stronger and thus be in a
better position to compete. Nevertheless, the continued existence of the multiple ownership rules
testifies to the concern that no one group should
control broadcasting stations to an unwarranted
degree. Diversity still remains a Commission goal.

The above discussion relates to the showing which must be made to meet basic qualifications, i.e., they represent multiple ownership standards which must be met even to have an application considered by the Commission. But the Commission also considers multiple ownership characteristics on a comparative basis. Thus, if applicant A for an FM license already holds an AM license for the same community, and applicant B holds no other broadcast interests, applicant B will, all other things being equal, be preferred. Applicant B may be preferred even if in another area of comparison, for example past broadcast experience, A would be found slightly superior. Industrial Business (1974). The fact that A's application complies with the multiple ownership rules allows A to be considered. It does not foreclose the issue. Actually, existing ownership of any nearby radio or television station will almost certainly doom a broadcast applicant in any comparative contest with another applicant who owns no such other media facility. The practical effect of the Commission's policies, as they now stand, is that the larger broadcast combinations allowed under the relaxed Commission ownership limits will be achieved through purchase of existing stations, rather than in competitive contests for new facilities.

f. Community Ascertainment Studies

The Commission has evolved a policy requiring broadcasters to become familiar with the community to be served, and particularly familiar with the needs and problems of that community. Although the broadcaster has by statute (47 U.S.C.A. § 326) discretion to choose the programming it wishes to present, it nevertheless must do so in light of the particular problems and needs of its community if it is to operate "in the public interest."

Although the Commission had at one time erected a highly formalized ascertainment process which applied to all types of broadcasting stations, its "deregulation" thrust has now eliminated the need for formal and specific ascertainment procedures. The broadcaster has discretion to utilize whatever ascertainment methodology seems appropriate; its obligation is "issue oriented" in that the broadcaster must provide programming relevant to the issues confronting its community. There are no specific procedures that must be followed; the licensee can become familiar with local issues in the manner it deems best. The only paperwork required is a listing in the station's public file of programs broadcast to meet the pressing issues the broadcaster believes to be most significant. Persons dissatisfied with a station's performance have the burden of demonstrating, at renewal time, the manner in which the station has failed its programming obligations. For new station applicants, the manner of ascertainment of public issues is neither a basic nor a comparative criterion.

g. Programming

Contrary to a widely held misconception, the Commission never established, even in its pre-deregulatory period, official minimum norms or requirements for any programming category. Although frequently asked to set minimum norms, the Commission has consistently refused to do so, mainly on First Amendment grounds. Section 326 of the Act forbids the Commission to act as a "censor." Setting up required minimums would, in the Commission's view, be tantamount to censorship. See Hubbard Broadcasting, Inc. (1974); Report and Order, 66 FCC 2d 419, 428–29 (1977); National Black Media Coalition v. FCC (1978).

Despite the absence of specific programming minimums, the Commission had evolved a series of unofficial "guidelines" which, prior to 1981, were used as application processing criteria. These "guidelines" became the standard that most applicants for a new or renewed license in fact used. The "guideline" became a de facto quota. As part of its "deregulation" effort, the Commission in 1981 abandoned use of the "programming guidelines" for radio stations (AM or FM) and in 1984 abandoned them for television stations. Programming for radio and television stations is now governed simply by the marketplace, subject to the right of listeners to attack a station's performance at renewal time.

The one exception to the FCC's general "hands off" rule is children's programming. Even here, the FCC, left to its own devices, refused to adopt specific limitations on commercial advertising, although repeatedly requested to do so. See Action for Children's Television v. FCC (1977). After much litigious skirmishing between the FCC and public interest advocacy groups, Congress stepped in and passed legislation (Children's Television Act of 1990, Public Law 101–437, 1990), which required the Commission to limit (through rulemaking) the duration of advertising on children's television programming to not more than 10.5 minutes per hour on weekends and not more than 12 minutes per hour on weekdays. Stations broadcasting more than the allowed limits can be (and have been) ordered to pay civil fines. 47 C.F.R. § 73.670. The FCC must also review applications for renewal of television licenses to consider the extent to which the licensee has complied with these standards and has served the educational and informational needs of children through its overall programming (47 U.S.C.A. § 303b).

The deregulatory trend of the last decade has shifted the balance of programming discretion significantly in favor of the broadcaster. As a result of the increase in media voices, new stations have come into being which specialize in niche programming. It is extremely difficult to quantitatively or qualitatively measure the programming difference made by the Commission's deregulatory efforts. Setting aside the special cases of children's programming, obscenity and violence, generally speaking, the American public seems to be satisfied with the FCC's deregulatory moves. At this writing, there seems little impetus to change this trend.

h. Equal Employment Showing

Since 1969 the Commission has required all applicants to adopt and file affirmative action equal opportunity programs to ensure non-discrimination against minority groups such as Blacks, Chicanos, Native Americans and Spanish surnamed and women. See 47 C.F.R. § 73.2080. This obligates the applicant to take specific and affirmative action in recruiting, advancement, and training to ensure equality of opportunity. Report and Order, 18 FCC 2d 240 (1969). Stringent reporting requirements may be imposed upon stations whose employment programs are in less than full compliance with the Rules. Bob Jones University, Inc. (1973).

The Commission has not adopted a required system of quotas, goals and time tables. There is no requirement that minority employment be specifically consistent with the percentage of minority or female population in the particular community. There is no case in which the Commission has denied an application because of imbalance in the work force. But the court of appeals has suggested that a renewal application might be denied where the percentage of minority or female employment is "outside the zone of reasonableness" when compared with the demographics of the community as a whole. Stone v. Federal Communications Commission (1972).

The Commission utilizes "guidelines" to determine whether a station's employment profiles merit routine approval of their renewal applications. It continually monitors equal employment opportunity performance by requiring stations with five or more full-time employees to file yearly employment profiles. See FCC Public Notice, EEO Processing Guidelines, 45 Fed.Reg. 16335 (Feb. 13, 1980).

Interestingly, the FCC is one of the few federal government regulatory agencies (outside of the Equal Employment Opportunity Commission) that supervises equal employment opportunities within its regulatory ambit. The Supreme Court, in NAACP v. FPC (1976), held that the grant of power to regulate "in the public interest" does not necessarily carry within it the power to regulate equality of employment. The latter is a power which must either be specifically granted by Congress or must necessarily derive from the nature of the regulated industry so that Congressional intent to delegate that power can be inferred. In the case of broadcasting, the Supreme Court noted in fn. 7 of NAACP v. FPC that the FCC has the power to oversee equal employment matters because employment is closely related to programming and programming is clearly a public interest consideration of which the Commission must be cognizant. The Commission has been even more active recently, imposing stiff fines on licensees for violation of Commission equal employment policies. Equal employment is one facet of the Commission's work which has not been deregulated.

3. Processing the Application

Section 307 of the Act provides that the Commission "shall grant to any applicant therefor" a license if the public convenience, interest or necessity will be served. Sections 307(a) and 309(d)(2) of the

Act allow the Commission to grant an application making the proper showing without evidentiary hearing, but Section 309(e) states that if (a) a substantial and material question of fact is presented or (b) the Commission "for any reason" is unable to make a finding that the grant would be in the public interest, then the application must be designated for "full hearing" with the "burden of proof" upon the applicant. The key with respect to factual disputes is that they must be material and substantial. Factual ambiguity that would not be significant even if resolved does not require hearing. See Stone v. Federal Communications Commission (1972). The importance of the second condition is that the Commission may be required to hold a hearing even if there are no factual disputes, if there are policy or public interest questions that can only be resolved after public evidentiary hearing. See Citizens Committee to Save WEFM v. Federal Communications Commission (1973); Citizens Committee v. Federal Communications Commission (1970). But instances of the latter type of hearing (i.e., where there are no substantial or material factual issues) are extremely rare.

4. Participation by Non-applicants in the Processing of Applications

The broadcast application process is not merely a duet between the Commission and the applicant. Others may have a significant role in the process, even if they are not themselves applicants. Generally, non-applicant participants are either (1) other broadcast stations that may be affected by a grant of the application, or (2) representatives of the public who may be affected.

a. Participation by Other Broadcast Stations

There are essentially two reasons why another broadcast station might be allowed to intervene in the application process:

(a) because a grant would itself act as a "modification" of the intervening station's license, thus requiring a hearing by statute; or

(b) because the intervening station might be a party economically "adversely aggrieved or affected" by a grant, thus being accorded intervenor's status.

An example of the first is the grant of the application to station A causing objectionable electrical interference (as defined in the FCC Rules) to station B. All AM stations have an area in which they are protected from interference. The normally protected contours of station B (as defined in the rules at the time of the grant to B) become part of B's license. Because Section 316(a) of the Act forbids a "modification" of B's license without a "public hearing," B is entitled to protest the grant to A and to be accorded a hearing on its protest. It should be noted, however, that the "modification" would occur only if the grant becomes effective during B's seven-year license term.

Aside from a Section 316 modification, an existing station might also intervene in Commission proceedings if it can demonstrate that grant of a pending application would have an adverse economic effect on it. The regulatory system allows other broadcasters to act as "private attorneys general," bringing to the Commission's attention shortcomings in applications by other applicants. Naturally, such action would not be altruistic, but would be spurred by potential economic injury to the intervening station. Because such intervention brings to the Commission's attention matters which it otherwise might miss, such intervention is allowed, so long as the prima facie fact of adverse economic impact is demonstrated. Importantly, however, the intervening station cannot urge economic injury to itself as a ground upon which to deny the pending application. The Commission is not required to shield stations from competition. The economic injury to the station only acts to allow it entry into the proceeding. Once in the proceeding, it must base its objection on public interest factors. See Federal Communications Commission v. Sanders Bros. Radio Station (1940).

b. Participation by the Public

Until the landmark decision by the United States Court of Appeals for the District of Columbia in Office of Communication of the United Church of Christ v. Federal Communications Commission (1966), the public played virtually no part in the licensing process. Standing to participate in that process was limited to persons who were "parties in interest," a classification limited by Commission practice and interpretation to other stations complaining of electrical interference or to those persons or stations claiming specific adverse economic injury. The interests of the listening public at large were to be represented by the Commission itself, which, by statute, was required to act only in the public interest.

United Church of Christ opened the Commission's forum to broader public participation. Rejecting the notion that only economic injury or electrical interference conferred participatory rights, and recognizing that the Commission may not always be able to reflect public sentiment as effectively as the persons actually affected, the court held that representatives of the public could participate in the licensing process upon a showing that a grant of the application sought would have a particular effect upon them. Any listener to a station, therefore, has potential standing to participate. But the Commission can protect the orderly character of its proceeding by refusing to allow the public to participate en masse, and by requiring that they do so through representative groups. And a citizen cannot gain entry merely by asserting a bare general listenership interest without alleging a specific injury to himself or herself. Unless injury in fact occurs to a person or a member of an organization which claims to speak in his or her name, the courts will refuse to grant standing to sue in court. American Legal Foundation v. FCC (1987). But a representative citizens group which can demonstrate a particular injury which a member might suffer as a result of the grant would have sufficient statutory "standing" to participate.

Since United Church of Christ, citizens' groups have participated with respect to thousands of applications. Public interest law firms have been organized specializing in the representation of minority group interests in application proceedings. Women's groups have been effective in attacking applicants as being unresponsive to women as listeners and employees. Ethnic groups have been allowed to participate on the grounds that particular applicants did not evidence sufficient awareness of their needs.

The form that such participation ordinarily takes is the filing of a "Petition to Deny" the application. If the Petition raises a substantial or material question of fact or a policy issue which the Commission cannot resolve on the basis of the information in the application alone, the application will be designated for hearing. The burden of proceeding with the evidence on the issue or issues raised in the Petition will be placed by the Commission upon the party best suited to do so. The ultimate burden of proof, however, remains with the broadcast applicant as to the grant of its application for license.

5. Comparative Qualifications—The Need for Choice

How does the Commission choose between competing applicants? This question arises in two contexts. The first concerns applicants for a new frequency. The second concerns an existing station seeking renewal of its license and a challenge by new competitors who desire to take the license away. These situations present different problems and we will discuss each separately.

a. The Non-renewal Situation

The Commission must often choose between applicants for the same new frequency, and the choice may depend not only upon the nature of the applicants but also upon the nature of the facility sought.

This can best be illustrated as follows. Two applicants might file to use the same AM frequency in different communities and, under the Commission's engineering rules, the frequency can only be used in one of them. Thus, the choice is not only between applicants, but between communities. Should the Commission choose the best qualified applicant? Or should it award the station to the applicant who seeks to serve the community with the greatest need?

The answer can be found in Section 307(b) of the Communications Act, which specifies that the Commission shall make such distribution of licenses "among the several States and communities as to provide a fair, efficient, and equitable distribution of radio service to each of the same." This statutory mandate, as interpreted by the Supreme Court (Federal Communications Commission v. Allentown Broadcasting Corp. (1955)), requires the Commission to determine first which community has the greatest need for the frequency and to award the station to the applicant seeking to serve that community, without making any comparison between the nature of the applicants with respect to their background, history, multiple ownership characteristics, and other considerations. So long as the applicant for the community of greatest need possesses basic qualifications, its application will be granted without considering comparative qualifications.

This mandate requires that the Commission establish criteria for determining relative need as among different communities. Generally speaking, the criteria are as follows:

(a) every community of substantial size is entitled to its own local transmission facility and, if it does not have one, will be presumed to have a greater need than another community that already has one or more local stations;

(b) the Commission desires to maximize competition and, given a choice, will prefer competition to its absence. Thus, the Commission will generally prefer to add a second station to one community in preference to adding a third or fourth to another since, by so doing, it would create competition where none exists; and

(c) if the contesting communities already have multiple broadcast stations, the Commission will then look to the applicant that will make more effective use of the frequency; this usually means the applicant applying for the community with the larger population, but may also involve other complex engineering valuations.

But sometimes the Commission simply cannot make the choice based upon a comparison of communities either because the communities demonstrate equal need or because the applicants seek to serve the same community. How then does the Commission choose between applicants? Until 1965, the criteria used to compare applicants were less than clear, and the relative weight accorded the criteria by the Commission was so inconsistently applied at times as to raise serious charges that the purported criteria were used merely to mask preconceived results. In 1965, to clarify and simplify the comparative process, the Commission set forth its present policy on comparative broadcast hearings. Policy Statement on Comparative Broadcast Hearings, 1 FCC 2d 393 (1965). Asserting its primary objectives to be (a) the "best practicable service" to the public and (b) a maximum diffusion of control of the media of mass communications, the Commission indicated the material comparative criteria to be:

(i) *Diversification of Control of Mass Communications.* This has become, in practice, the most important non-engineering criterion. All other things being equal (and even when all other things are not necessarily equal) the applicant who possesses no other broadcast interests will be preferred to the one who has other commercial media interests in the same area. An applicant with significant holdings in other mass media is at a comparative disadvantage.

(ii) *Full–Time Participation in Station Operation by Owners and Local Residence of Applicants.*
This factor had been considered to be of "substantial" importance since the Commission believed that "it is inherently desirable that local
responsibility and day-to-day performance be
closely associated" and that "there is a likelihood
of greater sensitivity to an area's changing
needs" to the extent that the proprietors participate in day-to-day operation. 1 FCC 2d at 395.
For decades, the applicant who lived in the community and who proposed to participate actively
in the station's operation was preferred to one
who would rely solely upon a hired staff. But the
importance of this criterion (familiarly known as
the "integration" criterion) appears to be at an
end. The Court of Appeals (D.C. Cir.) in December 1993 declared the integration policy to be
arbitrary and capricious (Bechtel v. FCC (1993))
thereby throwing the entire comparative process
into serious disarray.

It was in the context of the integration criterion
that the 20–year battle over whether to accord
preferences to minority groups and women was
fought. The 1965 Comparative Hearing Policy
Statement did not discuss whether minority groups
and women should receive preferences in comparative hearings. The Commission never considered
these as relevant criteria until the court of appeals
decision in TV 9, Inc. v. FCC (1973) where the court
decreed that the Commission could not ignore the
question of minority group status but, rather, must

take it into consideration as an "enhancement" feature in applying the "integration" criterion. If two applicants, for example, proposed that all of their owners would actively participate in station operations, but all of the owners of one applicant were black, whereas the owners of its opponent were white, it would be appropriate for the Commission to "enhance" the participation weight of the black applicant because it would be likely that the black applicant might be more sensitive to the needs of the black residents in the area. Subsequent to the TV 9 decision, the Commission on its own recognizance, applied a similar theory to women applicants and "enhanced" (i.e., gave added weight) to female ownership when comparing applicants who proposed that their owners would all work at the station. In closely contested cases, for over a decade it became routine for the Commission to award the frequency to the black or female applicant because of these enhancement preferences. Black and female enhancement was viewed as two sides of the enhancement coin.

This is no longer the case. Black and female preferences came under sharp constitutional attack as being race—and gender-based distinctions violative of the equal protection and due process clauses of the Constitution. Two District of Columbia Circuit Court of Appeals cases (Shurberg Broadcasting, Inc. v. FCC (1989) and Winter Park Communications, Inc. v. FCC (1989)) considered the constitutionality of preferences based on minority status. Shurberg specifically struck down as unconstitutional the FCC's "minority distress sale" policy, which allowed stations threatened with license revocation to sell their licenses to a minority applicant at a distress sale price. Yet the same Court (though a different panel) in Winter Park upheld the minority preference enhancement in FCC comparative cases. It was difficult to reconcile the reasoning of these minority enhancement cases decided the same year by different panels of the same Court. The issue was finally settled by a divided (5–4) Supreme Court in Metro Broadcasting, Inc. v. FCC (1990). Justice Brennan, writing for the majority in his last decision before retirement, stated that neither the minority comparative hearing preferences for minorities nor the minority distress sale policy was unconstitutional. Rather, they are "benign," "race-conscious" measures which serve important governmental objectives within the power of Congress and therefore, they pass constitutional muster. The public interest in enhancing program diversity is an important and appropriate governmental objective and there is an empirical connection between program diversity and minority ownership. Race-neutral measures have been found by the FCC to be insufficient to produce adequate program diversity; more expansive methods have been rejected by the FCC. Thus, the FCC has properly chosen the least restrictive alternative. Non-minority applicants cannot legitimately expect that their applications will be processed without consideration of the fact of minority ownership of their competitors. Of course, the Metro decision came at a time when the integration criterion was still being applied. In light of Bechtel, which struck down this criterion, it is unclear whether the minority preference will continue to live as a separate criterion.

Female preferences, however, are clearly at an end. The D.C. Court of Appeals (in Lamprecht v. FCC (1992)) struck down female preferences as violating both the equal protection and the due process clauses. The court, using the same criteria set out by Justice Brennan in Metro Broadcasting, did not find the connection between female ownership and programming that the Supreme Court and the FCC had found with respect to minority ownership and programming. Although the FCC had asserted that female gender preference was substantively related to program diversity, there was no record made in any proceeding to establish any meaningful link between female ownership and programming of any particular type. Absent such a record, female preference must constitutionally fail. Although the court remanded the case to the Commission to allow it to construct such a record if warranted, the Commission refused the invitation and instead, killed female preference rather than defend it in the Supreme Court.

(iii) *Proposed Program Service.* The Commission will *not* ordinarily use as a comparative criterion the proposed program services of competing applicants. This seems counter-intuitive because programming is, from the public's point of view, the most important aspect of a broadcast applicant's proposal. Why does the Commission fail to consider it at all? The reason derives from the FCC's experience that applicants generally propose similar program formats, and even if they differ, the "minor differences among applicants are apt to prove to be of no significance." 1 FCC 2d at 397. Moreover, comparing program proposals turns the application process into a "bidding" auction, with applicants vying to outpromise each other, with little likelihood that their programming would, in fact, be significantly different from the bulk of the programming presented by other stations. The Commission is particularly concerned that forcing it to compare different program formats casts it in the role of censor, and involves subjective qualitative judgments of the type that it would prefer not to make. The FCC has thus adopted a policy of ignoring changes in radio and television programming on the ground that there are a sufficient number of stations to allow that issue to be determined by the economic marketplace. This policy was affirmed by the Supreme Court in FCC v. WNCN Listeners Guild (1981). See, also, Report & Order, MM Docket No. 83–670, 98 FCC 2d 1076 (1984). The Commission will only consider programming differences between applicants where they are of such a magnitude that they represent different program universes, such as, for example, where one applicant proposes a classical music station, while another proposes a home shopping network. Even here, a special issue must be requested by the applicant seeking the comparative advantage.

(iv) *Past Broadcast Record.* The Commission uses an applicant's past broadcast record as a significant comparative factor only if the past record is either "unusually good or unusually poor." A past record that is "within the bounds of average performance will be disregarded." 1 FCC 2d at 398.

(v) *Efficient Use of the Frequency.* Where one or more competing applicants propose an operation that, for one or more engineering reasons, would be more efficient, this fact will be considered of significance in determining the preference.

(vi) *Other Factors.* The above framework does not exhaust the possibilities. Since the comparisons take place on a case-by-case basis, it would be impossible to list all situations which might arise. But it does indicate the nature of the pertinent criteria which the Commission considers. If an applicant desires consideration of another factor not specifically enumerated above, it must make a special request that the FCC do so.

The entire FCC comparative hearing process has come under sharp criticism as cumbersome, unnecessary, a fruitful ground for applicant deceit or dishonesty, unduly time consuming and expensive, and, on balance, indefensible since the process appears to have little effect on the ultimate programming product in the real world. No matter how the licensee is chosen, most broadcast programming appears disarmingly similar. What is the point, critics argue, in depending upon such criteria as local ownership and participation in management by owners when, in actuality, most owners (no matter how chosen) hire professional broadcasters to program and operate the station? Moreover, applicants have long since been schooled in "gaming" the system by putting together applications which on paper would fulfill all the Commission's comparative criteria (i.e., one owner being a local resident, another being a member of a minority group, all to be full participants in management), whereas, if chosen, these owners will undoubtedly hire professional broadcasters, thereby rendering their hearing promises irrelevant. Worse, the FCC has no effective way of insuring that its comparative criteria have any lasting meaning. Under the FCC's present policies, an applicant need merely operate its station one year after receiving the license and then it is perfectly free to sell it to the highest bidder, a purchaser who may bear no resemblance to the applicant who obtained the license as a result of the hearing. The lack of effective Commission follow-up control led the D.C. Court of Appeals in the Bechtel cases to ultimately declare the Commission's use of the integration policy improper. Partly as a result, the Commission is now reconsidering its entire comparative process. See Bechtel v. FCC (1992); Bechtel v. FCC (1993) and Reexamination of the Policy Statement on Comparative Broadcast Hearings (1992).

b. *The Renewal Situation*

What are the comparative factors when one of the applicants is not a newcomer, but instead, seeks a

renewal of its license in competition with a newcomer which seeks to replace it? Will the Commission apply the same criteria as it does when the
applicants are applying for a new facility, or will it
give a preference to an applicant who has demonstrated its ability by actually running the station
sought? This is a particularly vexing question because, on the one hand, giving preference to the
existing licensee would tend to freeze out newcom-
ers. On the other, ignoring past performance
would be unfair to a licensee who has spent considerable sums in building up its station, which might
not be recovered if its license were to be denied.
Moreover, such a policy might introduce an element
of instability in the broadcast industry which ultimately would not serve the public interest. But if
credit is to be given for past performance, how
much and in what way is it to be given?

The Commission first resolved this problem
(Hearst Radio, Inc. (WBAL) (1951)) by giving a
decisive preference to the renewal applicant. The
Commission reasoned that it was weighing a proven
past record against a mere proposal, and feared a
challenger might easily outpromise but not necessarily outperform an existing station. This policy,
of course, virtually ruled out successful challenges
at renewal time.

Although the Commission later became dissatisfied with the stringency of the Hearst policy, its
attempts to change that policy (at one point to
liberalize it and at another to tighten it) came to
naught. See, e.g., Greater Boston Television Corp.

v. Federal Communications Commission (1970); Citizens Communications Center v. Federal Communications Commission (1971). The present posture of renewal comparisons is essentially that embodied in Hearst, with this gloss: an applicant can rely on what has come to be known as a "renewal expectancy." The Administrative Law Judge will determine whether the incumbent was providing "minimal" or "substantial" service. If "minimal," the incumbent will not receive a comparative plus. However, if the incumbent is found to have rendered "substantial" service, its renewal expectancy will be recognized and it will be given a comparative preference of major, and probably decisive, significance. See Deregulation of Radio, 46 Fed.Reg. 13888, 13896 (1981); FCC v. National Citizens Committee (1978). This may be true even where the challenger is entitled to a significant preference in the area of ownership of mass media and would ordinarily have been preferred if both applicants had sought a new facility. See Central Florida Enterprises, Inc. v. FCC (1982). In determining whether service is "substantial," the Commission looks to (1) the amount (and times) of non-entertainment programming presented and whether it is directed to local needs and interest, (2) the amount of locally produced programming, and (3) the reputation of the station in the community. Formulation of Policy and Rules Relating to Broadcast Renewal Applicants, 4 FCC Rcd. 6363 (1989). Here again, only broad principles can be outlined. The resolution of individual cases (and particularly what will and will not be considered "substantial service") must depend upon the facts of each case.

The tension underlying the comparative renewal problem reflects the conflict between the desire for stability in the broadcast industry, and the view that a broadcasting license is a limited privilege which must be periodically renewed. There is a significant public interest component in stability because unless licensees can be reasonably assured that their heavy investment will not be rendered valueless after five or seven years, they might not make a long-term investment in public service programming. Rather, they will operate the station solely to maximize short-term profit. Yet, there is also a public interest benefit in insuring licensee responsibility through the veiled threat of loss of license in the event the broadcaster fails to fulfill its public service obligations.

During most of the Commission's regulatory history, the balance was weighed in favor of the latter consideration. Recent experience, however, particularly the extraordinarily lengthy and expensive proceedings characterizing license renewal challenges (and the potential for mischief in challengers filing only for the purpose of being "paid off") has made the Commission less enamored of the license challenge procedure as a prophylactic device. A one-time Chief of the Mass Media Bureau has been most vociferous: "[E]very effort to rid the public of this offensive process called comparative renewal should be made. The public interest demands it." Final Report of the Mediator/Facilitator in the RKO

Settlement Process, (unpublished report; available on request) (Feb. 3, 1987). Whether Congress will agree is yet to be seen; until now it has not.

6. The "Settlement Policy"

Perhaps nothing illustrates the shifting vagaries of Commission law and policy better than the tale of the Commission's policy on settlements of contested comparative hearings. One of the early Congressional fears was that the comparative hearing process (whether for determining a new license or for challenging an existing one) could be abused by applicants who filed not for the purpose of obtaining a broadcast station but, rather, simply for the purpose of extracting a cash payment in return for dismissing its application. Congress attempted to meet this problem by prohibiting any applicant from receiving a cash settlement for dismissing its application over and above its actual expenses in prosecuting the application. Because an applicant could, therefore, not make a profit simply by prosecuting its application, the likelihood of filing solely for that purpose would be eliminated.

The problem was that comparative hearings literally took years, cost huge amounts of money, and introduced a lengthy period of uncertainty as to who would be the ultimate licensee, without much demonstrated public interest benefit. It also tended to increase the likelihood and length of litigation, in contrast to the law's usual policy, which is to encourage resolution of conflict through settlement. Therefore, in 1981 and 1982, Congress repealed its prohibition against applicants receiving more than their legitimately expended costs (see Public Law 97–259, 96 Stat. 1087, 1095; Public Law 97–35, 95 Stat. 357, 737–38) and directed the Commission to encourage rather than discourage settlements of hearing conflicts. This legislative policy was soon put into effect (see Bison City Television 49 Ltd. Partnership (1983)) with the result that settlements in contested cases became the norm rather than the exception.

Alas, the policy promoting settlements, though somewhat effective in reducing the Commission's workload, nevertheless fostered other problems, primarily the problem of applicants filing applications with no serious thought of operating any broadcast station, but primarily for the purpose of extracting large settlement payments. Although filing an application simply for the purpose of settlement is in fact illegal, (47 U.S.C.A. § 311) nevertheless, it is extremely difficult to prove that an application was filed solely for that purpose. The problem was particularly vexing in the case of applications for renewal of licenses. Experience indicated that allowing settlements often did not substantially shorten or eliminate litigation since the parties would not settle until after extensive litigation had already taken place. All of this led the Commission to reinstate its preexisting policy of limiting settlement payoffs only to expenses actually incurred by the dismissing applicant. See Broadcast Renewal Applicants (Abuses in the Comparative Renewal

Process), 5 FCC Rcd. 3902 (1990); Comparative Broadcast Proceedings (Settlement Agreement Payments), 6 FCC Rcd. 85 (1991); Decisions on Reconsideration, 6 FCC Rcd. 2901 (1991).

7. Random Selection as a Licensing Mechanism

Congress and the Commission have expressed dissatisfaction with the traditional comparative hearing process as a mechanism to choose between competing applicants. The average delay caused by a comparative hearing is three years. The frequency lies fallow during the hearing. There are high tangible costs to the applicants (legal and engineering fees) and extensive costs to the Commission (engineering and legal manpower drains). See Notice of Inquiry, 45 Fed.Reg. 29335 (May 2, 1980).

Prior to 1981, the comparative hearing mechanism was mandated by statute. In 1981, Congress amended Section 309(i) of the Act (47 U.S.C.A. § 309(i)) to allow the Commission to utilize random selection (i.e., lottery) licensing mechanisms, but only after the Commission first determined the basic qualifications of applicants and established rules and procedures to ensure that persons "underrepresented in the ownership of telecommunications facilities will be granted significant preferences." (Omnibus Reconciliation Act of 1981, 95 Stat. 736–37).

After studying the possibilities of instituting such a mechanism, the Commission, in 1982, declined to do so primarily because it believed that requiring the Commission to determine basic qualifications of all applicants prior to holding a lottery "would not produce the operating economies which Congress sought to provide" (Report and Order, February 25, 1982, General Docket No. 81–768, 47 Fed.Reg. 11886 (Mar. 19, 1982)). The Commission also identified other problems:

1. The key to expeditious processing is reduction in the criteria used to establish "basic qualifications." Paradoxically, however, the easier it becomes to meet these criteria, the more applicants will apply, thus increasing the Commission's processing burdens.

2. The statutory provisions requiring "significant preferences" to persons who are "underrepresented" in the ownership of telecommunications facilities pose serious constitutional issues.

Congress responded by revising Section 309(i) of the Act in 1982 to give the Commission more flexibility in establishing a lottery mechanism. The 1982 legislation (Public Law 97–259, § 115) continues to require that the Commission, if it chooses to institute a lottery system, must grant "significant preferences" to applicants who would increase "diversification of ownership of mass media" and to any applicant "controlled by members of a minority group." No preferences are given to women.

Despite these difficulties, lotteries may very well be the wave of the future. Lotteries are already being used to award low power television frequencies, cellular radio frequencies and multipoint distribution system frequencies. The lottery system is still not used to award full service broadcast stations, but how long this policy will last is an open question.

CHAPTER XI

FCC CONTROL OF BROADCAST OPERATIONS

Although the Commission's primary function is and has been the licensing of broadcast stations, it has been involved from its inception, and increasingly in the past two decades, with the supervision of the manner in which stations are operated. Section 326 of the Act specifically forbids the Commission to "censor" material broadcast by a radio facility, and an overly broad reading of this restriction might make it appear that the Commission plays no part in the content of program material. Such is not the case; there are some areas in which, Section 326 notwithstanding, the Commission can and does control or influence program content. These areas include: (1) political broadcasting; (2) obscene, "indecent," and lottery programming; (3) so-called network "prime time" programming; (4) "anti-payola" and "anti-plugola" statutes; (5) regulations requiring separation between network ownership and program production; and (6) nebulous regulation by "raised eyebrow" in such areas as "family viewing time," drug lyrics and sexually stimulating radio programming. Also included was programming under the so-called "Fairness Doc-

trine" when the Commission was still enforcing
that doctrine.

A. POLITICAL BROADCASTING

From the inception of broadcast legislation, Congress has recognized the enormous potential of radio as a political tool. A major concern is that a
broadcast facility might improperly influence an
election by affording only one candidate access to its
audience. To prevent this possibility, Congress enacted what is now Section 315 of the Communications Act which provides that "If any licensee shall
permit any person who is a legally qualified candidate for any public office to use a broadcasting
station, he shall afford equal opportunities to all
other such candidates for that office in the use of
such broadcasting station," (47 U.S.C.A. § 315)
subject to certain specific exceptions. Although
clearly a statute which regulates program content,
it has survived attacks on its constitutionality. See,
e.g. Branch v. Federal Communications Commission
(1987). The section, as amended, also provides that
the rates charged each candidate must be equal and
that during election campaigns candidates must be
given the "lowest unit charge" that is offered by
the station to commercial advertisers for comparable time. The concept of equality extends not only
to rates but also to station business practices.
Thus, for example, a station cannot require one
candidate to pay by certified check while another is
allowed to pay by regular check in the normal
course of business. Alpha Broadcasting Corp.

(1984). Although rarely invoked, there are civil and criminal penalties for willful and knowing violations of the statute.

The political broadcasting statute (when applicable) is quite precise and leaves virtually no room for broadcaster discretion except in the area of news and news event coverage. It operates with a type of mathematical certainty not usually found in broadcasting regulation. Nevertheless, despite Congress' attempt at clarity, Section 315 law is often misunderstood because of its ad hoc application. Over the years, the statute has accumulated by accretion layers of interpretative rulings to the point where its intricacies have become quite arcane.

1. "Use"

Although it is generally thought that the "equal opportunities" provision of Section 315 applies to all election broadcasts, in fact, the provision is limited only to those circumstances where the candidate himself or herself "uses" the program. Section 315 thus does not apply to a broadcast or advertisement on behalf of the candidate where the material is not considered a "use." This is a critical distinction. Unless the broadcast is a "use," Section 315 simply does not apply.

The Commission's interpretation of "use" has changed over the years. Originally, the Commission held that "use" did not encompass, for example, an appearance by a candidate on news programs where the appearance was dictated by the licensee's news judgment. Allen H. Blondy (1957).

In 1959, however, the Commission radically departed from that concept, holding that a candidate's appearance (even on a news program) would be considered a "use" whenever his or her identity could reasonably be presumed to be known by the audience and where the appearance was of such magnitude to be considered an integral part of the program. Lar Daly, recon. den. (1959). Thus, a station staff person who was also a candidate could not appear at the station without invoking equal time obligations if his or her voice was distinctive or well known enough to be identifiable. See, e.g., National Urban Coalition (1970); Station WBAX (1969). This was true even where the appearance was not sought by the candidate so that, for example, when Ronald Reagan was a presidential candidate, stations that presented his 20 year-old movies during the political campaign incurred equal time obligations. Adrian Weiss Productions (1976).

In 1991, as part of a general recodification of its political broadcasting rules (Matter of Codification of the Commission's Political Programming Policies, (1991)) the Commission significantly narrowed its "use" interpretation so that a "use" now includes only candidate appearances that are controlled, approved, or sponsored by the candidate (or the candidate's authorized committee) after the candidate becomes legally qualified. The introduction of the concept of candidate approval and/or control as an element in the definition meant, for example, that film actor Reagan's movies would not be considered a "use" after he became a candidate, unless he specifically approved or controlled the presentation of the program. Similarly, the decision by a licensee to include a candidate on its news program would not be considered a use unless the candidate approved or controlled that decision. After experimenting with the narrower definition, however, the Commission (in 1994) elected to return to its more expansive 1959–1991 definition of "use."

The above discussion also illustrates another aspect of the "use" doctrine: a candidate's appearance will be considered a "use" even if the candidate is appearing for a completely unrelated purpose and never mentions his or her candidacy. Letter to United Community Campaigns of America, (1964). The classic example would be a station weatherperson, announcer or interview host who is also a candidate for local office. An appearance by any of them in their normal roles, in which they present the news or the weather, would nevertheless (assuming they can be identified) be considered a "use" entitling their opponent to equal time, even if they never mention their candidacy. See Newscaster Candidacy (1965); Station WBAX (1969); RKO General, Inc. (1970).

2. Legally Qualified Candidates

"Equal time" obligations come into play only upon "uses" followed by demands by "legally qualified candidates for public office." The determination of whether or not a user (or demander) is a legally qualified candidate for public office is made by reference to the law of the state in which the election is being held. Political Primer (1984). All elections are not for "public office." For example, the position of delegate to a party convention is not a "public office," even though the name of that person may appear on an election ballot. Russell H. Morgan (1976). Conversely, a candidate can be legally qualified even if his or her name is not on the ballot if such a person, under state law, is making a bona fide "write-in" campaign. Political Primer (1984). But in order to be a legally qualified candidate the person must publicly announce his or her candidacy, even if everyone expects the person to be a candidate. Thus, an incumbent president, for example, cannot be presumed to be a candidate for reelection until such candidacy is announced. Until that time, appearances by the incumbent president would not be considered a "use" triggering equal time requirements. Id. at 1480. And if a purported candidate is too young to serve even if elected, he or she could not demand equal time to respond to an opponent. Socialist Workers Party (1972). The question of whether a person is "legally qualified" can be quite complex, and the Commission will follow the laws of the particular state wherever possible. Committee for Mayor Bergin v. Station WATR–TV (1982). In cases of ambiguity, the Commission will be the ultimate arbiter of whether the person is a candidate. CBS, Inc. v. FCC (1981).

3. Exemptions From Equal Time Requirement

The stringency of the "use" doctrine as it then was interpreted by the Commission (i.e., any "appearance" by a candidate was a "use") led Congress in 1959 to create certain specific exemptions to the "equal time" doctrine. Thus, the equal time doctrine is not applicable where the appearance by the candidate takes place on any:

(1) bona fide newscast,

(2) bona fide news interview,

(3) bona fide news documentary (if the appearance of the candidate is incidental to the presentation of the subject or subjects covered by the news documentary), or

(4) on-the-spot coverage of bona fide news events (including but not limited to political conventions and activities incidental thereto). 47 U.S.C.A. § 315(a).

The exemptions were enacted in 1959 to avoid the situation where an appearance by an incumbent at a routine affair such as a ribbon cutting ceremony or a greeting of visiting dignitaries on a newscast could trigger demands for equal time by all of his or her opponents. See Columbia Broadcasting System, Inc. (1959). It was believed that applying the "use" doctrine in all its rigor would, in practice, force stations to ignore such events in their news programming even though, in the exercise of their editorial judgment, they would otherwise have presented such material.

The first three exemptions, i.e., newscasts, news interviews and news documentaries are rather straight-forward and have been further defined by extensive legislative history indicating their scope. Underlying them is the notion that such programs are essentially under the control of the station (and not the candidate) so that the candidate cannot misuse his or her appearance to gain an improper advantage. Indeed, the Commission considers such programs to be under the "control" of the station even if the newscasts, news interviews or portions thereof are created by persons other than station personnel; so long as the station retains the ultimate decision to run the program it is still in control. The inclusion of the concept "bona fide" in the exemption represents a restriction on the station. If the appearance on the news program is intended by the station to be aimed at favoring one candidate over another, the appearance would not be "bona fide" under the statute and thus would not be exempt.

The fourth exemption, however, "on-the-spot coverage of a bona fide news event" is less well defined in the legislative history and raises the question whether the definition of "bona fide" news event should be based upon the subjective determination of the broadcaster or upon an objective determination by the Commission. For example, two gubernatorial candidates have been invited by a local professional group to debate important issues. The debate is considered a "bona fide news event" by a local station which desires to carry it live as a matter of interest to its audience. Would the debate be an exempt program so that the station need not offer equal time to other candidates for the same office who are not invited to the debate? Similarly, if a station believed a presidential press conference to be a newsworthy item to be presented in its entirety, would the station's belief in the program's newsworthiness render it an exempt "bona fide news event"? The Commission first held in 1964 that the subjective judgment of the station was not dispositive and that the Commission would ultimately determine exemptions based on objective criteria such as whether the fact of candidacy was an integral part of the appearance or merely incidental thereto. Columbia Broadcasting System, Inc. (1964). The Commission later changed its mind. Now, at least with respect to debates and press conferences by candidates, it is the bona fide subjective judgment of the station which determines the exemption. If the station, in good faith, believes the debate or news conference to be newsworthy, it can cover these items without invoking the equal time rules for opposing candidates. Petitions of the Aspen Institute (1975), affirmed Chisholm v. Federal Communications Commission (1976). It can even sponsor the debate, so long as it does so without intending to benefit a particular candidate. Henry Geller (1983). This interpretation, however, has been limited to debates, press conferences and, on occasion, to speeches by incumbent officials on issues affecting the electorate. The Commission has been wary of extending the exemption much beyond these types of presentation. See King Broadcasting Co. (1991).

The Commission has also expanded its interpretation of "on-the-spot" coverage. While "on-the-spot" coverage was originally interpreted to mean that the event had to be broadcast within 24 hours, the Commission subsequently relaxed this restriction and now holds that a delayed broadcast of "reasonably recent events" could be considered "on-the-spot" so long as the determination was made by the station in good faith. Henry Geller (1983).

4. Reasonable Access (Section 312(a)(7))

Section 315 requires even-handedness, not access. Indeed, Section 315(a) specifically states that "No obligation is imposed under this subsection upon any licensee to allow the use of its station by any such [legally qualified] candidate." Technically, a station could avoid Section 315 entirely simply by refusing to allow any candidate to appear. But in so doing it would violate other sections of the Communications Act. Thus, with respect to *federal* candidates, Section 312(a)(7) of the Act specifically includes, as a ground for revocation of license, "willful or repeated failure to allow reasonable access to or to permit purchase of reasonable amounts of time for the use of a broadcasting station by a legally qualified candidate for Federal elective office on behalf of his candidacy." Federal candidates, thus, have a clear statutory right of access. CBS, Inc. v. FCC (1981). And although state and local candidates are not specifically mentioned under the access provisions of Section 312(a), the Commission has interpreted the general "public interest" standard of Section 307 of the Act to forbid any station from simply refusing to allow political candidates to use the station's facility in any way simply to avoid equal time obligations. Some access must be given to certain state and local candidates, although the rules in this respect are imprecise.

What represents "reasonable access" for federal and state candidates has not been precisely defined—the concept necessarily varies with the circumstances. But the Commission has set forth certain guidelines. If, for example, there are dozens of state or local candidates for state or local elective offices, the FCC has never required that every candidate for every office must be given access. A broadcast station is not a common carrier and access cannot be achieved on demand. A station can prune out election campaigns for minor offices and allocate time only for the major offices on the state and local level. This flexibility with respect to state offices arises because there is no specific requirement in the Act that all state or local candidates must be given access and the Commission has refused to create one. See Political Primer (1984); CBS, Inc. v. FCC, supra.

A station's discretion is much more limited with respect to federal offices. All federal candidates, under the strictures of the statute, must be given "reasonable access." But even here the station retains some discretion to determine the manner of access. Even under Section 312, a station is not required to *sell* programming or advertising time to candidates. Stations can, and some do, take the position that they will sell no program time to candidates, but instead will meet their "access" obligations by giving candidates a reasonable amount of free time. Political Primer (1984).

The federal candidate "reasonable access" provisions of Section 312(a)(7) have created complex and vexing questions due to the inherent ambiguity of the concept "reasonable." What seems perfectly reasonable to a station manager trying to maximize profits seems quite unreasonable to a candidate hoping to limit campaign expenses. Although requested to adopt formal rules spelling out "reasonable access," the Commission has consistently refused to do so, instead relying on the "reasonable good faith judgments" of its licensees. The Commission has, however, adopted certain guidelines articulating the essence of "reasonable access." (See Matter of Codification of Commission's Political Programming Policies (1991):

   a) Reasonable access must be provided to legally qualified federal candidates through the gift or sale of time for their "uses" of the station.

b) Reasonable access must be provided at least during the 45 days before a general or special election. The question of whether access should be afforded before these periods or before a convention or non-primary caucus will be determined by the Commission on a case-by-case basis.

c) Both commercial and noncommercial stations must make program time available to legally qualified federal candidates during prime time and other time periods unless unusual circumstances exist that render it reasonable to deny access.

d) Commercial stations must make spot announcements available to federal candidates in prime time. The same rule applies to noncommercial stations that utilize spot time for underwriting announcements. Where a noncommercial station normally broadcasts spot promotional or public or public service announcements only, it generally need not make those spot times available to political candidates.

e) If a commercial station chooses to donate rather than sell time to candidates, it must make available to federal candidates free time of the various lengths, classes and periods that it makes available to commercial advertisers.

f) Noncommercial stations may not reject material submitted by candidates merely on the basis that it was originally prepared for broadcast on a commercial station.

g) A station may not use a denial of reasonable access as a means to censor or otherwise exercise control over the content of political material, e.g., by rejecting it for nonconformance with any of the station's suggested guidelines.

h) Licensees may not adopt a policy that flatly bans federal candidates from access to the types, lengths, and classes of time which they sell to commercial advertisers. Noncommercial educational stations must provide program time which conforms to normal parts of the station's broadcast schedule.

i) In providing reasonable access, stations may take into consideration their broader programming and business commitments, including the multiplicity of candidates in a particular race, the program disruption that will be caused by political advertising, and the amount of time already sold to a candidate in a particular race.

j) Broadcasters may ban the sale of political advertising to federal candidates during news programs; the public interest is served by preserving the journalistic integrity of the licensee in its news programming and does not reasonably hamper access of federal candidates to broadcast time.

k) Licensees may sell a "news-adjacency" class of time to candidates, provided that such a class is sold at rates no higher then the sale of such time to most-favored commercial advertisers.

One final note. "Reasonable access" (being included in a portion of the statute pertaining to license revocation) does *not* apply to cable systems since such systems are not primarily licensed by the FCC but rather by state or local governments.

5. Lowest Unit Charge

Prior to 1971, Congress required only that stations treat political candidates in ways comparable to commercial advertisers. No station or cable system could charge a political candidate, whether federal or state, a greater amount than was charged for a comparable announcement presented on behalf of a commercial advertiser. The obvious intent was to prevent stations or cable systems from taking advantage of the necessity for political candidates to obtain advertising time during election campaigns.

For most of the year, the comparability criteria still holds true. However, in 1971 Congress amended Section 315 to require that during a specific election period (45 days preceding the date of a primary election and 60 days preceding the date of a federal or special election) a station may charge a political candidate no more than the lowest unit charge for the same class and amount of time for the same period. 47 U.S.C.A. § 315(b) (Cum.Supp. 1976). The station must, during this period, treat the candidate in a manner comparable to its most favored commercial advertiser. The difference between "comparability" and "lowest unit charge" may be illustrated in this way: if a station has an advertiser willing to commit itself to purchasing an advertising schedule which will run an entire year, the station might be willing to give that advertiser a quantity discount so that instead of paying a normal rate of, for example, $10 per announcement, the advertiser need only pay $6 per announcement. Under the comparability standard in effect during most of the year, the station need only give political candidates the $6 rate if the candidate also agreed to purchase a schedule of announcements for the entire year. Since both are being treated in a comparable manner, the equality terms of the Act have been met. However, under the lowest unit charge concept, enforced during the 45 or 60 day period prior to a primary or general election, a station would be required to offer the $6 rate, even if the candidate bought only one announcement, since this would be the "lowest unit charge" being made for the time in question. In other words, lowest unit charge requires a station to give a political candidate a quantity discount even if the candidate does not purchase the same quantity as would a commercial advertiser receiving the discount.

Even under the lowest unit rate the station still retains some flexibility. It may make distinctions between classes of time so that a candidate seeking, for instance, to purchase prime time advertisements to be run at a fixed time would be required to pay the lowest unit charge for such fixed prime time advertisements. Nevertheless, the lowest unit charge rule has given political candidates a significant price advantage in using broadcast facilities.

It must immediately be noted that the lowest unit rule, easily enough articulated in concept, has become increasingly complicated in actual operation, so much so that in a 1990 surprise FCC audit of major television stations, the Commission found that a majority of them violated the rule at one time or another during political campaigns. This revelation led to a series of suits by candidates in state courts seeking millions of dollars in rebates which, in turn, led the Commission ultimately to federally preempt the question of whether a station has violated the statute. Therefore, any candidate who now believes that a broadcast station has overcharged him or her is limited to seeking redress only at the FCC, and the FCC has established procedural rules governing such complaints, including limited discovery rights for claimants and the provision of requirements for rebates, if such are necessary. See Exclusive Jurisdiction, etc., Declaratory Ruling, 6 FCC Rcd. 7511 (1991).

During the surprise political audit and the ensuing litigation the Commission recognized that at least some of the violations were due to:

(a) the complexity of the problem coupled with the lack of up-to-date Commission guidance; and

(b) continuing changes in the manner in which stations sell advertising, particularly through creation of myriad "packages" with bonuses, rebates, different time periods, and an increasing tendency to sell advertising time on a virtual auction basis to the highest bidder.

This led the Commission in 1991 to articulate a series of lowest unit charge guidelines: Matter of Codification of Commission's Political Programming Policies:

(i) Stations must disclose to candidates all classes of time, discount rates, and privileges afforded to commercial advertisers. Furthermore, stations are required to sell such time to candidates upon request.

(ii) Stations must continue to apply the "most-favored advertiser" standard to factors which affect the value of an advertisement, including (but not limited to) priorities against preemption.

(iii) Stations are permitted to establish their own reasonable classes of immediately preemptible time so long as some demonstrable benefit besides price or identity of the advertiser (such as preemption protection, scheduling flexibility, or guaranteed time-sensitive make goods) distinguishes each class. The licensee must adequately define each class, disclose it, and make it available to candidates.

(iv) Stations may establish their own reasonable classes of "preemptible spots with notice" time, so long as they adequately define such classes, disclose them, and make them available to candidates.

(v) Stations may treat non-preemptible and fixed position as distinct classes of time, provided that they articulate clearly the differences between such classes, fully disclose them, and make them available to candidates.

(vi) Stations may not create a premium-priced, candidates-only class of time.

(vii) Stations must calculate rebates and provide them to candidates promptly.

(viii) All rates found in all package plans sold to commercial advertisers must be included in the station's calculating of the lowest unit rate.

(ix) Stations need not include in lowest unit charge calculations noncash merchandise incentives (e.g., vacation trips). Bonus spots, however, must still be calculated into lowest unit charge.

(x) Stations may not increase their rates during an election period unless the rate increase is an ordinary business practice.

(xi) Stations must provide make goods prior to the election if the station has provided a time-sensitive make good to any commercial advertiser during the year preceding the 45– or 60–day election period. All make-good spots must be included in the calculation of the lowest unit charge.

(xii) While there is no obligation to sell spots in a particular program to candidates, once a station has decided that it will sell spots in a program, daypart, or time period, it cannot inflate the price of the spot sold to a candidate beyond the minimum necessary to clear by claiming that all "preemptible time" is sold out.

The mere listing of these guidelines suggests the complexities inherent in the lowest unit rate rule.

It must also be emphasized that the lowest unit charge criterion is applicable only to a "use" by a legally qualified candidate. Appearances by spokespersons on behalf of a particular candidate would not fall within the lowest unit charge concept because, as discussed above, it would not involve an appearance by the candidate and thus technically would not be a "use." Political Primer (1984).

6. Censorship

Section 315(a) specifically provides that no licensee can have any "power of censorship over the material broadcast under the provisions of this section." A legally qualified candidate for public office is free to say anything, whether or not it relates to the candidacy, and whether or not the material is scandalous or in any other manner unsuitable for broadcast. The obvious intent behind this subsection is to allow candidates to use radio or television time free from the fetters of any other person or entity. As a quid pro quo for such freedom, the Supreme Court has held that no station can be sued for libel or slander arising from such use by a candidate, nor can it be acted against in any manner by a private person or by the government. Farmers Educational and Cooperative Union v. WDAY, Inc. (1959). This immunity from suit is, the Court declared, constitutionally required to insure free speech by candidates. The "no censorship" provision is so stringently interpreted that it would be considered improper for a station to request that a candidate provide it with a copy of the candidate's speech or other materials prior to broadcast, the Commission holding that such a condition might inhibit the candidate in his or her use of the facility. Western Connecticut Broadcasting Co. (1973).

There is one caveat to the "no censorship" clause. Although there has been no direct adjudicated case on the point, the Commission's staff has concluded in a memorandum to Congress that the prohibition against censorship would not apply to the broadcast of obscene material forbidden by the criminal code. Legislation to this effect has been introduced into both Houses of Congress, but not yet adopted. Even without legislation, it is likely that the Commission would take this position if an actual case came before it since otherwise it would be requiring a broadcaster to violate the criminal law in order to comply with Section 315. See Political Primer (1984). Query: Would a station be allowed to edit out (or channel to a "safe harbor" period), as indecent, the use of dead fetuses by an anti-abortion candidate? At least one federal district court has held that it can, proving once again that "indecency" may well be in the eye of the beholder. Gillett Communications v. Becker (1992).

It must be stressed that the "no censorship" provision applies only to a use by a candidate. It does not apply to a use by a spokesman on behalf of a candidate, and it did not apply to appearances by non-candidates under the "Fairness Doctrine when the Commission was still applying that doctrine."

7. Necessity for Timely Demand

Equal time rights, though available, can be lost through inactivity or delay. A candidate must make a request of a station for equal time within one week of the day of the first use giving rise to the right to equal opportunity in the use of the broadcast facility. 47 C.F.R. § 73.1940(e) (1981). If the person was not a candidate at the time of the first prior use, he is entitled to equal opportunity only with respect to uses made during the week prior to his announcement of his candidacy. Letter to Joseph H. Clark (1962).

There is no obligation on the part of the station to inform all other candidates, for purposes of equal opportunity, that a particular candidate is appearing on the station. It is assumed, and in essence required, that candidates will be vigilant on their own behalf. The only exception to this rule would be where the candidate—or user—is the licensee of the station involved. Under these circumstances, the Commission has held that the licensee is under an obligation to inform his opponent of the specific days that the licensee would be using the station for his candidacy. Letter to Emerson Stone, Jr. (1964). Absent such special circumstances, however, a licensee is under no obligation to inform candidates of uses by other candidates.

8. Political Editorializing

The Commission's Rules (47 C.F.R. § 73.1930 (1981)) contain special provisions relating to editorializing by licensees. These rules provide that where a licensee in an editorial either endorses or opposes a legally qualified candidate, the licensee must transmit to the other candidates within 24 hours notification of the date and time of the editorial, a script or a tape and an offer of reasonable opportunity for the candidate or his spokesperson to respond. Where such editorials are broadcast within 72 hours of the election, the licensee shall transmit the material sufficiently far in advance of the broadcast to enable candidates to have a reasonable opportunity to present a reply. This obligation only arises with respect to endorsements of candidates. It does not apply to editorials on issues not involving candidates such as, for example, municipal bond issues and referenda.

Although the political editorializing rules remain on the books, they came under heavy attack during the controversy over the continued application of the "Fairness Doctrine" (see below) and the Commission was urged to repeal them. The Commission sidestepped doing so but in light of its revocation of the "Fairness Doctrine," there is some question as to the continued viability of these rules.

9. The "Zapple Doctrine"

Although the "equal time" rule applies only to appearances by candidates, the Commission has created what has been termed a "quasi-equal opportunity doctrine," which relates specifically to appearances by spokespersons for candidates. Because appearances by such spokespersons on behalf of candidate A are not "uses," they do not vest any "equal time" rights in A's legally qualified opponents. However, under the "Quasi–Equal Opportunities Doctrine" (known as the "Zapple Doctrine"), when a station sells time to supporters or spokespersons of a candidate who urge the candidate's election, discuss the campaign issues or criticize an opponent, the licensee must afford comparable time to the spokesperson for an opponent. Letter to Nicholas Zapple (1970). If the first group of spokespersons purchases time, then the opposing group can also purchase time if it wishes to respond. If the first group is given free time, then the second group must also be given free time. The Zapple Doctrine is, in essence, a type of hybrid between the "Equal Time Doctrine" and what was known as the "Fairness Doctrine." But although it contains elements of "Equal Time," there are, nevertheless, important distinctions. The Zapple Doctrine does not apply to all parties and all candidates. A station may choose not to provide "fringe candidates or minor parties" with broadcast time under Zapple. First Report, Docket No. 19260, 36 FCC 2d 40 (1972). The Zapple Doctrine does not apply outside of campaign periods. And the Equal Opportunities Doctrine is mutually exclusive with the Zapple Doctrine. If a legally qualified candidate appears in the broadcast with his supporters, then the broadcast is a use under the Equal Time Doctrine and the Zapple Doctrine does not apply.

For further elaboration of the now quite complex evolution of political broadcasting, see Political Primer (1984); Matter of Codification of the Commission's Political Programming Policies (1991).

B. THE "FAIRNESS DOCTRINE"

Perhaps nothing better illustrates the deregulatory thrust of recent Commissions than its repudiation of what was one of the fundamental pillars of broadcast regulation: The Fairness Doctrine.

The Fairness Doctrine arose out of a series of FCC rulings which for over two decades were thought to have been codified by Congress in its 1959 Amendments to Section 315(a) of the Communications Act. P.L. 86–274, 73 Stat. 557. The 1959 amendments refer to the obligation of a broadcaster "to operate in the public interest and to afford reasonable opportunity for the discussion of conflicting views on issues of public importance." For over two decades, this language was construed to be legislative shorthand which enacted into positive law a dual licensee obligation: (a) to devote a reasonable amount of broadcast time to the discussion of controversial issues, and (b) to do so fairly, i.e., to afford reasonable opportunity for the presentation of opposing view-points. That interpretation was upheld by the Supreme Court. Red Lion Broadcasting Co. v. Federal Communications Commission (1969). See also 47 C.F.R. § 73.1910.

The entire "Fairness Doctrine" area was thrown into confusion by a 1986 United States Court of Appeals decision, Telecommunications Research and Action Center (TRAC) v. FCC (1986), in which the court held that the Fairness Doctrine was not, in fact, codified in the 1959 amendments. The court held that, rather than being a congressionally mandated statutory obligation, the Fairness Doctrine was the Commission's creation and its enforcement was left by Congress to the Commission, which was free either to apply the doctrine or eliminate it. The court decision was in one sense not surprising. The Commission itself had begun to question its long-standing interpretation of the 1959 amendments and, in a 1985 "Notice of Inquiry," had stated its belief that the Fairness Doctrine, as traditionally interpreted, was no longer necessary and was constitutionally infirm because of the increase in the number of broadcast stations and the emergence of new communications technologies, which assure the public access to a variety of viewpoints. See Notice of Inquiry Concerning General Fairness Doctrine Obligations of Broadcast Licensees, 102 FCC 2d 143 (1985).

The confusion was compounded when, in response to a court mandate, Meredith Corp. v. FCC (1987), that the Commission specifically consider the constitutionality of the doctrine, the FCC overturned decades of practice to hold that, in its present view, the Fairness Doctrine "contravenes the

First Amendment and thereby disserves the public interest." In re Syracuse Peace Council, Memorandum Opinion and Order (1987) at paragraph 98. The Commission reasoned that the Fairness Doctrine both chills speech and is not narrowly tailored to achieve a substantial or compelling government interest. It relied upon the growth of the electronic media which, in its view, removed the "scarcity" rationale of Red Lion. The Commission acknowledged that there still exists "allocational scarcity;" there are still more applicants for stations than spectrum space to accommodate them. However, the Commission now feels that this allocational scarcity cannot alone justify controls upon program content, with their "chilling effect" on editorial discretion. In the Commission's view, the effect of enforcement of the Doctrine acts to eliminate rather than foster coverage of controversial issues. Because of the increasing multiplicity of media the Commission now believes that the free marketplace would better insure a diversity of opinion than would rules imposed by the federal government. The FCC's decision repealing the Fairness Doctrine was upheld by the courts as an action within the Commission's discretionary authority. See Syracuse Peace Council v. FCC (1989); Arkansas AFL–CIO v. FCC (1993).

The Commission's decision caused sharp reaction from Congress, which immediately passed legislation enacting the Fairness Doctrine, as traditionally understood, into law. This legislation was vetoed by President Reagan. There are periodic indications that Congress might legislatively reenact the doctrine. As yet, this has not happened.

The elimination of the Doctrine has led some to argue that the "public interest" standard is now devoid of substantive meaning. The Commission, however, took great pains in its Fairness Doctrine decision, and its Order on Reconsideration (Syracuse Peace Council (1988)) to separate the question of the desirability of the Fairness Doctrine from the issue of licensee responsibility under the "public interest" standard of the Act. The "public interest" standard requires that licensees broadcast programming in response to public issues in the community and failure to do so can raise serious questions at renewal time. The formal Fairness Doctrine may be outdated but the public interest obligations of broadcast licensees (which gave it life) still remains in force.

In this context (i.e., the general "public interest" standard), the charge is often made that a particular news program is "slanted" or "biased." Here, the Commission has held that direct intervention into the thought processes of broadcast newspersons could well have an extremely "chilling effect" in an area explicitly protected by the First Amendment. Absent some direct, extrinsic evidence of deliberate news slanting, the Commission will not entertain complaints concerning the "fairness" of news presentations. Hunger in America (1969); Central Intelligence Agency (1985).

1. Personal Attack Rule

The Personal Attack Rule (47 C.F.R. § 73.1920) was born as an aspect of the Fairness Doctrine. It related to the right of a person attacked by a broadcast licensee to gain access to the broadcast facility to defend himself or herself. The Personal Attack Rule is quite precise and specific. It holds that when, during the presentation of views on a controversial issue of public importance, an attack is made upon the honesty, character, integrity or like personal qualities of an identified person or group, the licensee shall, within a reasonable time and in no event later than one week after the attack, transmit to the person or group attacked (1) notification of the date, time and identification of the broadcast; (2) a script or tape of the attack; and (3) an offer of a reasonable opportunity to respond over the licensee's facilities. The rule does not apply to:

1. attacks on foreign groups or foreign public figures;

2. personal attacks made by legally qualified candidates, their authorized spokesmen, or persons associated with them; and

3. bona fide newscasts, bona fide news interviews or on-the-spot coverage of bona fide news events.

The rule only applies to a personal attack broadcast during the presentation of views on a controversial issue of public importance. Galloway v. FCC (1985). A person attacked at some other time will have no redress from the Commission but must look to the law of defamation for remedy. Straus Communications, Inc. v. Federal Communications Commission (1976). Moreover, the attack must be as to the person's honesty, character, integrity or like personal qualities if the rule is to be invoked. An attack, for example, upon a person alleging that a person's ideas are "stupid" would not be considered a personal attack for the purposes of the rule. Mrs. Frank Diesz (1971). The complainant must show that the person or group attacked was identified with sufficient specificity that the listening or viewing public would have been able to discern the specific person or group. Fairness in Media (M.M.B.1985). If the Personal Attack Rule applies, the person attacked has an absolute right to appear in his or her own defense. The station has no discretion to require that the defense be made by another person.

Paradoxically, the Commission did not overturn the Personal Attack Rule in its August, 1987 repudiation of the Fairness Doctrine. Because the Personal Attack Rule is really only an aspect of the Fairness Doctrine, there is little logic in continuing the rule once the doctrine has been abandoned. But as yet, the Commission has not repealed it.

C. OBSCENITY, INDECENCY AND VIOLENCE

Although not contained in the Communications Act of 1934, the Criminal Code of the United States

(18 U.S.C.A. § 1464) contains a specific prohibition against broadcast stations presenting any material which is "obscene," "indecent," or "profane." Rarely invoked, the "obscenity" section of the statute has been held constitutional because obscenity is not protected by the First Amendment. Illinois Citizens Committee for Broadcasting v. Federal Communications Commission (1974).

The standard used by courts with respect to "obscenity" on radio or television is that followed in the normal "obscenity" case, i.e., whether the material taken as a whole is patently offensive and appeals to an average person's prurient interest without serious literary, artistic, political, or scientific value when considered in connection with contemporary community standards. Miller v. California (1973). In practice, the courts have applied a more expansive concept of prurience to broadcasting than that applied to other forms of media. But there are few reported cases and the outlines of such standards for broadcasting have not yet been fully delineated. The courts have approved Commission prohibition of explicitly sexual programming where, during daytime hours, listeners freely discussed their sexual practices in a normal "disc jockey" format readily accessible to children. See Illinois Citizens Committee v. Federal Communications Commission, supra. Beyond this, the line between protected programming and "obscenity" is far from clear. In recent years, the Commission has evidenced a reluctance to become involved in obscenity determinations. While recognizing its concurrent jurisdiction to enforce federal anti-obscenity statutes, it has nevertheless determined to leave to local prosecutors the responsibility of identifying and prosecuting violators of such statutes. Video 44 (1986).

Not so with respect to "indecency." The "indecency" standard as it relates to broadcasting has also been upheld as a constitutionally proper exercise (under certain circumstances) of the state's police power. FCC v. Pacifica Foundation (1978). Significantly, the Supreme Court has allowed the Commission to give the concept of "indecency" a broader definition than that of "obscenity." Material that is "patently offensive," and either "sexual" or "excretory" may, if broadcast during times when children are presumed to be in the audience, be punishable even if not "obscene." The Pacifica Foundation case is instructive because the Court had previously defined the concept of "indecency" to be coextensive with "obscenity" if presented in books and films. Pacifica is an excellent example of the court applying different statutory and constitutional standards to broadcasting, primarily because of broadcasters' ease of access to children and the difficulty of parental supervision.

For almost a decade after Pacifica, the Commission, in practice, limited its definition of "indecency" to the specific "seven dirty words" at issue in that case. Between 1975 and 1987 no broadcasts were found actionable under this narrow interpretation. In 1987, however, the FCC gave notice that in the future it would apply the indecency standard more broadly and take action if such material was broadcast at a time of day when there is "reasonable risk" that children were in the audience. Unfortunately, the Commission gave no guidelines as to what would be considered "reasonable risk" and it warned broadcasters that adult programming after 10 p.m. (which it heretofore had suggested was safe) might not, in fact, be safe. See New Indecency Enforcement Standards To Be Applied to All Broadcast and Amateur Radio Licenses, 2 FCC Rcd. 2726 (1987). Such ambivalence invited a court test, which came immediately and which resulted in a remand by the court to the Commission. Although the appellate court rejected an attack on the Commission's definition of "indecency" on grounds of vagueness and overbreadth, nevertheless, it vacated action against two post–10 p.m. broadcasts on the grounds that the Commission was constitutionally required to create a "reasonable safe harbor" during which programming which might be indecent with respect to children could nevertheless be broadcast to adults. The court mandated the Commission to develop a precisely defined "safe harbor" after compiling an appropriate factual hearing record on which to do so. See Action for Children's Television v. FCC (1988).

Before the Commission could begin these "safe harbor" hearings, Congress intervened and passed a rider to an appropriations bill requiring the Commission to promulgate regulations to enforce the indecency provisions of the Criminal Code on a 24–hour–per–day basis. (Public Law No. 100–459,

§ 608, 102 Stat. 2228 (1988). Concluding that Congress had left it no discretion, the Commission thereupon promulgated a rule prohibiting all broadcasts of indecent material and enacting no safe harbor.

Another appeal immediately followed and the court again struck down the Commission's approach. The court noted that, in the interim, but after the 1988 Congressional rider, the Supreme Court (Sable Communications v. FCC (1989)) had invalidated a Commission total ban on indecent commercial telephone messages, holding that even indecent material can be proscribed only if government chooses the least restrictive means of so doing. Although the Constitution will allow regulation by the Commission of "indecent" programming, the Commission cannot prohibit it altogether. It must enact some type of safe harbor for adults, as the court has repeatedly held. See Action for Children's Television v. FCC (1991); Action for Children's Television v. FCC (1993). That judgment was vacated, however, when a petition for rehearing en banc was granted.

As of this writing, the Commission has not held the hearing on which to build a record supporting a "safe harbor" period. It has continued to fine stations for presenting indecent material during daylight hours when it can be legally presumed that there is a reasonable risk that children will be in the audience. See Evergreen Media Corp. (1991). Indeed, it has levied draconian fines on stations broadcasting the "Howard Stern" show during daytime hours. What the ultimate safe harbor will be remains unclear.

Another troublesome First Amendment area is that of televised violence. Some critics have long demanded government control over the depiction of violent events on television, but neither the Commission nor Congress has ever enacted such legislation. The Department of Justice has extended waivers of the antitrust laws to allow networks to cooperate in voluntary joint efforts to control violence. The difficulty with legislation is that it inevitably raises First Amendment questions of censorship, vagueness, over-breadth, and the "chilling effect" on creative talent and ideas. There also remains the nagging question of whether controls would have any real effect on violence (particularly when there is no such control imposed on movies or cable programming). The apparent rise in violent crime among youth (particularly random violent crime) in 1992 and 1993 led to a resurgence of the demand for such controls.

Spearheaded by Congressmen who threatened to enact legislation unless the television industry policed itself, these threats were taken quite seriously by the industry, particularly when they were endorsed by Attorney General Janet Reno. The industry has agreed to review the issue and take steps to voluntarily alleviate Congressional concern. Whether the industry can defuse the issue and, if not, whether legislation will ever be enacted (and whether it could withstand court review) remain open questions.

D. LOTTERIES

The federal criminal code generally prohibits any station from broadcasting any information concerning a lottery. 18 U.S.C.A. § 1304. Section 73.1211 of the Commission's rules essentially follows this criminal code section. A lottery is any game or contest which contains the elements of prize, chance and "consideration." These elements are construed in terms of a type of federal common law of lotteries followed by the Federal Communications Commission, the Post Office Department and the Department of Justice. See Federal Communications Commission v. American Broadcasting Co. (1954). This area of the law can become quite complex particularly in determining whether "consideration" is present. The federal common law of "consideration" means a monetary or other detriment to the participant in the contest rather than merely a benefit to the contest operator. For example, the requirement of the listener mailing in a post card to a station would not be considered "consideration," even though the station may thereby "benefit" by obtaining a list of members of its audience or by the contest enlarging the station's audience. Federal Communications Commission v. American Broadcasting Co., supra; cf. Caples Co. v. Federal Communications Commission (1957).

There are two exceptions to the general lottery ban. A station is now allowed to broadcast any information about a state authorized lottery so long

as the station is located in a state which has its own
official lottery.   It can also broadcast advertisements of lotteries conducted by non-profit organizations or by commercial organizations using lotteries
as an ancillary promotional activity.   18 U.S.C.A.
§ 1307, 47 C.F.R. § 73.1211(c)(1).   Additionally, a
station may broadcast information concerning a
fishing contest if such contest is not conducted for
profit.   18   U.S.C.A.   § 1305;   47   C.F.R.   § 73.-
1211(c)(2).

The "state-authorized lottery" exception raises
an interesting dilemma: A station in a state which
does not allow state lotteries cannot broadcast commercials for a legal lottery run by an adjacent state,
while a station in the adjacent state can broadcast
lottery information into the state that has no legal
lottery.   This was covered by the Supreme Court in
United States v. Edge Broadcasting Co. (1993), discussed in Chapter IX, pp. 303–304.

E.   PRIME TIME ACCESS RULE
AND THE "FINSYN" RULE

The Commission, over the years, has evolved a
series of policies which have specific impact upon
the material presented by a network affiliated
broadcast station.   Networks are, generally speaking, organizations which have been created for the
purpose of producing and distributing programming
to individual stations and also to act as advertising
clearance centers for all network affiliated stations.
Although networks can (and do) act as licensees of

individual stations, the networks themselves are not licensed by the Commission and the Commission has no power directly to regulate their operations. But the Commission can and does indirectly regulate the networks through its power over the licenses of individual stations. This regulation is apparent in the so-called "Network Rules" which prohibit any individual station from entering into contracts with networks which contain certain provisions that the Commission finds offensive to the public interest. 47 C.F.R. §§ 73.132 (AM radio), 73.232 (FM radio), and 73.658 (television) (1981). These prohibitions forbid network contract clauses that would prevent the licensee from broadcasting the programs of any other network, or that would prevent another station in the affiliate's area from broadcasting a network program if the affiliate declines to broadcast it. The Rules also require that television network affiliation terms be no longer than two years (§ 73.658(c)), and that the television affiliate be granted the right to reject network programs that it believes unsatisfactory (§ 73.658(e)).

Among the most important of these rules are provisions covering television prime time programming. The "Prime Time Access Rules" reflect a concern with the lack of local programming activity among network affiliates. They provide (§ 73.658(k)) that television stations owned by or affiliated with a national television network in the 50 largest television markets shall devote during the four hours of prime time (7–11 p.m. Eastern Time and Pacific Time and 6–10 p.m. Central Time

and Mountain Time) no more than three hours to
the presentation of programs from a national network, including programs that formerly had been
presented on national networks. The only exception is that certain categories of programs need not
be counted toward the three-hour limitation such as
(1) programs designed for children, public affairs
programs or documentary programs; (2) special
news programs and political broadcasts; (3) regular
network news broadcasts up to one-half hour when
immediately adjacent to a full hour of locally produced news programming; and (4) run-overs of
sporting events and network broadcasts of national
sports events or other programs of a special nature.
In practical effect, the Prime Time Access Rule
means that three hours of the four-hour-prime time
period will be devoted to network entertainment
programs, one-half hour will be devoted to network
news programming and the remaining one-half
hour will consist of either non-network produced
entertainment programs or special documentary or
public affairs features. The Prime Time Access
Rule represents as definite a restriction on program
content as the courts have countenanced. It has
been justified as appropriate regulation in the public interest and not program censorship otherwise
prohibited by Section 326 of the Act. Mt. Mansfield
Television, Inc. v. Federal Communications Commission (1971).

In 1970, the FCC placed significant restrictions
on the ability of the then established television
networks (ABC, CBS, and NBC) to (a) own televi-

sion programming produced (or co-produced) by others and (b) engage in the business of "syndication" (the sale of programming exhibition rights to television stations). These restrictions were intended to limit network control of television programming generally and thereby encourage the development of independent program producers. The FCC believed that program diversity would be better served by fostering the growth of independent producing entities (not controlled by the networks) who would grant networks only the exhibition rights to prime-time entertainment programs, reserving to the independent producers the rights to sell exhibition rights to others. Because of the networks' almost monopolistic power to control access to the nationwide television audience, it was feared that networks could dominate the production and distribution end of television simply by demanding ownership and syndication rights in programs produced by independents, using as a lever the networks' power to act as gatekeeper. Accordingly, the FCC adopted rules which effectively froze the networks out of the prime time entertainment program production business and out of the (even more lucrative) syndication business. This significant restriction of network power was also allowed by the courts as appropriate economic regulation in Mt. Mansfield, supra, and was incorporated into anti-trust consent decrees entered into by the networks and the Department of Justice. The Commission's attempt to create production diversity was successful. The ensuing decades saw the growth of program producing units independent of network control, based primarily in the Hollywood motion picture studios. Program syndication by the independent producers to non-network-owned stations grew. At the same time, however, the growth of non-network programming outlets (primarily cable systems and cable programming networks) loosened the networks' power to act as gatekeeper to the national television audience (from 1970 to 1992 the networks' share of the listening audience decreased from over 90% to less than 60%).

The networks bitterly fought to repeal the financial interest and syndication restrictions and in 1991, the Commission relaxed (although it did not repeal) these Rules. Report and Order, 6 FCC Rcd 3094, as modified at 7 FCC Rcd 345 (1991). The FCC's relaxation order proved unpersuasive to the Court of Appeals for the Seventh Circuit, which remanded the case for a fuller explanation as to why the FCC rejected certain of the networks' arguments and why its limited 1991 relaxation satisfied the Commission's goals of program and outlet diversity. Schurz Communications v. FCC (1992). The Commission thereupon relaxed these rules still further (Second Report and Order, 8 FCC Rcd 3282, reconsidered at 8 FCC Rcd 8270 (1993)), although still retaining a remnant of them.

The result of the Commission's relaxed restrictions is to allow, to a significant extent, the re-entry of the networks into the prime-time television entertainment programming production and syndication business, thus allowing the production and distribution arms of the industry to come into closer common control. There are no longer any restrictions on networks holding a financial interest in any type of network television programming (whether or not the network produced or co-produced the program) or owning syndicated rights in such network programming. The only restriction with respect to network programming is that even if the networks own syndication rights to prime-time entertainment network programming, their syndication role must be "passive." Networks are prohibited from actively being the syndication agent. The active role must be played by an independent party, the reason being the possibility that if allowed to actively syndicate, the network still might improperly use its power as a network (which even if diminished is still considerable) to disadvantage competing or non-network affiliated stations.

Networks are also prohibited from owning financial interests or syndication rights for *non-network* first-run programs (such as the Oprah Winfrey Show) unless the network itself produced the program solely in-house and even here the networks' syndication role must be passive. This is the FCC's last remaining effort to separate production from distribution. Even these restrictions appear destined to disappear. The restrictions will be reviewed and will sunset in 1995 unless the Commission affirmatively finds that they should be continued. F.R. §§ 73.659–73.662.

F. SPONSORSHIP IDENTIFICATION RULES: "ANTI–PAYOLA" AND "ANTI–PLUGOLA" REQUIREMENTS

Congress and the Commission have expressed concern that the airwaves not be used by "hidden persuaders." Although most sponsors purchase time specifically to identify themselves and/or their products, there are occasions when persons wish to use programming time anonymously to further their own purposes. Such use can occur in a number of ways. Record promoters may offer money to disc jockeys to induce them to play their records ("payola") or to advertise certain activities ("plugola") without the public being aware that such material is being broadcast for pay. Other examples include broadcasting paid political matter or material concerning controversial issues without identifying the person or group presenting the material.

Because it is believed important that the audience be aware of the person paying the piper, Section 507 of the Communications Act and Section 73.1212 of the Commission's Rules stipulate that any person who pays or receives money or other valuable consideration for including any material as part of programming to be broadcast over a station must report that transaction to the licensee or licensees over whose facilities the program is aired. In turn, under Section 317 of the Act and Section 73.1212 of the Rules, the licensee is required to identify over the air, clearly and concisely, the person making the payment, and the fact that payment was made.

The sponsorship identification rules have caused some particular anomalies in the public broadcasting field where commercial sponsorship, per se, is prohibited, while identification of "sponsors" is required by Section 317 of the Act. The Commission has resolved this anomaly by holding that a public broadcaster is required to identify the name of a donor, and may even refer to the donor's product or service, but may not "promote" the product or service in the sense of urging viewers to purchase it. See Educational Broadcasting Stations (Promotional Announcements) (1982); Educational Broadcasting Stations (1984). Admittedly, the line between "identifying" and "promoting" becomes rather thin. The Commission has recently become more active in policing the sponsor identification rules with respect to public broadcast stations and has fined a number of them for engaging in what clearly is "commercial" promotional matter rather than merely identification of public broadcast benefactors.

Section 73.1212(d) of the Rules also requires that if any material or service is given to a station as an inducement to use such material or service in the broadcast of political matters or during the discussion of controversial issues of public importance, an announcement must be made indicating the material or service that was received by the station and identifying the person or entity which provided that material or service.

G. CONTESTS

Both Congress and the Commission have adopted standards of conduct governing broadcast contests. Section 73.1216 of the Rules mandates that a station must fully and accurately disclose the material terms of any contest which the station presents and the contest must be conducted in the manner advertised. The material terms include, inter alia, entry qualifications, eligibility restrictions, deadline dates, prize information, basis for valuation of prizes and tie-breaking procedures.

Section 508 of the Communications Act provides that, in contests of "intellectual knowledge, intellectual skill or chance," it is illegal to supply any contestant with any special or secret assistance, to persuade or intimidate a contestant from refraining from using his knowledge or skill or to engage in any prearrangement or predetermination of the outcome.

H. PUBLIC BROADCASTING

There is one striking exception to the general rule that American broadcasting follows the marketplace wherever possible. The exception is the growth and development of what has come to be known as "Public Broadcasting," i.e., a wide-ranging coalition of nonprofit (both private and governmental) broadcast stations operated by state governments, private and state colleges, private nonprofit organizations, religious groups, etc. The single unifying factor in this diverse group (other than their non-profit status) is their mission which is, in large part, to broadcast material which would *not* ordinarily be demanded by the commercial marketplace. These stations are, in effect, programmed for specialized audiences. They were created precisely to fill the lacunae inevitably left by mass market tastes.

That such a system exists is due to the foresight of the Congressmen and Commissioners who specifically fought for and ultimately adopted a policy of reserving from the commercial allocation system certain frequencies (both radio and television) specifically to be used by noncommercial entities for "educational" uses. Although at first limited to educational licensees (colleges, high schools, state university systems, etc.) these were later joined by other types of nonprofit licensees. The public broadcasting base evolved beyond televised classrooms and sunrise semesters to a whole range of cultural programming, including operas, literary presentations, concerts, "how to" shows, plays, nature documentaries and ultimately into the diverse public broadcasting network known as PBS.

The basic Public Broadcasting structure is quite simple: stations operating on the frequencies reserved for noncommercial use must be licensed only to nonprofit entities and cannot broadcast "commercials" promoting or advertising goods and services. The stations are to be supported not through the purchase of specific portions of time by commercial entities in return for advertising the goods and services of those entities, but instead, by:

(a) public funding through donations by private individuals and businesses;

(b) public funding through government sources; and

(c) sale of programming and related materials to the public (such as, for example, the sale of the cassettes of the popular "Civil War" series).

Although the line between "identification of donations by commercial businesses" and "the promotion of goods and services by commercial announcements" can become very blurred, nevertheless, the difference between commercial broadcasting stations and public broadcasting stations is usually readily apparent to viewers.

Aside from the reservation of operating frequencies for noncommercial use, the principal federal governmental role in Public Broadcasting is twofold:

a.   Through the Department of Commerce, the Federal Government has established a matching grant program (not subject to judicial review) under which the Federal Government will give matching grants (up to 75%) to noncommercial stations for the purpose of purchasing equipment and for other capital costs; and

b.   Making available, through the Corporation for Public Broadcasting, significant funds to public stations and networks for the production and distribution of programming to be presented on public broadcasting stations.

The Corporation for Public Broadcasting is a private, nonstock corporation chartered by the federal government, all of whose Board of Directors are appointed by the President. The Corporation, however, is not a government agency in the same sense as the FCC or FTC. It receives its funding through government grants and then proceeds to carry out its own grant programs as would any other private foundation or endowment. It operates under the rules established in its enabling statute (47 U.S.C.A. §§ 396–399B) which requires, inter alia, that grants shall be made available "with strict adherence to objectivity and balance in all programs or series of programs of a controversial nature" (47 U.S.C.A. § 399(g)(1)(A). But the FCC has no jurisdiction or authority to enforce the statutory rules governing the Corporation. Nor does any member of the public have the power to do so; the Public Broadcasting Act creating the Corporation did not confer a private right of action upon any private group or individual. See Network Project v. Corporation of Public Broadcasting (1977). The only governmental body overseeing the Corporation's work is Congress which, of course, has the power to revise or amend the Corporation's enabling statute.

The statutory provision concerning the need for "objectivity and balance" and a corresponding statutory provision (47 U.S.C.A. § 399) that no public broadcasting station may support or oppose any candidate for public office, illustrates the tension

between the need for government funding on the
one hand and the First Amendment on the other.
Ordinarily, he who pays the piper calls the tune.
But the First Amendment's prohibition against government regulation of the media places severe restrictions on the government-payor. Where does
illegal government action end and appropriate government oversight of public funding begin? This
vexing question comes up in many guises (such as,
for example in the National Endowments for the
Arts and Humanities) and it arose in the Public
Broadcasting field in Section 399 of the Communications Act. As originally drafted, Section 399 prohibited public broadcasting stations from engaging
in "editorializing" or in supporting or opposing any
candidate for public office. The prohibition against
"editorializing" was attacked on First Amendment
grounds and struck down as unconstitutional by the
Supreme Court in FCC v. League of Women Voters
of California (1984). The Court, by a 5–4 margin,
held that the broad ban on editorializing by stations
merely because they receive Corporation for Public
Broadcasting funds was a content-based restriction
going beyond anything necessary to protect against
the risk of undue governmental interference into
public affairs. Interestingly, however, the prohibition against endorsing (as distinct from editorializing in favor of) candidates for public office still
stands; it was not specifically at issue in the League
of Women Voters case. And a strong dissent by
Justice (now Chief Justice) Rehnquist argued that
stations which take government funding can legiti-

mately be required to conform to the restrictions placed by Congress upon that funding, even with respect to editorializing, a position which, although not in the majority in 1984, nevertheless ultimately became the law with respect to federal funding for family planning clinics as regards their abortion counseling. See Rust v. Sullivan (1991).

It must be recognized, of course, that in one sense Congress has the ultimate power of censorship. It can cut off CPB funding completely or at least reduce it significantly. Just such an attack on CPB funding was recently mounted by some who argued that in times of budget deficits there is simply no warrant to fund public broadcast programming rather than other more pressing governmental needs. The attempt was defeated by the full Congress, a significant demonstration that public funding of public broadcasting programming is indeed popular. The visionaries who saw a public need and desire for some nonmarket-driven programming appear to have been vindicated.

CHAPTER XII

CABLE AND NEW TECHNOLOGIES

A. TELEVISION BY CABLE

CATV (cable television) arose because of inherent
limitations in commercial television. Television is
merely the wireless transmission of visual and aural
material over the air. Because of its physical characteristics, the distance that the television signal
can travel over the air is limited. This fact, together with the Commission's television allocation policy whereby only a limited number of frequencies
were assigned to designated cities throughout the
country, posed significant reception problems for
many residents of outlying areas, or areas on the
fringe of larger cities. The problem was exacerbated by the fact that even some of the larger cities to
which frequencies were assigned were only assigned
three VHF channels, and some only two; thus there
were large areas of the country that could receive
no more than two or, at most, three signals. Because television signals only travel a line-of-sight
path, there were some communities located in
mountainous terrain that could not even obtain
adequate reception from the two or three stations
that they theoretically should have been able to
receive over the air.

The solution to the problem for many of these communities was to erect extremely tall receiving towers at the highest point in the area to pick up the off-the-air signals and then retransmit the signals over wires run from the tower to various homes (subscribers). Typically, the home subscriber would pay a one-time installation fee for the wiring and a monthly fee for the service.

Although the original CATV systems were intended mainly to fill in the blanks within stations' normal coverage areas, it soon became apparent that CATV could also bring in service from distant cities which, under the Commission's allocation plan, were never intended to render service to that particular cable community. Thus, for example, a city such as Kingston, New York, located 90 miles from New York City, was never intended by the Commission to receive off-the-air service from the New York City television stations; the Commission intended Kingston to be served by the closer Albany, New York, facilities. However, cable television could bring in all of the New York stations, an obvious benefit to the residents of Kingston, but also a possible economic detriment to the Albany station, which could have its "natural audience" in Kingston fragmented. Moreover, CATV system operators could offer other communications services, including programming services such as sports events and feature films. This latter capability caused many to begin referring to CATV as "cable television," implying that the new service was much more than merely a community antenna.

Cable television also posed legal problems:

(a) Was cable television subject to FCC jurisdiction? It was not in existence when the Communications Act was passed, and might be considered merely a receiving rather than a transmitting unit, thus not "broadcasting."

(b) If the Commission did have jurisdiction, did the federal government preempt the field of regulation so that state or local governmental bodies were deprived of jurisdiction over such systems? This question was particularly important since cable television systems required local construction of wire lines and thus had a significant effect on the local citizenry;

(c) If jurisdiction was to be shared between a federal and local agency, how should the power to regulate cable be allocated?

(d) How was the Commission to reconcile the new technology of cable and its potential for carrying distant signals over the entire country with the existing Commission policy of station allocation?

(e) How did cable television comport with the copyright laws?

1. Jurisdiction

a. History

At first, the Commission refused to take jurisdiction over cable on the grounds that its power to do so was in question and that it did not feel the impact of cable television at the time was sufficient to invoke discretionary jurisdiction. Frontier Broadcasting Co. v. Collier (1958). In 1966, the Commission changed course and adopted the first general federal regulation of cable systems, asserting that some overall comprehensive federal regulation was necessary to meet the Commission's responsibility to promote, maintain, and supervise an effective television service throughout the country. Second Report and Order, 2 FCC 2d 725 (1966). The Commission's power to assert jurisdiction under its general grant of power from Congress and in the absence of specific legislation concerning cable television was affirmed by the Supreme Court in United States v. Southwestern Cable Co. (1968). The Commission's jurisdiction was limited, however, "to that reasonably ancillary to the effective performance of the Commission's various responsibilities for the regulation of television broadcasting."

Some clarification of what the Court meant by reasonably ancillary came in United States v. Midwest Video Corp. (1972) when, by a 5–4 vote, the Court upheld regulations that required specified cable systems to originate local programming. But the Chief Justice (who voted with the majority) took pains to point out that in making such a requirement the Commission appeared to be reaching the limits of its authority under the Communications Act. Actually, the Commission had voluntarily stepped back from its position during the course of the Midwest litigation. It suspended the mandatory program origination rule and never reinstated it.

The Chief Justice's remarks were prophetic. The mandatory program origination rules appear to have been the high water mark of Commission cable regulation. Not long thereafter, the court of appeals struck down Commission rules restricting the ability of cablevision systems to present certain feature films and sports programs, holding that such regulation was beyond the power of the Commission because it was not "reasonably ancillary" to the Commission's long-term regulatory goals and responsibilities. Home Box Office, Inc. v. FCC (1977). And in 1979, the Supreme Court struck down the Commission's rules requiring cablevision systems to offer separate channels for public, educational and government use ("PEG channels"), as well as at least one channel available on a lease basis for commercial use ("leased access channels"), on the grounds that these provisions also went beyond the Commission's regulatory powers. FCC v. Midwest Video Corp. (Midwest Video II) (1979).

In cable, unlike in broadcasting, the Commission accepted a bifurcated jurisdictional scheme that also allowed state and local authorities regulatory authority over cable. Under this scheme state or local authorities issued the franchise or license for the specific cable operator, imposing whatever obligations they thought necessary. For example, access channel requirements, similar to those held beyond the Commission's jurisdiction in Midwest Video II, were common in franchising agreements. The franchise agreements were, however, subject to certain minimal FCC limitations, such as a ceiling of 5% of gross revenues on franchise fees.

By the early 1980s, there was a great deal of controversy over the jurisdictional scheme that had developed. Cable operators felt that some franchising authorities were making excessive demands. Of even greater concern was the question of renewal. With no renewal standards or guidelines and no specific requirement of renewal expectancy, cable operators were worried about what would happen when initial franchise agreements expired.

Meanwhile, the FCC was becoming more aggressive in asserting its jurisdiction at the expense of the state and local authorities. For example, the Commission preempted rate regulation of premium cable services (pay services such as HBO). The preemption of franchising requirements for SMATV was seen as a foreshadowing of even more preemption in the cable area. See New York State Commission on Cable Television v. FCC (1984).

Then in 1984, the FCC received strong support for its authority to preempt state and local regulation of cable in Capital Cities Cable, Inc. v. Crisp (1984) (application of Oklahoma ban on alcoholic beverage advertising to out-of-state signals carried on Oklahoma cable systems held preempted by FCC signal carriage regulations). Further limitations on state and municipal franchising authority seemed inevitable.

b. *The Cable Communications Policy Act of 1984*

Cable operators, represented by the National Cable Television Association (NCTA), and state and local authorities, represented by the National League of Cities (NLC), sought legislative relief. Eventually a compromise bill was drafted and, in late 1984, enacted into law as the Cable Communications Policy Act of 1984 (P.L. 98–549, 47 U.S.C.A. § 151 et seq.).

The 1984 Cable Act created Title VI of the Communications Act, 47 U.S.C.A. §§ 521–559, setting explicit rules for cable that clearly delineated the jurisdictional division between the FCC and state and local authorities. Franchising authority still rested with state and local authorities. In addition, they were given explicit authority to require PEG channels. In contrast, leased access channels were mandated by the Act itself, with the number of leased access channels dependent on the overall number of channels provided by the cable system. Franchise authorities could not, however, regulate cable as a common carrier, nor could they require specific video programming services. Specific guidelines for franchise renewal were set out, giving extensive protection to the incumbent franchisee. There were also guidelines for franchise modifications that permitted an operator to appeal the denial of requests for modification.

c. *The Cable Television Consumer Protection and Competition Act of 1992*

Cable flourished under this new regulatory structure. By 1992, cable service was available to 96 percent of the nation's homes. Approximately 60 percent subscribed to cable. However, consumer complaints regarding both rates and service had also increased dramatically. Responding to these complaints, Congress passed the Cable Television Consumer Protection and Competition Act of 1992. P.L.102–385, 47 U.S.C.A. § 151 et seq.

Whereas the 1984 Cable Act could be viewed as cable-friendly, the 1992 Cable Act was anything but. It required rate regulation for the vast majority of cable systems, imposed several measures designed to improve the competitive position of broadcast television stations, and directed the FCC to develop mandatory customer service standards for cable systems. It also gave the FCC greater authority to oversee state and local regulation.

2. Cable System Ownership

At the heart of all cable regulation is the government's ability to choose who will be permitted to offer cable television service. As previously noted, this is subject to a bifurcated jurisdictional scheme. State and local authorities award cable franchises subject to federal limitations. These limitations include concentration rules and restrictions on the demands franchising authorities can make on franchisees. For example, franchising authorities are not permitted to establish requirements for video programming or other information services. (47 U.S.C.A. § 544). Both initial franchising proceedings (47 U.S.C.A. § 541) and renewal (47 U.S.C.A. § 546) proceedings must conform to procedures set out in the Communications Act. Cable companies are prohibited from selling cable systems within 36 months of their acquisition. (47 U.S.C.A. § 617).

Finally, the Communications Act imposes some requirements of its own. For example, § 612 requires each cable system with 36 or more channels to set aside a percentage of its channels for commercial lease. The percentage depends on the total number of channels available on the system (See 47 U.S.C.A. § 541).

a. *Franchising*

Among the more common provisions in cable franchise agreements are requirements that the franchisee make service available to all homes in the franchise area ("universal service") and that they install state-of-the-art technology. Franchising authorities will usually require cable operators to designate a portion of their channel capacity for public, educational and governmental use. Other than the right to prohibit programming that is obscene or otherwise unprotected by the U.S. Constitution, cable operators have no editorial control over these "PEG" channels.

Prior to the 1992 Act, most franchising authorities awarded only one franchise in any given area. Cable companies were forced to bid against each other for what was essentially de facto monopoly.

(The 1992 Act prohibits the award of exclusive franchises.) This allowed the franchising authorities to extract the maximum in terms of service and equipment. For many years cable companies were loath to challenge franchising regulations—probably because of fear that such an action would damage the challenging company's chances of obtaining the franchise. Then in 1984 Preferred Communications Inc. sought to bypass the City of Los Angeles' franchising regulations by asking various utility companies to provide space on their poles for the express purpose of constructing a cable system. The companies refused because Preferred had not obtained a cable franchise from the city.

Preferred then brought an action seeking to have the cable franchising regulations declared unconstitutional under the First and Fourteenth Amendments. Los Angeles' successful motion to dismiss for failure to state a claim upon which relief could be granted was appealed by Preferred. In a strongly worded opinion, the court of appeals reversed the district court's grant of the motion to dismiss. Preferred Communications, Inc. v. City of Los Angeles (1985).

Although the Supreme Court affirmed the appellate court's decision, it did so on very narrow grounds. Justice Rehnquist's majority opinion stated that the activities engaged in by cable television companies clearly implicated First Amendment activities but then noted, consistent with the Court's new hierarchical approach to the Amendment, that "[E]ven protected speech is not equally permissible in all places and at all times." He also noted that the construction and operation of a cable television franchise involved a mixture of speech and conduct, thus presenting special questions regarding the right of the state to regulate the non-speech elements involved. The Court was unwilling to decide the appropriate degree of First Amendment protection to be afforded cable without the more complete factual record that an actual trial could provide. Justice Blackmun concurred to emphasize that the proper First Amendment standard for cable was still undetermined. City of Los Angeles v. Preferred Communications, Inc. (1986).

Although it may be dangerous to draw too many conclusions from what is really a very limited opinion, it appeared as though the Court was leaning toward granting cable less protection under the First Amendment than that enjoyed by the print media. Rehnquist's opinion also suggested that the Court might adopt the O'Brien test. This approach was first used by the United States Circuit Court of Appeals for the District of Columbia in Home Box Office, Inc. v. FCC (1977). HBO had challenged a series of regulations prohibiting cable systems from presenting certain film or sports presentations which were available on "off-the-air" or "free" television. In addition to finding the rules both beyond the FCC's jurisdiction and arbitrary and capricious, the court found them unconstitutional. The court held that Red Lion was inapplicable because cable was not limited by the physical scarcity of the electromagnetic spectrum. Viewing the anti-siphoning rules as regulation where the restriction on speech was incidental to the purpose of the regulation, the court chose to apply the O'Brien test: "If such regulations 'further an important or substantial government interest; ... and if the incidental restriction in alleged First Amendment freedoms is no greater than is essential to the furtherance of that interest,' then the regulations are valid." See United States v. O'Brien (1968). Under this test the rules were found to be grossly overbroad.

Meanwhile, without a clear Supreme Court holding on the First Amendment status of cable, lower courts continued to produce inconsistent holdings on this issue. One district court judge rejected a First Amendment attack on the franchise fee and access channel provisions of a franchise agreement, applying the standard for broadcasting set out in Red Lion. "In its effort to preserve an uninhibited marketplace of ideas, government is entrusted with protecting the First Amendment rights of cable television viewers." Erie Telecommunications, Inc. v. City of Erie (1987).

A different approach was taken by the court of appeals in Chicago Cable Communications v. Chicago Cable Commission (1989). In determining the constitutionality of a requirement that the cable system supply 4 ½ hours per week of local programming, the court applied the O'Brien test. Because localism was a substantial government interest and the 4 ½ hours per week requirement an incidental burden, the court found the requirement constitutional. The court also seemed influenced by the natural monopoly characteristics of cable.

Still other courts used a mix of O'Brien and strict scrutiny analysis. For example, in the Preferred remand the court set up two categories of franchise requirements. The O'Brien test was applied to those requirements imposing an incidental burden on speech. These included awarding a de facto exclusive franchise, prohibiting transfer of the franchise without the city's consent and requiring universal service. Strict scrutiny was applied to restrictions "intended to curtail expression." Among these were mandatory PEG channels and a state-of-the-art technology requirement. Preferred Communications, Inc. v. City of Los Angeles (1990). The court of appeals upheld the lower court's finding that de facto exclusive franchising violates the First Amendment.

b. Concentration Rules

Both the 1984 Cable Act and the 1992 Cable Act imposed restrictions on cable ownership. Earlier Commission rules prohibiting a television broadcast licensee from owning a cable system within its signal coverage area or a common carrier from owning one within its telephone service area were codified in the 1984 Cable Act. Network ownership of cable systems was also prohibited, although television network ownership of cable networks is not. For example, ABC is a part owner of ESPN. At the same time state ownership restrictions were preempted.

A few years later, the FCC decided to relax both the network-cable and telephone-cable crossownership rules. The new network-cable crossownership rules permit television networks to own cable systems. However, a television network's cable systems cannot exceed 10 percent of the homes passed by cable nationwide or 50 percent of the homes passed by cable within any ADI. Television networks are still prohibited from merging with or investing in major MSOs. Common Ownership of Cable Television Systems and National Television Networks (1992).

Telephone companies are now authorized to transmit video programming on a common-carrier basis. The new "video-dialtone" rules still prohibit telephone companies from exercising editorial control of video programming carried under these rules. Transmission capacity must be offered on a non-discriminatory basis. Neither the telephone company carrying programming pursuant to the video dialtone rules nor the customer supplying the programming is subject to franchising requirements. Telephone–Cable Cross–Ownership (1992). The FCC's decision was affirmed on appeal. NCTA v. FCC (1994).

In 1993 a U.S. District Court held that the crossownership rules were unconstitutional as applied to one of the regional Bell operating companies. Chesapeake and Potomac Telephone Company of Virginia v. United States (1993). Applying an O'Brien analysis, the court addressed two asserted government interests: "promoting competition in the video programming market and preserving diversity in the ownership of communications media." The court quickly rejected the first interest because the crossownership prohibition reduced the number of outlets through which programming could be transmitted and thus, reduced rather than enhanced competition in the video programming market.

With regard to the second asserted interest, the court found that given the FCC's video dialtone decision, the telephone companies were already in a position to monopolize the video transmission market. Thus, there was not a reasonable fit between the asserted government interest and the means chosen to advance that interest.

c. *Rate Regulation*

As noted previously one of the first areas of regulation preempted by the FCC was rate regulation of premium cable channels. The 1984 Cable Act went further and prohibited rate regulation except where there was a lack of effective competition. Even where there was a lack of effective competition only basic cable rates could be regulated.

The FCC initially defined effective competition as the presence in the market of at least three off-the-air television signals. However, the circuit court found the definition arbitrary and capricious. American Civil Liberties Union v. FCC (1987).

On remand, the FCC defined effective competition as the availability of three or more off-air signals in all geographic areas served by the cable system. The three signals did not have to be the same ones throughout the cable system's service area. Cable Communications Policy Act Rules (Signal Availability Standard), 3 FCC Rcd. 2617 (1988). Under this definition less than 4 percent of all cable systems were subject to rate regulation.

Three years later the FCC changed the definition again. Effective competition required meeting one of two alternative conditions. The first was the availability of six off-air signals throughout the entire area served by the cable system. The second was the presence of an independently owned, competing multichannel video service available to a minimum of 50 percent and subscribed to by a minimum of 10 percent of the homes in the cable system's area. Effective Competition, 6 FCC Rcd. 4545 (1991).

Despite the new definition, complaints about unreasonable cable rates continued, prompting Congress to enact a much more stringent system of rate regulation as part of the 1992 Cable Act. As was the case with the 1984 Cable Act, cable systems subject to effective competition are exempt from rate regulation. Effective competition is defined as meeting one of three conditions. The first is "fewer than 30 percent of the households in the franchise area subscribe to the cable service of a cable system." The second is that the franchise area must be "served by at least two unaffiliated multichannel video programming distributors each of which offers comparable video programming to at least 50 percent of the households in the franchise area; and the number of households subscribing to programming services offered by multichannel video programming distributors other than the largest multichannel video programming distributor exceeds 15 percent of the households in the franchise area." The third is that "a multichannel video programming distributor operated by the franchising authority for that franchise area offers video programming to at least 50 percent of the households in that franchise area." 47 U.S.C.A. § 543.

Section 623 of the Act directed the Commission to issue regulations ensuring that rates for basic cable on systems not subject to effective competition are reasonable. The actual regulation is to be done by franchising authorities, unless a franchising authority does not do this consistent with the FCC's regulations. In those cases the FCC can claim jurisdiction and regulate rates for systems franchised by that authority. However, the FCC has decided that where a franchising authority opts not to regulate (as opposed to regulating improperly) the FCC will not claim jurisdiction.

In April 1993, the Commission adopted a series of regulations governing cable rates. These regulations established three classes of rates—basic, premium and other. For basic cable the FCC created a table of benchmarks "based on the average September 30, 1992 rates of systems subject to effective competition." Basic rates that are below the applicable benchmark are to be presumed reasonable. Basic rates that exceed the benchmark must be reduced by 10 percent or to the benchmark, whichever is higher. Once these initial rates are set, they become subject to a price cap which will be adjusted annually. Cable Rate Regulation, 8 FCC Rcd. 5631 (1993).

Premium channels, services offered on a per-channel or per-program basis, are not subject to this provision. Finally, the FCC was required by the 1992 Cable Act to establish a system for resolving complaints about other cable rates, i.e., those that are neither basic or premium. The Commission announced it would use the same table of benchmarks to determine the reasonableness of these rates. However, the FCC must receive a complaint from a subscriber before it starts this process.

When the Commission's rate regulations took effect, many cable customers found that the expected reduction in their rates did not materialize. In response to public outcry and Congressional pressure, the Commission revised its table of benchmarks. As of May 15, 1994, cable systems not subject to effective competition had to set their rates so that their regulated revenues did not exceed their September 30, 1992 revenues, reduced by 17 percent, as opposed to the 10 percent reduction imposed by the Commission's original rate regulation.

Section 623 also prohibits cable operators from requiring subscription to any tier above the basic tier as a condition of receiving programming offered on a per-channel or per-program basis. However, systems that cannot comply due to technical limitations are exempted until either the limitation is eliminated or October 5, 2002, whichever comes first.

3. Copyright Problems

One of the earliest legal problems to be faced with the advent of cable television was whether a cable system, by the act of receiving a program broadcast over the air and then sending the program by wire to various subscribers, was undertaking a "performance for profit," thereupon subjecting itself to liability either to the television station whose program it was re-transmitting, or to the copyright holders of the work being presented on the station. It was argued by the cable interests that cable systems were not "performing" in the sense contemplated by the copyright laws since they were merely receiving material sent out over the air by stations which had already paid a copyright fee. Imposing liability on the cable system would, the argument ran, result in double payment to the copyright holder. Others argued that whether or not copyright fees should be paid depended upon whether the cable system merely filled in the blanks within a station's normal service contour or whether the cable system extended the range of a station's service beyond the normal service contour.

The Supreme Court dealt with the issue in two landmark cases absolving cable systems of copyright liability for material picked up over the air and then sent through wire, on the ground that this was not a "performance" but merely a mechanical, passive act no different in quality than the erecting by a single person of an extremely tall receiving antenna to improve his or her own reception. Because such an act did not subject the individual to copyright liability, the provision of such a service for profit did not change the quality of the act for copyright purposes under the then existing copyright act. Fortnightly Corp. v. United Artists Television, Inc. (1968); Teleprompter Corp. v. Columbia Broadcasting System, Inc. (1974).

a. The Compulsory License For Retransmission of Broadcast Signals

The Fortnightly and Teleprompter decisions led Congress to enact significant revisions of the copyright statute. Under the Copyright Act as it now reads, cablevision systems are free to retransmit television signals containing copyrighted materials without obtaining permission of the copyright holder. There is no fee for retransmission of local broadcast signals. However, systems must pay a compulsory license fee for retransmission of distant signals. Originally, the amount of that fee, and the manner in which the fee was to be disbursed, were determined by the Copyright Royalty Tribunal (CRT), a statutory body created by Congress for this purpose. With the 1994 elimination of the CRT, these duties have been delegated to the Library of Congress. See 17 U.S.C.A. § 111.

The compulsory license has proven quite controversial. Not only were broadcasters dismayed at receiving no compensation for local retransmission, but they were also dissatisfied with the CRT's distribution formulas. The Motion Picture Association of America (MPAA), which represents those holding copyrights in televised motion pictures and syndicated programs, has consistently been awarded the lion's share of the license fees. Broadcasters have received very little by comparison.

b. *Retransmission Consent*

Broadcasters consistently argued that the compulsory license should be replaced by a system known as retransmission consent. As the name implies, cable operators would be prohibited from retransmitting broadcast signals without first securing the broadcaster's consent. Broadcasters assumed that cable operators would be willing to pay for retransmission rights.

The 1992 Cable Act created a retransmission consent option for broadcasters, but it is applicable only to carriage by local cable systems, carriage for which broadcasters received no compensation under the compulsory license. Each television station can choose between must-carry status, discussed below, and retransmission consent. A broadcaster who opts for retransmission consent must then negotiate for carriage with each local cable system. Any cable system unable to obtain the broadcaster's consent is prohibited from retransmitting that broadcaster's signal. Every three years broadcasters have the option of changing their status.

The underlying assumption was that higher-rated stations would opt for retransmission consent, while the others would retain must-carry status. Retransmission consent was not what broadcasters had hoped it would be. For the most part cable companies refused to pay cash for retransmission consent. As the deadline for obtaining consent approached, several broadcast groups found a compromise that proved acceptable to both sides. If a cable operator agreed to carry a cable channel from the broadcast owner, the broadcaster would agree to allow retransmission of its broadcast signal. For example, Hearst and Cap Cities/ABC reached agreements with a number of MSOs, including Continental Cablevision and Jones Intercable, whereby the cable operator agreed to pay for and carry ESPN2 (co-owned by Hearst and Cap Cities/ABC). In turn, Hearst and Cap Cities/ABC granted those cable companies retransmission consent for their broadcast stations. Other broadcasters, including CBS, gave retransmission consent without receiving anything in return.

4. Signal Carriage Rules

The potential impact of cable television upon the Commission's television allocation scheme has two aspects. First, the importation of distant signals might fragment the audience of the local television station since the local station would now be required to compete with "outside" signals not originally anticipated in the Commission's allocations policy. This is the so-called "distant signal" problem.   Second, unless the local cable system is required to carry the signals of the local stations, viewers who choose to subscribe to the system usually would not be able to receive the signal of the local station because they would probably disconnect their regular antennae.

To complicate matters further, the cablevision impact upon independent, non-network and UHF television stations is paradoxical. To the extent cablevision systems carry local, non-network, UHF stations, the cablevision system helps them by eliminating most of the technical advantages which off-the-air VHF reception possesses over UHF reception.   On the other hand, to the extent these systems carry distant signals and cable networks, they tend to fragment the audience and therefore harm local non-network UHF facilities.

a.   The "Must–Carry" Rules

The Commission in 1972 attempted to resolve these issues and integrate cablevision in the television scheme by enacting a series of rules aimed at protecting local stations.   These rules essentially fell into two categories: "Must Carry"—rules requiring cable systems to carry local stations—and "May Carry"—rules limiting the number or type of competing signals cable systems may carry.   We will return to the latter later in this chapter.

The must-carry rules were designed to ensure that cable subscribers would still receive the local broadcast stations and that these stations would have the same signal quality as competing signals. They remained in effect until 1985.

The constitutionality of the must-carry rules went unchallenged for years, probably because most cable operators believed them to have been a trade off for the compulsory license. Thus, they feared that if the must-carry rules were eliminated, the compulsory license would be in jeopardy. As a result the must-carry rules were in place for over a decade before a court was asked to decide their constitutionality. In Quincy Cable TV, Inc. v. FCC (1985), the court declared the must-carry rules, as written, unconstitutional under the First Amendment. The case involved two petitions. Quincy Cable, located in Quincy, Washington, was appealing an FCC order requiring it to carry some Spokane, Washington television stations as well as a $5,000 forfeiture for its failure to comply with the Commission's order. Turner Broadcasting System (TBS) was appealing the Commission's denial of TBS's petition to have the must-carry rules eliminated.

The court began by stating that the more limited scope of First Amendment protection enjoyed by the broadcast media as a result of Red Lion is not appropriate for cable. The court rejected any application of the scarcity rationale, noting that cable does not use the airwaves to deliver its programming to its subscribers. The court also rejected an economic scarcity argument based on the idea that cable is a natural monopoly. Not only was the court skeptical of cable's status as a natural monopoly, suggesting that the pattern of one cable system to a market was primarily a result of municipal franchising policies, but the court observed that economic scarcity had been rejected as a ground for infringing First Amendment rights in Miami Herald Pub. Co. v. Tornillo (1974).

The court found it unnecessary to decide whether the rules should be examined under the O'Brien test or some more exacting level of scrutiny, because in the court's analysis the rules failed even the more relaxed O'Brien test. The court held that the Commission had failed to prove that the rules served an important government interest. Although the Commission asserted that the interest served by the rules was preserving free, locally-oriented television, it failed, at least in the court's eyes, to prove it. Even though substantial deference to the Commission's expertise is required, the court concluded that after twenty years of regulation, something more than unsubstantiated assumptions and speculations was needed to support the Commission's conclusions.

The court went on to state that even if it assumed that the rules served the asserted government interest, they would still fail the O'Brien test as overinclusive. In the guise of protecting local broadcasting the rules were protecting local broadcasters regardless of the quality of their service or the number of stations in the market. The rules imposed no requirement that a station offer at least a minimum amount of local programming or demonstrate that its programming was not completely duplicative of another already in the market.

Finally, the court of appeals majority indicated that it had "not found it necessary to decide whether any version of the rules would contravene the First Amendment," leaving the door open for the Commission to draft new rules.

The Commission ceased enforcement of the old rules in September 1985. Then in August 1986, under pressure from Congress, the Commission announced a new set of must-carry rules. The purpose of the new rules, according to the Commission, was to provide time to educate consumers as to the availability of a device, an A–B switch, that would allow them to easily switch between an antenna for broadcast reception and the cable feed. Reinforcing the transition concept, the Commission included a five-year sunset provision in the rules.

These rules were also struck down on appeal. Again the court found it unnecessary to determine the appropriate level of scrutiny because the rules failed even the O'Brien test. In the court's view the FCC neither proved that consumers were ignorant of A–B switches nor that, without must-carry rules, cable systems would drop local broadcast stations. Therefore, there was no proof that the must-carry rules furthered a substantial government interest. In addition, the court found no evidence that it would take five years to learn about A–B switches and thus, the rules were not narrowly tailored. As in Quincy, the court emphasized that it was not declaring must-carry rules per se uncon-stitutional. Century Communications Corp. v. FCC (1987).

The 1992 Cable Act contained provisions requir-ing the FCC to promulgate two new must-carry rules, one for commercial stations, the other for non-commercial stations. With regard to commer-cial stations, cable systems with 12 or fewer chan-nels must carry at least three local broadcast sig-nals. Larger systems must carry all local commer-cial stations up to a maximum of one third of the system's total number of channels. Where the number of local commercial stations exceeds this maximum, the cable operator may choose which stations to carry. In so doing the operator cannot choose a low-power TV station unless all full-power stations are carried, and if a network affiliate is chosen, it must be the affiliate of that network closest to the system's head end. 47 U.S.C.A. § 534. In addition, each broadcast station carried pursuant to the requirements of § 614 must be carried on either the channel number on which it is broadcast, "the channel on which it was carried on July 19, 1985, or the channel on which it was carried on January 1, 1992, at the election of the station." Carriage on any other channel must be mutually agreed upon. 47 U.S.C.A. § 534(b)(6).

As far as noncommercial stations are concerned, systems with 12 or fewer channels must carry one local noncommercial educational television station. Systems with 13–36 channels must carry all local noncommercial educational television stations up to a maximum of three. Systems with a channel capacity greater than 36 must carry all local noncommercial educational television stations. 47 U.S.C.A. § 535.

As required by § 23 of the 1992 Cable Act, challenges to both must-carry provisions were heard by a special three-judge panel of the United States District Court for the District of Columbia. In Turner Broadcasting System Inc. v. FCC (1993), the district court, 2–1, granted summary judgment holding the rules constitutional.

Judge Jackson found that in enacting the must-carry provisions of the 1992 Cable Act, "Congress employed its regulatory powers over the economy to impose order upon a market in dysfunction, but a market in a commercial commodity nevertheless." In his view the commodity being regulated was the means of delivery of video signals to individual receivers, not the actual signals themselves. Thus, the 1992 Cable Act was nothing more than "industry-specific antitrust and fair trade practice regulatory legislation."

Recognizing however, that First Amendment values were implicated, Judge Jackson held that the O'Brien test was the appropriate standard to be applied. He found that the record compiled by Congress when combined with the deference the court should accord Congress was adequate to sustain a finding that there was a substantial government interest in sustaining local broadcasting. Again noting the deference due Congress, he found the must-carry rules were narrowly tailored to achieve the substantial government interest in sustaining local broadcasting. Finally, the rules did not unduly burden cable operators because they retained editorial control over the majority of their channels.

Judge Sporkin also viewed the case as dealing with economic regulation that only minimally implicated the First Amendment. He dismissed the cable operators' argument that the rules impermissibly interfere with their editorial discretion, finding that their editorial discretion does not rise to the level of detail-oriented, content-based decision making exercised by newspaper editors. Similarly, he rejected the programmers' argument that the rules favored one class of speakers—local broadcasters—over others, holding that it was only necessary that the statutory classification bear a rational relationship to a substantial government interest.

In dissent, Judge Williams took a very different approach. He focused on the leased access channels required under § 612 of the 1992 Act. If, in fact, cable operators are capable of exercising monopoly power over the delivery of video signals, the requirement that they lease a percentage of their channels to unaffiliated programmers provides an adequate remedy. In contrast, the must-carry rules favor a specific class of speakers, one that is required by the FCC to "provide programming responsive to issues of concern to its community." Judge Williams' view, this means that the must-carry rules are content-based and, as such, require strict scrutiny.

Applying strict scrutiny to the must-carry rules, he found two interests that the government claimed were furthered by the rules. The first was diversity, which is arguably a compelling interest. However, the rules are not a narrowly tailored means of advancing that interest. Increasing the number of access channels would be a less burdensome method of increasing diversity.

The second interest asserted by the government to be served by the must-carry rules is the preservation of local broadcasting. For the purpose of his analysis, Judge Williams divided this interest into two parts. One is Congress' desire to ensure the availability of local programming. The other is the need to ensure that noncable subscribers have access to video programming. Judge Williams doubted whether the desire for local programming could ever reach the level of a compelling government interest. Even if it could there is a less restrictive means of assuring local content. The government could subsidize the provision of local programming.

Turning to the need to ensure that noncable subscribers have access to video programming, he found that the figures cited by the government did not constitute evidence that, absent must-carry, there would be widespread failure of over-the-air stations. Even if cable systems should drop a lot of broadcast stations (which Williams believed to be highly unlikely) leading to a serious drop in advertising revenues, a less restrictive solution would be to expand the number of leased access channels and, if necessary, subsidize the cost of leasing for local broadcast stations.

The Supreme Court vacated the judgment and remanded the case for further proceedings. Turner Broadcasting System, Inc. v. FCC (1994). A bare majority of the Court, in an opinion written by Justice Kennedy, decided that the rules were subject to the intermediate level of scrutiny set out in O'Brien. The Court rejected the less vigorous Red Lion—broadcast—level of scrutiny because spectrum scarcity and signal interference do not exist with cable.

The Court also rejected strict scrutiny because in its view the must-carry rules are content neutral. The rules distinguish between speakers based on the method of transmission as opposed to content. Because most cable subscribers either take down their TV antennas or allow them to fall into disrepair, cable operators effectively control access to the 60 percent of the television households that subscribe to cable. Breaking this "bottleneck" control (not the favoring of a particular content) was Congress' objective in adopting the rules, and justifies the differentiation in treatment between broadcast and cable.

Applying O'Brien, the Court found that the rules further three important government interests unrelated to the suppression of free expression. These are "(1) preserving the benefits of free, over-the-air local broadcast stations, (2) promoting the widespread dissemination of information from a multiplicity of sources, and (3) promoting fair competition in the market for television programming."

Turning to the questions of whether the must-carry rules advance these government interests, and whether they burden speech no more than necessary to achieve those interests, the majority split 4–1. Justices Kennedy, Souter, Blackmun and Chief Justice Rehnquist held that, even giving Congress' predictive judgments the substantial deference required, the government had not adequately proven either. They noted that there was no evidence presented "that local broadcast stations have fallen into bankruptcy, turned in their broadcast licenses, curtailed their broadcast operations, or suffered a serious reduction in operating revenues as a result of their being dropped from, or otherwise disadvantaged by, cable systems." In addition, the government had failed to provide "any findings concerning the actual effects of must-carry on the speech of cable operators and cable programmers." Therefore, because genuine issues of material fact remained, summary judgment should not have been granted.

Justice Stevens argued that in fact the government had provided adequate evidence that they do not burden more speech than necessary to advance those interests. He would therefore have voted to affirm the lower court's judgment. Because so voting would mean that no disposition of the case would command a majority of the Court, however, he concurred in the judgment vacating and remanding for further proceedings.

Justice O'Connor, joined by Justices Scalia, Thomas and Ginsburg, dissented. She argued that the must-carry rules were clearly not content neutral, and thus should be subject to strict scrutiny. She noted that the findings enumerated in the 1992 Act cited "[p]references for diversity of viewpoints, for localism, for educational programming and for news and public affairs." In her view, these findings prove that the government interests are not compelling, and thus the rules are unconstitutional.

Even assuming arguendo that the rules are content neutral, O'Connor would still find them unconstitutional because they are overbroad. "They disadvantage cable programmers even if the operator has no anticompetitive motives, and even if the broadcasters that would have to be dropped to make room for the cable programmer would survive without cable access."

Justice Ginsburg wrote a separate dissent, adopting the reasons contained in Judge Williams' dissent from the district court judgment. She characterized the rules as "an unwarranted content-based preference." She also termed the harm the rules are supposed to prevent "imaginary."

Perhaps the most important effect of Turner is the clear rejection of the broadcast standard of scrutiny as appropriate for cable. Instead, in determining the constitutionality of cable regulation, the O'Brien standard should be used for content-neutral regulations imposing only an incidental burden on speech, and strict scrutiny for content-based regulations. Of course, determining whether a given regulation is content neutral or content based (and teasing out the elements of the O'Brien standard) will still prove difficult.

A number of questions remain, however. For example, if the Regional Bell Operating Companies are permitted to compete directly with cable systems, either through video dialtone, discussed supra, or by operating their own video programming distribution service, does this change the justifications for the must-carry rules? What if DBS, discussed infra, is successful? How would the advent of 500-channel cable systems affect the Court's analysis? Obviously the rapidly changing communication technology landscape will continue to present Congress and the courts with difficult questions.

b. The "May–Carry" Rules

The may-carry rules took several forms. One, no longer in effect, was a limit on the number of signals from distant stations that a cable system could transmit. This limit varied according to market size and the number of available over-the-air signals within the market.

A second restriction on distant signals involves syndicated programming. Generally, syndicated programming is sold on a market-exclusive basis, but the importation of syndicated programming made it impossible to guarantee market exclusivity. The Commission therefore requires cable systems in major markets to black out distant syndicated programs when local commercial stations own the exclusive rights to the broadcast of these programs.

Any station that has obtained local exclusivity can enforce that against local cable systems. Stations are also permitted to obtain and enforce national exclusivity. This provision, which benefits superstations, also exempts such stations from the territorial exclusivity rule discussed at p. 436, supra. Syndicators may also enforce exclusivity contracts for the first year after the initial syndication. See United Video, Inc. v. FCC (1989).

One may-carry rule that remains is the network nonduplication rule. It is aimed at the problem that arises when the same cable systems carry "local" and "distant" stations which may both be broadcasting the same network program. Because such duplication through the use of cable television could have a detrimental economic effect on the local station that had obtained exclusivity for the program under its network agreement, the Commission enacted rules which require that cable systems with more than 1000 subscribers delete the network programs of duplicating distant stations under certain circumstances. When the Commission reinstituted the syndication exclusivity rules, the network non-duplication rules were expanded from simultaneous network programming to all network programs. See 47 C.F.R. §§ 76.92–76.99 (1981). The deletion is made in accordance with certain priorities set forth in the Commission's Rules: a "local" television station has the right to require the deletion of a duplicating network program from the signal of a lower priority station. See 47 C.F.R. § 76.92. In order to invoke such protection the station requesting deletion must formally notify the cable system.

In sum, the only programming restrictions that still remain upon the type of material that can be presented on cablevision systems relate to the syndication exclusivity rules (See 47 C.F.R. § 76.161), the non-duplication protection afforded network programs (47 C.F.R. §§ 76.92–76.99 (1981)), and those portions of the Commission's rules placing a blackout upon the cablecasting of sports events taking place locally (See 47 C.F.R. § 76.67) (1981).

5. Content Regulation

The Commission has imposed upon cable systems certain operating requirements similar to those imposed upon broadcast stations. Thus, despite the fact that cable may not be considered "broadcasting" in the usual sense, nonetheless, to the extent cable systems originate their own programs, the Commission's Rules require that these systems follow all of the "equal time" and "lowest unit rate" political broadcast regulations promulgated pursuant to Section 315 of the Communications Act, adhere to the rules concerning the Personal Attack and Political Editorial Rules, not transmit obscenity, even on the so-called "access" channels, identify all material that is sponsored, and maintain certain records. Unlike the various attempts by both state and federal government to limit cablecasting of indecent material, these restrictions have engendered very little litigation.

Most of the constitutional challenges to content regulation of cable have involved laws aimed at limiting the carriage of indecent programming. Ex-

cept for the clear authority of Miller v. California
(1973), chapter IV, supra, to ban obscenity over
cable, it is not yet clear whether any other sexually-
oriented programming may be proscribed.

Supporters of such indecency restrictions argue
that they can be constitutionally applied to cable for
the same reasons that the Supreme Court held
similar restrictions are constitutional when applied
to broadcasting. See FCC v. Pacifica Foundation
(1978). Opponents contend that the Pacifica rationale is only applicable to broadcasting and that the
appropriate precedent is Erznoznik v. Jacksonville
(1975) in which a local ordinance banning all nudity
on drive-in movie screens visible from the street
was held unconstitutionally overbroad.

In Cruz v. Ferre (1985), a Miami ordinance banning the distribution of obscene and indecent programming over cable was struck down on overbreadth grounds. The court distinguished Pacifica
on the basis of differences between broadcasting
and cable. Cable requires the affirmative decision
to subscribe and juveniles can be protected through
the use of lockboxes that permit parents to lock out
channels and put them out of reach of their children.

Even if these differences did not exist, the court
would still have found the ordinance unconstitutional because it banned indecent programming outright. In Pacifica the U.S. Supreme Court had
indicated that indecent programming might be permissible in appropriate time periods or programming contexts. No such allowances were made in
the Miami ordinance.

Similarly, in Jones v. Wilkinson (1986) the court of appeals affirmed a lower court decision striking down the Utah Cable Television Programming Decency Act. However, one member of the court argued in his concurrence that Pacifica was the appropriate standard by which cable indecency regulations should be judged. He then found that the Act could not even meet the more relaxed Pacifica standard. The U.S. Supreme Court affirmed without issuing any opinion. Wilkinson v. Jones (1987).

The 1992 Cable Act contained several provisions aimed at limiting cablecasting of indecent material on either leased access channels or PEG channels. The FCC was required to promulgate regulations requiring cable operators to place on a single channel all indecent programming intended to be carried on leased access channels and to block access to that channel absent a written request for access from the subscriber. Also required by the 1992 Act were regulations permitting cable operators to prohibit obscene or indecent material on cable channels.

In compliance with these provisions of the 1992 Cable Act the Commission adopted indecency rules for leased access channels, Cable Access Channels (Indecent Programming) (1993), and PEG channels, Cable Access Channels (Indecent Programming) (1993). Both were successfully challenged on First Amendment grounds. Alliance for Community Media v. FCC (1993). However, that judgment was vacated when a petition for rehearing en banc was granted.

B. HIGH DEFINITION TELEVISION
(HDTV)

Although a plethora of new systems for delivering television programming (cable, MDS, DBS, and SMATV, all discussed later in this chapter) have been developed, one thing has remained constant—the television picture itself. The last major change was the advent of color decades ago.

All this could change with the development of High Definition Television (HDTV). The key difference between HDTV and the current U.S. broadcast standard is that HDTV has approximately double the number of scan lines (1100–1200 as opposed to 525). The result is a sharper, brighter, clearer picture with deeper, more vibrant colors. In addition HDTV uses a five-to-three aspect ratio as opposed to the four-to-three currently in use. Proponents of HDTV claim that its quality approximates that of 35 mm. film.

When the FCC began considering the advent of HDTV service, there were a number of questions that had to be answered before the new service could become a reality. Should a technical standard be selected, and if so, which one should it be? Should the new service be compatible with the current television standard? How much spectrum should be assigned to this service? Who should be authorized to provide HDTV?

In a series of decisions issued between 1988 and 1993, the Commission has answered most of these questions. HDTV will utilize the existing television broadcast spectrum. Current television licensees will receive the initial HDTV licenses. HDTV will not be required to be compatible with existing television service.

In order to provide an orderly transition to HDTV, broadcasters will be given an additional 6 MHz in which to broadcast HDTV. Within as short a time span as possible, licensees will be expected to simulcast 100 percent of their programming on their original channel and their HDTV channel. Once HDTV becomes the prevalent medium, broadcasters will be required to surrender their original channel.

As far as a standard is concerned, the Commission suggested that the proponents of the four competing systems that remained in 1993 should merge their systems, using the best aspects of each. They have done so, and it is expected that the Commission will adopt this combined system as the HDTV standard sometime in late 1994 or early 1995.

C. MULTIPOINT DISTRIBUTION SERVICE (MDS)

By the early 1980s, despite the emergence of cable television and pay television, and despite the nationwide saturation of receivers, there were still approximately 1.2 million households that had no access to television service and there were approximately 4 million households that received only one or two channels (see 47 Fed.Reg. at 1967, Jan. 13, 1982). There were additional millions of households that received only three or four channels. In an attempt to alleviate the shortage, alternative technologies have been developed.

The multipoint distribution service (MDS) is one such technological alternative. In its early years, this service typically consisted of a microwave transmitter and antenna at the transmitting site broadcasting over a microwave frequency omnidirectionally covering a line of sight area of approximately 10 to 20 miles. The signal was then received by a receiving antenna at a particular site. The signal was converted from the microwave frequency to a lower frequency compatible with the customer's television set. The signal was passed from the downconverter through a cable to the customer's set on a VHF channel which was vacant in the community (see 45 Fed.Reg. 29350 at ¶ 24 (May 2, 1980)).

Economically, the arrangement was as follows: the transmitting equipment was licensed to an entity which acted as a common carrier. The licensee as a common carrier did not have control over the programming presented on the channel. Persons wishing to present programming over the system (called "subscribers") leased air time on the transmitter and made the programming available for transmission. Time was usually sold to a programmer on a block basis. The subscriber also typically owned the receiving antenna and the downconverter. The subscriber then contracted with the customer for delivery of the program to the customer's set. In essence, the transaction was very close to a point-to-point transmission, using the air waves rather than a wire.

Originally, most markets had only one or two microwave channels available for MDS service. They were allocated via the comparative hearing method with all its attendant delays and expenses. Then in 1983 the Commission reallocated eight of the 28 instructional television fixed service (ITFS) microwave channels to MDS. ITFS (MDS Reallocation), 48 Fed.Reg. 33,873 (July 15, 1983). At the same time, the FCC authorized MDS operators to lease extra channel capacity from ITFS operators and changed its method of allocating MDS channels from the comparative hearing to a lottery system. The expanded service created by the rule changes is called multichannel multipoint distribution service (MMDS). It is often referred to as "wireless cable."

In 1987, noting that MMDS was for the most part being used to deliver broadcast-type services, the Commission decided to allow MMDS operators to choose the regulatory model to be applied to them based on the type of service provided. 47 C.F.R. §§ 21.900–21.908.

Because the service developed as a "common carrier" service neither licensees nor subscribers (i.e., programmers) were subject to the equal time or fairness rules, the access rules for political candidates, or the other doctrines which control broadcast operations. Unlike cable system operators MDS operators do not have to obtain a franchise grant from a state or town because the FCC has preempted state and local regulation of MDS. See New York State Commission on Cable Television v. FCC (1982).

As a competitor of cable, MMDS has several advantages. Installation is much less expensive, especially in urban areas where cable must be placed underground. Because there are no franchising requirements, MMDS does not have to provide expensive community services such as access channels and studios. Long expensive franchising battles are not required and an MMDS operator can offer service to all the surrounding communities.

On the other hand, even with the new channels made available, MMDS is limited to less than thirty-five channels, whereas some urban cable systems have the capacity to provide 100 or more. By using recently developed digital compression technology, MMDS systems may soon have up to 300 channels. The same techniques are expected to permit 500–channel cable systems. Perhaps more important, cable is already established in many communities and it may be difficult for MMDS operators to convince existing cable subscribers to switch. The best opportunities for MMDS appear to be in those communities that either have no existing cable service or have old, limited-capacity systems.

D. SATELLITE MASTER ANTENNA TELEVISION (SMATV)

One of the earliest alternatives to cable, satellite master antenna television (SMATV) is really a cable

system that does not cross a public right of way or
connect separately owned buildings. See FCC v.
Beach Communications (1993). A SMATV operator
sets up one or more earth stations on an apartment
building or residential complex. The programming
received by these earth stations is distributed
throughout the building or complex by wire.

In 1983, the FCC preempted state and local entry
regulations for SMATV. The Commission's decision was affirmed in New York State Commission
on Cable Television v. FCC (1984). As a result
SMATV is an essentially unregulated industry.

Because a SMATV system cannot cross a public
right of way, SMATV is limited to large apartment
buildings, hotels and private residential complexes.
In those areas it has several advantages over other
services. The absence of any franchising requirements allows immediate entry into the market.
Like MMDS, SMATV cannot be required to provide
access channels and studios, thus reducing the cost
of operation. However, unlike MMDS, SMATV has
no limit on channel capacity.

E.   DIRECT BROADCAST
SATELLITES (DBS)

As satellite communications technology improved,
both the cost and size of earth stations capable of
receiving satellite transmissions decreased. As a
result direct transmission to individual homes appeared to be both technologically and economically

feasible. In 1980, the Commission began conducting inquiries into how best to initiate such a service. See Notice of Inquiry, 45 Fed.Reg. 72,719 (Nov. 3, 1980).

Among the questions that needed to be addressed were the type of service to be offered (pay or advertiser-supported), the number of satellites and channels to be used, and the frequencies to be allocated to the service. Permanent answers had to await the decisions of an international conference allotting frequencies and orbital slots to the Western Hemisphere nations.

However, in an attempt to hasten the development of this new service the Commission in July, 1982 issued interim guidelines for DBS operators. Licenses would be granted for five years, and licensees would be required to meet international guidelines. DBS services with broadcast characteristics would be subject to the broadcast sections of the Communications Act, but not subject to non-statutory Commission policies with the exception of the Commission's equal employment opportunity rules. DBS operators offering common carrier-type services were to be subject only to the common carrier sections of the Act. The interim guidelines were challenged in National Association of Broadcasters v. FCC (1984) and were upheld except for the exemption from the broadcasting sections of the Communications Act of programmers leasing DBS channels.

In response to the Court's decision, the FCC changed its method of classifying subscription video programming services from a content-based system to an intent-based system. This meant that these subscription services would not be subject to broadcast regulations despite their offering broadcast-like services because the programmers' intent would be to limit access to their signals. Subscription Video (1987).

The 1983 international conference set aside 12.2 to 12.7 GHz for DBS and awarded orbital slots. Other allocation questions were left for a 1985 conference which in turn left them for another conference scheduled for 1988. At that conference it was decided to resolve allocation disputes through flexible, multilateral planning meetings.

In 1983 United Satellite Communications, Inc. (USCI) became the first company to offer DBS service. Less than two years later, after huge losses, USCI discontinued its service. Meanwhile, a number of the other companies that had originally applied for licenses to offer DBS service abandoned their DBS plans.

The advantages of direct broadcast satellites had appeared obvious. A single satellite could provide programming to a large area of the country. Most importantly, satellites offered a way to serve those areas of the country (primarily rural) where cable cannot be profitable due to high per-subscriber installation costs.

Unfortunately, less immediately apparent were some of the key disadvantages. DBS service turned out to be very expensive because of the costs involved in putting satellites in space. There were not enough potential subscribers to make advertiser-supported service feasible. Instead subscribers had to pay several hundred dollars to buy a receiving dish in addition to a monthly charge of more than $20/month for a limited number of channels. Thus, in those areas where cable was available, DBS could not compete. The uncabled areas were insufficient to support DBS by themselves.

New technology has improved the outlook for DBS. High-powered satellites will permit the use of smaller, less expensive receiving equipment. Digital compression techniques will enable DBS operators to offer hundreds of channels. Hughes Aircraft has formed a new subsidiary, DirecTv, Inc., which is scheduled to begin DBS service in 1994. Whether the new technology will improve the economics of DBS service to the point where it can survive is difficult to judge.

The 1992 Cable Act imposed some content regulation on DBS, including equal opportunity and reasonable access. See discussions of §§ 315 and 312(a)(7), pp. 400–413, supra. In addition, the Act required DBS to make available non-commercial educational and informational channels at reasonable rates, and provide service to local communities. These provisions were found unconstitutional in Time–Warner v. FCC (1993).

One concern voiced by each of these alternative delivery systems, MMDS, SMATV and DBS, has been access to programming. The question is whether program vendors have been unfairly favoring cable operators, by far their biggest customers. One provision in the 1992 Cable Act requires the Commission to conduct a rulemaking proceeding to "establish regulations governing program carriage agreements and related practices between cable operators or other multichannel video programming distributors and video programming vendors."   47 U.S.C.A. § 535.

F.   HOME SATELLITE DISHES (TVRO)

Still another competitor for cable spawned by developments in satellite communications is the television receive only dish (TVRO). As the size and cost of these dishes dropped, people began buying them for their backyards. With a dish it became possible to pick up a seemingly endless number of programming feeds. The two most important types of signals available were cable programming services and network television feeds.

Earlier purchasers of these TVRO systems were mostly those who lived in remote areas. Unserved by cable or in many cases even by conventional broadcasting, these people had no other way to obtain video programming. However, as the prices of the equipment dropped, people in more populated areas became increasingly interested. The large number of available signals as well as the lack of any cost beyond the initial purchase price made them an attractive alternative to cable.

As the number of backyard dishes increased, cable operators, cable programmers and television network executives all became concerned. The cable operators and cable programmers had obvious economic concerns—dish owners were not likely to subscribe to cable and they were not paying the programmers for their services. The networks had a different concern. Much of what the dish owners were receiving was raw programming material, for example, news reports being sent back to the network studios or programs being transmitted from the network to the local affiliates without the local commercials inserted.

These concerns were addressed in The Cable Communications Policy Act of 1984 which amended section 605 of the Federal Communications Act specifically to prohibit unauthorized reception of any *encrypted* satellite cable signal, as long as there is a marketing mechanism available for those who wish to purchase the service.

In 1986 various cable programming services began scrambling their signals. The industry agreed on a standard for scrambling, which means a dish owner only has to buy one converter no matter how many programming services are desired. As a result the Commission concluded that there was no need for it to set a standard. Satellite Cable Programming (Universal Encryption Standard), 5 FCC Rcd. 2710 (1990).

A great deal of controversy continued to surround scrambling. Many of the services initially designated local cable companies as the only ones authorized to market their programming to dish owners. The prices set for these services were almost always as much or more than the cost of the service when delivered by cable, even though the cost of delivery is less.

The Society of Private and Commercial Earth Stations (SPACE), a trade association for dish owners, claimed that the cable programmers set prices artificially high and used cable operators as marketers in order to protect the cable operators, who are, of course, their largest customers.

There were several difficult questions involved here. Although it was obvious that the dish owners shouldn't be able to obtain the programming free, neither should the price be prohibitive. If TVROs were to provide a competitive alternative to cable, how could cable operators be the sole distributors of satellite delivered programming? Did retransmitting broadcast stations directly to dish owners violate copyright? What about network programming? Why should dish owners have access to programming other than the finished product aired by network affiliates? And what about the rural dish owner who does not otherwise have access to network programming?

Congress addressed some of these questions in the Satellite Home Viewer Act of 1988. The compulsory copyright license was extended to satellite retransmission of independent stations. Satellite retransmission of network stations is also covered, but only for dish owners who are otherwise unable to receive the network's programming. 17 U.S.C.A. § 111.

The Act also required the FCC to apply the syndicated exclusivity rules to satellite carriers to the extent it was feasible. The FCC determined that it was not feasible. Syndicated Exclusivity Requirements for Satellite Carriers (1991).

G. ELECTRONIC PUBLISHING
(TELETEXT)

Another new technology whose promise has far exceeded its performance is electronic publishing. It is possible, utilizing previously unused portions of television signals (the Vertical Blanking Interval (VBI) or the space between frames) to transmit textual information. A decoding unit can take the information in the VBI and display it on the television screen. Closed captioning for the deaf is a simplified version of this process.

Original proposals for this service often known as teletext or videotext analogized it to an electronic newspaper. Viewers would be able to call up news, sports, and weather, as well as restaurant reviews, airline schedules, and concert ticket availabilities at the touch of a button. They could then make plane reservations and order concert tickets or merchandise by phone. Interactive cable versions of the service would even allow the entire transactions to be done by cable.

In 1983 the FCC authorized the use of the broadcast VBI for teletext. Teletext service would be regulated as either broadcast or common carrier depending on the nature of the service. No specific teletext standard was set. The Commission declined to apply the equal time or fairness rules to broadcast-like teletext services and also refused to require cable systems to carry the teletext portion of stations, even when required to carry the stations themselves under the must-carry rules.

The equal time and fairness aspects of the ruling were appealed. In Telecommunications Research Action Committee v. FCC (1986) the court held that because teletext was a broadcast service, it had to be subject to § 315 of the Communications Act. However, the court found that the fairness doctrine was not codified in § 315 as many had thought and therefore, the Commission had the authority to exempt teletext from its application.

INDEX

References are to Pages